In the Form of a God

Studies in Early Christology

Series editors: Michael Bird, David Capes, and Scott Harrower

The purpose of the Studies in Early Christology (SEC) series is to foster public research in a range of disputed questions relating to early Christology with a view to clarifying the issues, furthering the debate, and—most of all—offering compelling accounts of the emergence of early Christology/Jesus devotion by Christian groups in the Greco-Roman world. The ambition of the series is to attract leading researchers in the fields of Second Temple Judaism, Hellenistic Religion, New Testament, Christian Origins, and patristic studies, with a view to exploring how various Christologies and patterns of devotion to Jesus emerged and why they took on the shape that they did. The series will include monographs by emerging scholars, contributions from senior researchers, and conference proceedings on salient topics related to early Christology. The editors of the series invite submissions for consideration that contribute to discussions on early Christology, demonstrate a sophisticated knowledge of primary sources, interact thoroughly with secondary literature, and use appropriate methodologies.

In the Form of a God

The Pre-existence of the Exalted Christ in Paul

Andrew Perriman

CASCADE *Books* · Eugene, Oregon

IN THE FORM OF A GOD
The Pre-existence of the Exalted Christ in Paul

Studies in Early Christology

Cascade Books
An Imprint of Wipf and Stock Publishers
199 W. 8th Ave., Suite 3
Eugene, OR 97401

www.wipfandstock.com

PAPERBACK ISBN: 978-1-6667-3067-8
HARDCOVER ISBN: 978-1-6667-2247-5
EBOOK ISBN: 978-1-6667-2248-2

Cataloguing-in-Publication data:

Names: Perriman, Andrew, author.

Title: In the form of a god : the pre-existence of the exalted Christ in Paul / by Andrew Perriman.

Description: Eugene, OR: Cascade Books, 2022 | Series: Studies in Early Christology | Includes bibliographical references and index.

Identifiers: ISBN 978-1-6667-3067-8 (paperback) | ISBN 978-1-6667-2247-5 (hardcover) | ISBN 978-1-6667-2248-2 (ebook)

Subjects: LCSH: Jesus Christ—Pre-existence. | Jesus Christ—Person and offices. | Bible. Epistles of Paul—Theology. | Jesus Christ—Exaltation. | Bible. Epistles of Paul—Criticism, interpretation, etc.

Classification: LCC BS2651 P47 2022 (print) | LCC BS2651 (ebook)

11/21/22

In memory of James D. G. Dunn

Contents

Abbreviations

Journals and reference works

AB	Anchor Bible
BBR	*Bulletin for Biblical Research*
BDAG	Walter Bauer, Frederick W. Danker, W. F. Arndt, and F. W. Gingrich. *Greek-English Lexicon of the New Testament and Other Early Christian Literature.* 3rd ed. Chicago: University of Chicago Press, 2000
BDF	Friedrich Blass and Albert Debrunner. *A Greek Grammar of the New Testament and Other Early Christian Literature.* Translated and revised by Robert W. Funk. Chicago: University of Chicago Press, 1961
BNTC	Black's New Testament Commentaries
CBQ	*Catholic Biblical Quarterly*
CGL	*The Cambridge Greek Lexicon.* Cambridge: Cambridge University Press, 2021
FGrH	Felix Jacoby, *Die Fragmente der griechischen Historiker.* Berlin: Weidmann, 1923
HBT	*Horizons in Biblical Theology*
HTR	*Harvard Theological Review*
JBL	*Journal of Biblical Literature*
JETS	*Journal of the Evangelical Theological Society*
JSNT	*Journal for the Study of the New Testament*
JTS	*Journal of Theological Studies*
LSJ	Henry George Liddell, Robert Scott, and Henry Stuart Jones. *A Greek-English Lexicon.* 9th ed. Oxford: Oxford University Press, 1940

NETS	*A New English Translation Of The Septuagint*. Edited by Albert Pietersma and Benjamin G. Wright. Oxford: Oxford University Press, 2014
NICNT	New International Commentary on the New Testament
NICOT	New International Commentary on the Old Testament
NIGTC	New International Greek Testament Commentary
NTS	*New Testament Studies*
OGIS	Wilhelm Dittenberger. *Orientis Graeci Inscriptiones Selectae*. Leipzig: Hirzel, 1903
PG	J. P. Migne, ed. *Patrologia Graeca*. Paris, 1857–1886
PGM	K. Preisendanz. *Papyri Graecae Magicae*. Leipzig: B. G. Teubner, 1931
PNTC	Pillar New Testament Commentary
RB	*Revue Biblique*
TDNT	*Theological Dictionary of the New Testament*. 10 vols. Edited by Gerhard Kittel. Translated by Geoffrey W. Bromiley. Grand Rapids: Eerdmans, 1964

Apocrypha and Septuagint

Bar	Baruch
Ep Jer	Epistle of Jeremiah
1–2 Esd	1–2 Esdras
Jdt	Judith
1–4 Macc	1–4 Maccabees
Sir	Sirach/Ecclesiasticus
Tob	Tobit
Wis	Wisdom of Solomon

Old Testament Pseudepigrapha

2 Bar.	2 Baruch (Syriac Apocalypse)
4 Bar.	4 Baruch (Paraleipomena Jeremiou)
Dem.	Demetrius (the Chronographer)
1 En.	1 Enoch (Ethiopic Apocalypse)
2 En.	2 Enoch (Slavonic Apocalypse)

Gk. Apoc. Ezra	Greek Apocalypse of Ezra
Jos. Asen.	Joseph and Aseneth
Jub.	Jubilees
L.A.B.	Liber antiquitatum biblicarum (Pseudo-Philo)
L.A.E.	Life of Adam and Eve
Let. Aris.	Letter of Aristeas
Odes Sol.	Odes of Solomon
Pr. Jos.	Prayer of Joseph
Pss. Sol.	Psalms of Solomon
Sib. Or.	Sibylline Oracles
T. Ab.	Testament of Abraham
T. Adam	Testament of Adam
T. Benj.	Testament of Benjamin
T. Jac.	Testament of Jacob
T. Job	Testament of Job
T. Jos.	Testament of Joseph
T. Levi	Testament of Levi
T. Reu.	Testament of Reuben
T. Sol.	Testament of Solomon

Philo

Abraham	On the Life of Abraham
Alleg. Interp.	*Allegorical Interpretation*
Cherubim	*On the Cherubim*
Confusion	*On the Confusion of Tongues*
Creation	*On the Creation of the World*
Decalogue	*On the Decalogue*
Dreams	*On Dreams*
Drunkenness	*On Drunkenness*
Embassy	*On the Embassy to Gaius*
Eternity	*On the Eternity of the World*
Flight	*On Flight and Finding*
Giants	*On Giants*

Good Person	*That Every Good Person Is Free*
Heir	*Who Is the Heir?*
Joseph	*On the Life of Joseph*
Migration	*On the Migration of Abraham*
Moses	*On the Life of Moses*
Names	*On the Change of Names*
Planting	*On Planting*
Posterity	*On the Posterity of Cain*
Prelim. Studies	*On the Preliminary Studies*
QE	*Questions and Answers on Exodus*
QG	*Questions and Answers on Genesis*
Rewards	*On Rewards and Punishments*
Sacrifices	*On the Sacrifices of Cain and Abel*
Spec. Laws	*On the Special Laws*
Unchangeable	*That God is Unchangeable*
Virtues	*On the Virtues*
Worse	*That the Worse Attacks the Better*

Josephus

Ag. Ap.	*Against Apion*
Ant.	*Jewish Antiquities*
J.W.	*Jewish War*
Life	*The Life*

Other Greek and Latin texts

Aeth.	Heliodorus, *Aethiopica*
Aj.	Sophocles, *Ajax*
Alc.	Euripides, *Alcestis*
All.	Heraclitus, *Allegoriae (Quaestiones homericae)*
Anab.	Arrian, *The Anabasis of Alexander*
Anaplus	Dionysius of Byzantium, *Anaplus Bospori*
An. procr.	Plutarch, *De animae procreatione in Timaeo*
Anth.	Stobaeus, *Anthology*

Ant. or. Preface	Dionysius of Halicarnassus, *De antiquis oratoribus. Preface*
Artapan.	Artapanus
Bacch.	Euripides, *Bacchae*
Bib. hist.	Diodorus Siculus, *Bibliotheca historica*
Cael.	Aristotle, *De caelo*
Carm.	Horace, *Carmina*
Chaer.	Chariton, *Chaereas and Callirhoe*
Chrys.	Euripides, *Dramatic Fragments, Chrysippus*
Corp. herm.	*Corpus hermeticum*
Def. orac.	Plutarch, *De defectu oraculorum*
Dem.	Dionysius of Halicarnassus, *De Demosthene*
De rerum	Lucretius, *De rerum natura*
Descr.	Pausanias, *Graeciae descriptio*
Din.	Dionysius of Halicarnassus, *De Dinarcho*
El.	Sophocles, *Elektra*
Eugnostos	*Eugnostos the Blessed* (Nag Hammadi Codex III,3)
Eur.	Moschus, *Europa*
Fals. leg.	Demosthenes, *De falsa legatione*
Geogr.	Strabo, *Geographica*
Hel.	Euripides, *Helena*
Hom. Hymns	*Homeric Hymns*
Il.	Homer, *Iliad*
Leg.	Cicero, *De legibus*
Leuc. Clit.	Achilles Tatius, *The Adventures of Leucippe and Clitophon*
[Lib. ed.]	Plutarch, *De liberis educandis*
Library	Apollodorus, *The Library*
Library	Diodorus Siculus, *The Library of History*
[Mundo]	Aristotle, *De mundo*
Med.	Marcus Aurelius, *Meditations*
Mem.	Xenophon, *Memorabilia*
Metam.	Ovid, *Metamorphoses*
Metaph.	Aristotle, *Metaphysica*
Nat. d.	Cicero, *De natura deorum*
Od.	Homer, *Odyssey*

Orat.	Aelius Aristides, *Orationes*
Orig. World	*On the Origin of the World* (Nag Hammadi Codex II,5)
Pel.	Plutarch, *Pelopidas*
Pers.	Aeschylus, *Persians*
Phaed.	Plato, *Phaedo*
Phaedr.	Plato, *Phaedrus*
Phil.	Plutarch, *Philopoemen*
[Philopatr.]	Lucian, *Philopatris*
[Plac. philos.]	Plutarch, *De placita philosophorum*
Pol.	Aristotle, *Politica*
Princ. iner.	Plutarch, *Ad principem ineruditum*
Pro imag.	Lucian, *Pro imaginibus*
Quaest. plat.	Plutarch, *Quaestiones platonicae*
Resp.	Plato, *Republic*
Rom.	Plutarch, *Romulus*
Symp.	Plato, *Symposium*
Them.	Plutarch, *Themistocles*
Tim.	Aeschines, *Against Timarchus*
Tim.	Plutarch, *Timoleon*
Top.	Aristotle, *Topica*
Vit. Apoll.	Philostratus, *Vita Apollonii*
Vit. Pyth.	Iamblichus, *De vita Pythagorica*

Early Christian writings

1 Apol.	Justin, *First Apology*
Comm. Apoc.	Victorinus, *Commentary on the Apocalypse*
Comm. Luc.	Eusebius, *Commentary on Luke*
De ador.	Cyril of Alexandria, *De adoratione*
Dei cogn.	Dio Chrysostom, *De dei cognitione (Or. 12)*
Dial.	Justin, *Dialogue with Trypho*
Did.	*Didache*
Ep.	Isidore of Pelusium, *Epistles*
Haer.	Hippolytus, *Refutation of All Heresies*

Hist. eccl.	Eusebius, *Historia ecclesiastica*
Hom. Gen.	Origen, *Homiliae in Genesim*
Inst.	Lactantius, *The Divine Institutes*
Ps.-Clem. Hom.	*Clementine Homilies*
Ps.-Clem. Rec.	*Clementine Recognitions*
Vit. Const.	Eusebius, *Life of Constantine*

Rabbinic texts

Gen. Rab.	*Genesis Rabbah*
Ketub.	*Ketubbot*
Yebam.	*Yevamot*

1

Introduction

THE BASIC QUESTION IS a straightforward one: did Paul hold to the view that *before* he was sent to Israel in the likeness of sinful flesh, Christ Jesus existed actually and personally in heaven from eternity? If we are persuaded that the answer to that question is yes, we may want to ask in what "form" he pre-existed, what the manner of his pre-existence was, what the nature of his relationship to God was. Then we may start wondering about the *origins* of the belief and the language in which it is expressed. After all, no one in the New Testament claims that the pre-existent heavenly Christ was ever seen or encountered as such in the way that the resurrected and exalted Christ was seen and encountered—in the Spirit, in visions, in worship, perhaps through some manner of mystical ascent.

So how did the belief arise? Scholarship has entertained a range of possibilities. Has the exalted Lord been projected back into eternity because eschatology is necessarily mirrored in protology, as Martin Hengel and others have argued?[1] Has Paul drawn on Jewish ideas regarding the paradoxical visibility of the Glory of God, the quasi-independent role of divine Wisdom in creation, or the pre-existence of the apocalyptic Son of Man? Has he identified Christ with one or other of these familiar entities? Did some Jews, in any case, believe in a pre-existent messiah? Did he have reason to think of Christ as one of the heavenly sons of God, as an angelic figure, even as the representation of God's own gigantic humanlike form? Or is the conceptual background to the belief to be found nearer the Hellenistic end of the dazzling religious spectrum that colored the ancient Mediterranean world? Are there emerging gnostic narratives that account for it? Has the Jewish messiah metamorphosed into a pagan god who breaks in from the heavenly realm in the manner of Zeus or Apollo?

Much of this book will be taken up with this first series of questions, though the enquiry cannot be as linear as I have suggested here. We are

1. Hengel, *Cross*, 67; cf. Hurtado, "Pre-existence," 746.

1

bound to approach the problem *from somewhere*—with a more or less dog-matic, more or less critical, more or less informed, more or less transpar-ent assortment of preconceptions. We begin with a narrow focus on one or other of a handful of discrete texts, christological gemstones prised from their settings by interpretive tradition. What order do we take them in? To what extent can they be taken to be mutually interpretive? We then have to decide how far to zoom out, how much additional Pauline material to take into consideration, how much of the wider story to tell, in order to read the texts properly, which will bring more exegetical and theological assumptions and expectations quietly into play. Finally, given the limited amount of information available on the surface of our texts, we are inevi-tably drawn into the work of reconstructing the external contexts of Paul's thought, Jewish and Greek, thus setting in shimmering motion a fascinating but extremely complex pattern of interactions between the words on the page and multifarious domains of semantic possibility.

If it turns out, on the other hand, somewhere along the way—spoiler alert!—that the answer to the question is no, we have to decide whether that constitutes a theological *problem* or a christological *opportunity*. Probably the scope of our study is too restricted for a negative outcome to be regarded as a serious threat to classical trinitarian belief, which has several other biblical and theological legs to stand on. In that case, the particular line of enquiry may appear to be a dead end. There is no further need to speculate about the manner of Christ's pre-existence or the provenance of the belief; let us get on with more useful tasks. But there must be a reason why the passages under consideration have lent themselves to the development of that conviction. Among them are some key texts for Pauline Christology—Gordon Fee, for example, highlights the general importance of 1 Cor 8:6, Phil 2:6–11, and Col 1:13–17.[2] If it turns out that the pre-existence of Christ is not at issue here, how does a rethinking of these texts contribute to our understanding of the story that Paul was telling or the agenda that he was pursuing? What does a negative conclusion contribute to our understanding of his Christology? That question would certainly need to be pressed.

I have a few other informal observations to make about method as we travel to the exegetical coal face to dig out an answer to our question—an obsolescent metaphor, in this day and age, if ever there was one. First, Fee begins his study of Paul's Christology—an investigation into the *person* of Christ—by registering a number of methodological difficulties. The first is that Paul makes no distinction between who Christ was or is and what Christ did. The *work* of Christ, however, is defined immediately in soteriological

2. Fee, *Christology*, 16–20.

terms: "If Christ is the singular passion of Paul's life, the focus of that passion is on the saving work of Christ."[3] That seems to me already to have stumbled into the ditch which is the fourth difficulty identified by Fee—namely, that "One can hardly, nor should one be expected to, come to these letters with a *tabula rasa*, a clean slate that has no presuppositions."[4] Why emphasize the *past* saving event of Christ's death? Why not the *future* convulsive event of his inheritance of the nations? My own core presupposition, in this respect, is that the good news that Paul proclaimed, first to Jews, then to gentiles, across the Greek-Roman world—the *oikoumenē*—was that the God of his fathers was preparing to overthrow the old pagan hierarchies and establish a new political-religious order through and in his Son.[5] This entails a narrowing of perspective: I take it that Paul is thinking *historically and contingently* for the most part, not cosmically and universally, and that this has important implications for his Christology. The view will be tested along the way to some extent, but the reader should be aware that this perspective on Paul's "singular passion" frames the study from the outset.

To be sure, the Jewish apostle says that "Christ died for *our* sins"— perhaps specifically for the sins of *his* people (1 Cor 15:3; cf. Gal 4:4). It is not his death, however, but his resurrection from the dead that is proclaimed and is critical for the faith of those who believe in him, because it is the condition for a series of future events: the "day of our Lord Jesus Christ," his *parousia*, the resurrection of the dead in Christ at the *parousia*, the reign of Christ in the midst of his enemies, the final dissolution of all rule, authority, and power, the destruction of the last enemy, death, and the transfer of the kingdom back to God the Father so that he "may be all in all" (1 Cor 1:8; 15:12, 22–28). The exemplary faith of the Thessalonians slots neatly into this storyline: at considerable risk they have abandoned their idols to "serve the living and true God, and to wait for his Son from heaven, whom he raised from the dead, Jesus who delivers us from the wrath to come" (1 Thess 1:9–10). The gentile saints in Rome have come to glorify God for his mercy to his people and actively to put their hope in the "root of Jesse" who eventually *will rule the nations* (Rom 15:8–12). In this narrative the saving death of Jesus is, frankly, of secondary importance: it

3. Fee, *Christology*, 1–2. We have a similar problem with the complaint of Bowman and Komoszewski that "if Christ did not exist before his human life, then he is a revelation of the nature of God only in the sense that in his words and actions we see how God wants us to live" (*Putting Jesus*, 82). That begs more than one question. Did Paul understand it to be the purpose of Christ to reveal the nature of God? Was Christ sent to Israel in order to show us how to live?

4. Fee, *Christology*, 4.

5. See Perriman, *Future of the People of God*.

ensured the survival and expansion of God's people, it nullified the sting of death for those who followed him, but the real goal, the real hope, the real object of faith, was future régime change and the concomitant transformation of the ancient world.

Secondly, while we are on the subject of presuppositions, Crispin Fletcher-Louis expresses a common opinion: "Time and again, a high Christology . . . in Paul is presented as a presupposition that Paul assumes his readers will share."[6] In addition to the not-entirely-frivolous quibble that the whole point of a presupposition is that it is *not* "presented," there is the serious methodological question of how we are to infer the nature and shape—indeed, the very existence—of such a presupposition if it is nowhere stated or discussed. Some time back Jerome Murphy-O'Connor raised concerns about the *Vorverständnis* or pre-understanding of exegetes for whom the notion of pre-existence in Phil 2:6 "seems to be derived from an uncritical acceptance of the current consensus, an acceptance that is facilitated by the dogmatic understanding of Christ as the Second Person of the Trinity . . . ."[7] I am not much occupied with the hermeneutical—or indeed theological—problem in this book; my interest is much more in the storytelling. But the question will lurk disconcertingly in the background.

It *could* be an assumption of Paul's argument in 1 Cor 8:6, for example, that Christ has always been part of the divine identity as it is expressed in the Shema (Deut 6:4). But the verse could equally presuppose the belief that the risen Christ has been *given* the authority to exercise certain functions associated with "lordship." The question is: which of these two presuppositions has the best textual support? Oddly, we are then in the position of having to weigh the unstated presupposition of Christ's preexistence against the quite extensive, if debated, evidence in Paul and in the New Testament generally that Christ became the "one Lord" on the basis of his resurrection from the dead (e.g., Matt 28:18; Acts 2:36; Rom 14:9; 1 Cor 15:27; Phil 2:9–11; Eph 1:20–21; Heb 2:8; 1 Pet 3:22). We are left wondering why Paul thought it necessary to affirm explicitly and to defend at some length the resurrection and exaltation of Christ (Rom 1:4; 6:9; 4:24–25; 1 Cor 6:14; 15) but felt that he could safely *assume* that his readers agreed with him about Christ's pre-existence and incarnation, which certainly were not explicit elements in the gospel that he preached (1 Cor 15:1–5; Rom 1:1–4; Gal 1:11–16; 1 Thess 1:9—2:2).

6. Fletcher-Louis, *Christological Origins*, 34; cf. Fee, *Christology*, 92, 500–501.

7. Murphy-O'Connor, "Anthropology," 31. He quotes Bartsch: "To see the oldest evidence of this idea in the Christ hymn is scientifically justifiable only when all other possible interpretations have been exhausted." Also Wanamaker, "Philippians 2:6–11," 179.

Thirdly, setting aside those texts that say "all things" were made through or in Christ (1 Cor 8:6; Col 1:15–16), and which need to be discussed, it appears that Paul's interest in the original act of creation is rather limited. In Rom 1:19–25 creation is a given reality which for the Greeks has served not as a window on to the "power and divinity" of the creator but as a source of materials for the manufacture of idols. It is an argument not about the *beginning* of creation but about its subsequent misappropriation by a particular culture.[8] Created things hope to be liberated from their captivity to such futility and corruption and to share in the "freedom of the glory of the children of God" (Rom 8:19–22). Paul knows that the woman was created from and for the man (1 Cor 11:8–9), but he is more interested in the "new creation" and "new things" that have come about in Christ (2 Cor 5:17; Gal 6:15; cf. Eph 2:10, 15; 3:9; 4:24). He shows no interest in making inferences from his future-oriented program to answer questions about how the cosmos first came into existence. The point here is that we would expect even a *presupposed* pre-existence to entail an active conceptual framework, one that makes sense in relation to the structures and trajectories of Paul's predominantly eschatological outlook.

Fourthly, it hardly needs to be said that the purported pre-existence statements are made in the context of Paul's mission among Jews and gentiles in Asia Minor and Greece. But the implications of that may be less obvious. On the one hand, Paul proclaimed a risen and exalted Lord, who through the Spirit could be powerfully present to believers but who existed invisibly in heaven in a "spiritual body" (1 Cor 15:42–46). For gentiles, but perhaps also for most Jews who listened to Paul, the prior career of the prophet-messiah from Nazareth—going back a few years now—was of little relevance. At least, from where they stood in time and space any journey of retrospective enquiry would arrive first, perhaps with something of a jolt, at the life and actions of an early first-century Jew in far off Palestine, who appeared to have had little interest in the world beyond Israel's borders. Here was the immediate unknown quantity, the dark fog seen in the rear-view mirror from which the movement had emerged—the *pre-existence* of the now exalted Christ. On the other hand, we may need to allow for the possibility that Paul's language about the Christ in whom many non-Jews now believed reflects a distinctly non-Jewish perspective, not so much because he has reworked a primitive Jewish Christology in Hellenistic categories, but because he occasionally had *rhetorical* cause to view Christ through pagan or post-pagan eyes. We have no access to the minds of the Greek converts in the Pauline churches, but it is likely that

---

8. See Perriman, *Future of the People of God*, 32–36; Perriman, *End of Story*, 93–96.

their intuitive take on the historical Jesus diverged from the standard Jew-ish-Christian witness—and in ways that may still surprise us if my reading of Phil 2:6–8 has anything to recommend it.

Finally, much of the exegetical discussion considered proceeds on the basis of analysis of more or less relevant Jewish and Greek literary materials. The methodology is unavoidable, but I find that texts are not always read well. No doubt I will make my own mistakes, but it seems important to justify the extensive and sometimes quite detailed reading of the disparate sources. Accuracy is obviously important, but such reading is also the only means we have, within the limits of this sort of research, to reconstruct the imaginative world of Paul and his Jewish and Greek readers—to get a *feel* for how the language worked. The aim, therefore, will be as much to evoke the *stories*—the heaving sea of stories—in which the language is at home as to pin down lexicological relationships, as much to grasp the *manner of the storytelling* as to fix conceptual boundaries.

All that said, I will take a rather conventional exegetical approach to the interpretation of the relevant texts: I will present and evaluate the arguments of those who defend the idea of Christ's pre-existence in one form or another, and affirm, amend, or provide a counter proposal where appropriate.

On two occasions Paul says that God "sent" his Son, to be "born of woman" and "in the likeness of sinful flesh" (Gal 4:4; Rom 8:3). He does not say that God sent the Son *from heaven into the world*, but it has appeared to many commentators that these assertions *presuppose*—that word again—an incarnational Christology. The detailed arguments will be considered in chapter 2.

In chapter 3 we look at a small group of disparate texts under the ru-bric of the "eschatological wisdom of God." It has become a widely held view in recent years that in 1 Cor 8:6 Paul has deliberately assimilated Christ, as the one Lord through whom all things came into being, into the Shema, the foundational confession of the oneness of Israel's God. The identification of the "spiritual Rock that followed them" with Christ in 1 Cor 10:4 is often interpreted quite literally as an assertion of the presence of Christ with the Israelites in the wilderness. The statement in 2 Cor 8:9 that Christ was rich but became poor has been read as a metaphor for the incarnation. Finally, it has been suggested by some that in 1 Cor 15:47 and Rom 10:6–7 Paul's argument entails the prior existence of a "heavenly man," who then appeared on earth as Jesus. The assertion in Col 1:15–16 that "all things" were created in, through, and for Christ might have been considered here, but given the reservations about authorship it seems better to deal with it separately; and in certain respects, it will provide a fitting narrative climax to our study.

We then come to the most important text for this debate—the statement in Phil 2:6-7 concerning Christ Jesus, "who, though he was in the form of God (*en morphēi theou*), did not count equality with God a thing to be grasped, but emptied himself, by taking the form of a servant, being born in the likeness of men." That is how the ESV renders the long relative clause, and we will have to make do with it for now. But translation is fraught with difficulty at every turn, and it will take us chapters 4 to 7 just to work through the interpretation of the phrase *en morphēi theou*. Is it a reference to some essential aspect of the being of God? Is the thought perhaps of Christ's earthly or heavenly human form? Does it presuppose a heavenly archetype such as an angel or the "Son of Man" figure of Jewish apocalyptic thought? Or should we abandon the traditional view that this is the form of the one God and suppose instead that *en morphēi theou* means "in the form of *a god*"? In chapter 8, I will point out an overlooked but crucial implication of Roy Hoover's argument about the idiomatic meaning of the *harpagmos* clause (translated in the ESV as "did not count equality with God a thing to be grasped") and then consider how we might reconstruct the circumstances under which Jesus made this fateful decision.

I will refer both to the Philippians passage and to Col 1:15-20, in chapter 9, as encomia rather than as "hymns," though I recognize that this somewhat prejudges the question of whether a divine or human figure is being praised. In his recent study of the "christological hymns" in the New Testament Matthew Gordley acknowledges with respect to the Philippians text that "if one does not see preexistence in the opening lines, then . . . one would need to conclude that this was an encomium of an exalted human rather than a *hymnos*." Indeed, he makes the point later that "this praise of Jesus follows the pattern for an encomium."[9] In the Colossians passage Christ is described as "image of the invisible God," "firstborn of all creation" or "of every creature," and as the one in, through, and for whom "all things were created." Each of these epithets has been understood to allude to or assert his pre-existence. I keep an open mind about the authorship of Colossians, but the thinking expressed in it seems sufficiently Pauline in character to treat the passage as a continuation of our reading of the undisputed texts.[10]

In the final short chapter I will endeavor to pull together the findings and ask about the implications for our general understanding of Paul's Christology and mission.

9. Gordley, *Christological Hymns*, 95, 99-100.

10. See Pascuzzi, "Reconsidering," for a cautious defense of Pauline authorship on the grounds that "Paul's letters were occasional and that they were collaborative creations."

My own translations of ancient texts are marked with an asterisk beside the reference and should be treated with some suspicion—as, of course, should all translations. Unless otherwise stated, I have used the ESV for biblical texts; NETS for the Septuagint; C. D. Yonge, *The Works of Philo, Complete and Unabridged*; W. Whiston, *The Works of Flavius Josephus, Complete and Unabridged*; J. H. Charlesworth, *The Old Testament Pseudepigrapha*; *The Dead Sea Scrolls: A New English Translation*, edited by M. O. Wise, M. G. Abegg Jr., and E. M. Cook; and the online Loeb Classical Library for most other Greek and Latin texts. Translations from original German and French works are also mine.

2

The Son Sent to Israel

ON TWO OCCASIONS PAUL speaks, in strikingly parallel fashion, of God sending his Son.[1] According to the condensed argument of Gal 4:1–7, God sent out his Son 1) in the fullness of time, 2) "born of a woman, born under the Law," 3) to redeem those under the Law 4) from servitude under the Law, so that 5) they might share in his sonship, and 6) receive the Spirit of the Son, and 7) cry, "Abba! Father!" The same narrative may be assembled from Rom 5–8: God sent his Son 1) at the right time (Rom 5:6), 2) "in the likeness of sinful flesh" (8:3), 3) to set free those subject to the Law of sin and death (8:2) 4) from servitude under the Law (cf. Rom 7:1–6), so that 5) they might become "sons of God" 6) by virtue of the Spirit of Christ, which dwells in their hearts and 7) enables the cry, "Abba! Father!" (8:9–17).

Several reasons—also seven, coincidentally—have been put forward for thinking that the "sending formula" in these two passages presupposes the pre-existence of the Son.[2] 1) The phrase "in the fullness of time" is sometimes thought to have a supra-historical frame of reference that invites a transcendent understanding of the sending of the Son. J. Louis Martyn argues that "the Son's sending is an invasion of cosmic scope, reflecting the apocalyptic certainty that redemption has come from outside, changing the very world in which human beings live, so that it can no longer be identified simply as 'the present evil age' (Gal 1:4). In this sense the Son

---

1. Hengel emphasizes the syntactical parallelism between the two statements (*Cross*, 10–11).

2. Fee, *Christology*, 214–16, 245–47; Ridderbos, *Paul*, 68–69; Gathercole, *Preexistent Son*, 28–29. Hurtado lists Gal 4:4 as one of a small number of passages in the undisputed letters which "reflect and presuppose the idea of Jesus' preexistence" in the view of an "overwhelming majority of scholars" (*Lord Jesus Christ*, 119). For German opinion see Kuschel, *Before All Time*, 272–73. Söding says that the sending statements are unrelated to the "pre-existence Christology" of 2 Cor 8:9 and Phil 2:6 in terms of tradition history but "in the context of Paul's theology acquire pre-existence-Christological implications" ("Gottes Sohn," 66).

is an other-worldly figure who has his origin in God."[3] 2) The compound verb *exapostellō* in Gal 4:4, translated by Simon Gathercole as "send forth," is reckoned to give "a much stronger impression of mission from God or from the heavenly council."[4] 3) This "sending out" of the Son is followed by the "sending out" of the Spirit (Gal 4:6), and it has seemed natural to think that in both cases the sending is from heaven. Much has been made of the parallel with the sending out of wisdom followed by the sending of the Holy Spirit in Wisdom of Solomon 9:10, 17. 4) That God sends emphatically "his *own* Son" (Rom 8:3) has been taken to indicate an especially intimate relationship or a "significant degree of similarity" between God and Jesus.[5] 5) Fee argues that the use of *genomenon* in the two participle clauses in Gal 4:4 ("*genomenon* from a woman, *genomenon* under the Law") suggests "coming into existence" rather than simply "being born."[6] 6) The expressions "*genomenon* of a woman" and "in the likeness of sinful flesh" have been understood in incarnational terms. If the sending is associated with the *birth* of Jesus, then it is likely to entail, in the words of Pannenberg, an "entering into earthly circumstances and relations . . . . Sending thus presupposes preexistence."[7] Scholars have found it difficult otherwise to account for what appears to be a statement of the obvious.[8] 7) Moreover, the clauses are likely to be "posterior to the main verb": Jesus is first sent, then he comes into existence. To reverse the order, Fee thinks, would miss the point of the statement: "God's Son was sent into our human condition precisely because only thus could redemption be effected." We will consider these arguments in order but then also ask whether Paul's sending formula owes anything to Jesus' parable of the vineyard, as a reworking of the biblical tradition of the prophets sent in vain to uncooperative Israel (2 Chr 36:15–16; Jer 7:25–26).

In the Fullness of Time

The sending out of the Son in Galatians comes as the climax to a narrative about Israel's subjection to the Law as to a guardian, which in Paul's mind

3. Martyn, *Galatians*, 408; cf. Waddell, *Messiah*, 121–22.

4. Gathercole, *Preexistent Son*, 29; cf. Waddell, *Messiah*, 122.

5. Yarbro Collins and Collins, *King and Messiah*, 120; Fee, *Christology*, 245–46.

6. Fee, *Christology*, 215–16; cf. Bates, *Gospel Allegiance*, 52.

7. Pannenberg, *Systematic Theology* 2, 369n133, drawing on Hahn. Gathercole thinks that "in the likeness of sinful flesh" suggests that "in the action of the Father's sending, the Son takes on a condition (the flesh) which he had not previously possessed" (*Preexistent Son*, 29).

8. E.g., Fee, *Christology*, 215: "What is striking about the phrase 'born of a woman' is how unnecessary it is to the argument as a whole"; cf. Betz, *Galatians*, 207.

was tantamount to slavery (Gal 3:19—4:4). This climax is also the coming of the "fullness of the time"; and we recall from 1:4 that the redemption of those under the Law by Jesus' death was a deliverance "from the present evil age." How we understand this temporal aspect of Paul's argument has some bearing on the interpretation of the sending out of the Son. If this is taken to be a pivotal moment in cosmic time—in F. F. Bruce's words, the "nodal point of salvation-history"—it is likely that we will construe the sending as an event "from outside," as Martyn says.[9] There are reasons, however, to prefer a more down-to-earth, historical understanding of this critical point in time.

In Jewish usage analogous statements about the fullness or fulfilment of time invariably have reference to existing or foreseeable historical circumstances. Jeremiah is told that the land will be desolate and the people will be "slaves among the nations seventy years." But at the "fulfilment" of the 70 years God will punish the Babylonians and "make them an everlasting waste" (Jer 25:12 LXX); and when the 70 years are about to be "fulfilled," he will visit the exiles and bring them back to the land (Jer 36:10 LXX = 29:10 MT). This already constitutes a substantial parallel to Paul's narrative in Galatians: a period of slavery is fulfilled and brought to an end when God acts to redeem his people, the main difference being that for Paul God does not visit in person but sends out his Son for the purpose.

For Daniel the "hours of the time of completion" comes after a protracted seventy weeks of years, with a detailed historical dénouement in view (Dan 8:19*, 9:24–27 LXX). The thought is reproduced widely in the apocalyptic literature with reference to the hope that the current oppression of Israel will be ended and Jerusalem glorified among the nations. Enoch tells his son, for example, that those who keep the Law in the last days must "wait patiently in all the days until (the time of) those who work evil is completed, and the power of the wicked ones is ended" (1 En. 108:2; cf. Tob 14:5; 4 Ezra 4:23–37; 7:28; 2 Bar. 29:8—30:1; 39:1—40:3). The conviction that the Dead Sea community has come into existence "at the time appointed" or "for the times appointed" and that a tumultuous end to the current evil conditions is coming "at the times appointed" is found throughout the Qumran texts (e.g., 1QHa 7:27–30; 1QS 4:18–19, 22–23; 1QM 1:8–10; 3:7; 14:4–5, 13–18; 1QpHab 7:1–17).

In the context of Paul's argument about the provisional jurisdiction of the Law, "the fullness of *the* time" should signify the moment when this period of Israel's history was brought to an end by the sending out of the

9. Bruce, *Galatians*, 194. For a more detailed statement of the argument here see my forthcoming *CBQ* article "When the Fullness of the Time Came: Apocalyptic and Narrative Context in Galatians."

Son to "redeem those under the Law" (Gal 4:5*). The *chronology* of the argument is too strong to suppose that in verse 4 Paul switches abruptly from a historical to a supra-historical time frame: 430 years elapsed from Abraham to the giving of the Law, which was to remain in force until "the seed to whom it was promised should come" (Gal 3:19*, 24); and throughout this time of minority the Jews were held captive under an enforced guardianship or tutelage, being little better off than the Greeks, who "were enslaved to things which by nature were not gods" (Gal 4:8*). In effect, "the fullness of the time" is the "date fixed by the father" for terminating the administration of the Law.[10] The sending out of the Son to redeem those under the Law, therefore, is on a par with the original sending out of Moses (Exod 3:12) as a mediator between YHWH and his people (Gal 3:19).

The expression "the present (*enestōtos*) evil age" in Gal 1:4 should also not be read as a reference to the whole of fallen human history—the "totality of human life dominated by sin and opposed to God."[11] The thought is not the same as in Gal 4:4, but it introduces the idea of a *current* crisis at the outset that disposes us to reframe the whole argument of the letter historically. The perfect participle *enestōtos* already suggests that the evil that defines this age is a *recent* development. It distinguishes the period not only from what will come after but also from what went before.[12] This is the sense in 1 Cor 7:26, where *tēn enestōsan anagkēn* means either the distress that is about to come or the distress that has recently come upon them, because it has to account for the novel recommendations about marriage. The contrast between "things present" (*enestōta*) and "things to come" (*mellonta*) puts the emphasis on the currently experienced circumstances (Rom 8:38; 1 Cor 3:22). The author of 2 Thessalonians warns his readers not to be taken in by any communication to the effect that "the day of the Lord has come (*enestēken*)" (2 Thess 2:2); and in the last days, "there will come (*enstēsontai*) times of difficulty" (2 Tim 3:1).[13]

10. Gourgues argues that Paul uses *chronos* because he has in mind the completion of a period of time, specifically the period of Israel's subjection to the Law ("Plénitude," 103–4). He cites a number of papyri in which *chronos* is used with *plēroō* to speak of the fulfilment of the term of a loan. It is incorrect, therefore, to understand Gal 4:4 in an absolute sense "as a sort of summit in the design of God."

11. Fung, *Galatians*, 41.

12. According to BDAG s.v. ἐνίστημι 337, *enistēmi* has reference especially to "circumstances prevailing or impending, with contextual stress on the temporal feature of someth. taking place in a sequence."

13. The division of the sanctuary into two sections is a "parable for the present time (*ton kairon ton enestēkota*)" (Heb 9:9*). This "time" is either the period of the temple's existence or the present transitional period: "By this the Holy Spirit indicates that the way into the holy places is not yet opened as long as the first section is still standing" (9:8).

This seems invariably to be the case with *enistēmi* in temporal expressions. In the Septuagint it is used for the year or month or winter that has now come upon people (1 Kgs 12:24; 1 Esd 5:46; 9:6; 13:6; 4 Macc 2:8), war coming upon a nation (1 Macc 8:24; 12:44), the misery that came upon the Jews (2 Macc 6:9), and the present crisis (*tois enestōsin*) provoked by Ptolemy's determination to enter the sanctuary of the temple (3 Macc 1:16). Josephus speaks of the time of a feast being "at hand" (*enstasēs*) (*Ant.* 13:304; cf. 17:213). The phrase "in the present time" (*en tōi enestōti kairōi*) is contrasted with "in the time past" (*Ant.* 16:162). Physical sensations, according to Philo, have their existence "solely with reference to the present moment (*kata ton enestōta chronon*)," as distinct from past or future events (*Alleg. Interp.* 2 42). The "present time" (*ton enestōta . . . chronon*), in which God speaks to Abraham, is contrasted with the future revelation of that which is promised (*Migration* 43). Harvests and seasons "happen" (*enistatai, enstēi*) at a particular time of the year (*Spec. Laws* 1 183, 186). There is nothing remotely dualistic about the usage: these are moments and periods in ordinary linear time.

I think we must say, therefore, that the sending of the Son happens not at some arbitrary, pivotal moment in human history but is contingent in two respects. It brings the period of "enslavement" to the Law as a system for the management of Israel's propensity to transgress to an end; therefore, there is no sense in gentile converts taking upon themselves the works of the Law. But more immediately, it is a response to the "present evil age" of pagan domination. God sends out his Son, an "offspring" of Abraham, to deliver his people from an especially dire period in Israel's history, analogous to the crises of apostasy, oppression, and resistance described in the apocalyptic texts. This was exactly the "right time" (*kata kairon*)—before it was too late, in other words—for Christ to die in hope of saving weak, ungodly, and antagonistic Israel from the wrath of God (Rom 5:6–9).

The sending out of the Son

The verb *exapostellō* normally means "send out" or "send away." Pharaoh, for example, must "send away the sons of Israel from his land" (Exod 6:11; frequently in Exod 3–14; 1 Sam 6:6; Philo, *Drunkenness* 77; *Confusion* 94). The somewhat archaic English translation "send forth" has a theological bias that risks prejudging the matter. In the Septuagint and literature of Hellenistic Judaism the instances of God sending out or away with *exapostellō* fall into a number of distinct categories.

1. God sends his people here and there, for one purpose or another. He sends them out from Kadesh-barnea to inherit the land (Deut 9:23); he sends David away (1 Sam. 20:22); he sends his people away to walk in their evil practices (Ps 80:13 LXX); he sends away priests captive and overthrows mighty ones (Job 12:19); he sends out his prisoners from the pit (Zech 9:11); he sends his people away to the land of the Chaldeans (Jer 24:5; cf. Bar 4:11; Pss. Sol. 17:12); he will send Hananiah away from the face of the earth (Jer 35:16).

2. Individuals are sent out to perform a specific task. God sends out Moses to bring his people out of Egypt (Exod 3:12; Ps 104:26 LXX; Mic 6:4); he sends out his messenger Samuel to select and anoint David (Ps 151:4 LXX); he sends out a prophet to the sons of Israel to address their fears regarding the Midianites (Judg 6:8); the angel of the Lord sends out Gideon to deliver Israel (Judg 6:14); God will send out those who have been saved (probably Jews) to the nations to declare his glory (Isa 66:19); he will send out insolent men against the Chaldeans (Jer 28:2 LXX).[14] Kings may be sent out by God for some political or military end: "in those days the Lord began to send out against Judah Rezin king of Syria and Pekah son of Remaliah" (2 Kgs 15:37*); the king of Egypt says to Josiah, "I have not been sent out against you by the Lord God, for my war is at the Euphrates" (1 Esd 1:25); and a certain king will be sent out from God against Nero to "destroy all the great kings and noble men" (Sib. Or. 5:106–9).

3. Prophets are commonly "sent out" to rebellious Israel. At the time of Zedekiah's rebellion against Nebuchadnezzar God "sent out by the hand of prophets, sending (*apostellōn*) his messengers early on," in the hope of saving the people and the sanctuary, but both the priests and the people of the land "kept mocking his messengers and disregarding his words and poking fun at his prophets until the Lord's wrath went up against his people until there was no cure" (2 Chr 36:15–16). Jeremiah will "go to all to whom I send you out" (Jer 1:7*). Ever since he brought his people out of Egypt, God has "sent out all my slaves the prophets to you by day, and early in the morning I also sent (*apesteila*), and they did not obey me" (Jer 7:25–26). God says to Ezekiel, "Son of man, I am sending you out to the house of Israel, those who are embittering me" (Ezek 2:3–4; 3:5). The remnant of the people listened to the words of the prophet Haggai, "as the Lord had sent him to them" (Hag 1:12). Zechariah says that when YHWH restores his scattered people to Jerusalem, the people "shall recognize that the Lord Almighty has sent me to you" (Zech 2:15 LXX = 2:11 MT; cf. 4:9). The Lord sends out words "by his spirit by the hands of the former prophets" (Zech

14. Oswalt, *Isaiah 40–66*, 688–89.

7:12; cf. Obad 1). God sends out his messenger (*angelon*), who will "oversee the way before me, and the Lord whom you seek will suddenly come to the shrine" (Mal 3:1). The *angelos* who is sent out is not the same as the *angelos* of the covenant who is coming to judge unrighteous Israel.[15]

4. Supernatural beings, either "real" or visionary, are sent out. Zechariah sees a man on a red horse with three others, who have been sent out to patrol the earth (Zech 1:8–11). The "chief captain" Michael is sent out to Abraham to comfort him (T. Ab. A 8:11), but this is part of an elaborate narrative, in the style of a Hellenistic romance, in which Michael shuttles back and forth between heaven and earth. Similarly, Asenath blesses God, who sent out an angel ("the chief of the house of the Lord and commander of the whole host of the Most High") to rescue her from darkness and bring her into light (Jos. Asen. 14:8; 15:12). Conceivably, Peter's assertion that "the Lord sent out his angel and delivered me from prison" (Acts 12:11*) evokes a similar literary paradigm. More common is the use of the simple *apostellō* for the sending of an angel (e.g., Gen 24:7, 40; Exod 23:20; 33:2; 1 Chr 21:15; 2 Chr 32:21; Dan 3:95; 4:13, 23; 2 Macc 11:6; 15:22–23).[16]

5. Harm and well-being are sent out in various forms, both concrete and abstract, without any suggestion that they are sent *from heaven*. God sends out death among his people (Lev 26:25), "lack and hunger and exhaustion" (Deut 28:20), hornets against the Amorites (Josh 24:12), an evil spirit to stir up trouble between Abimelech and the men of Shechem (Judg 9:23), arrows to scatter his enemies (Pss 17:15; 143:6 LXX), help from Jerusalem (Ps 19:3 LXX), light and truth to lead the king (Ps 42:3 LXX), plagues and "his anger's wrath" among the Egyptians (Pss 77:45; 104:28; 134:9 LXX; cf. Exod 9:13; Philo, *Giants* 17), "satisfaction" to the souls of his people in the wilderness (Ps 105:15 LXX), a rod of his power from Zion to rule in the midst of his enemies (Ps 109:2 LXX), fire into the cities of Judah to devour their foundations (Hos 8:14; cf. Amos 1:4, 7, 12; 2:2, 5), death to Israel in the

---

15. The identity of the "messenger" is disputed. According to Verhoef, "Most interpreters agree that the 'messenger' would be a human being. They also identify him with Elijah, whom the Lord will send before the coming of his day and who then would reconcile fathers and sons . . ." (*Haggai and Malachi*, 287–88). Cf. Hill, *Malachi*, 265. For the view that the "messenger of the covenant" is the "angel of Yahweh," see Smith, *Micah-Malachi*, 328.

16. Otherwise, the semantic difference between *apostellō* and *exapostellō* seems slight. The compound form perhaps carries the idea either of sending *from a center or away into remote and scattered places* (cf. Exod 7:16; 11:17). But the difference may be no more than stylistic: see the parallel constructions in Esth 9:19, though the plural "to those nearby" with *exapostellontes* suggests that a wider sending *out* or distribution is intended; and Jer 7:25 LXX (cf. 2 Chr 36:15–16): "I have also sent out (*exapesteila*) all my slaves the prophets to you by day, and early in the morning I also sent (*apesteila*) . . . ."

wilderness in the manner of the plagues in Egypt (Amos 4:10), a famine of hearing the word of the Lord (Amos 8:11), grain, wine, and oil for his people (Joel 2:19), locusts against them (Joel 2:25), and deadly snakes (Jer 8:17). He sends out his "four grievous punishments, sword and famine and harmful animals and death" upon Jerusalem (Ezek 14:21), a curse against the priests (Mal 2:2), and a commandment to the priests (Mal 2:4). God will send out his spirit, and living things will be created to renew the face of the earth (Ps 103:30 LXX). Fire is sent out from above to destroy mountains and woods (Ep Jer 61). An owl is sent out by God as a sign that Agrippa will soon be released from captivity and "promoted to the highest dignity and power" (Josephus, *Ant.* 18:200). Only occasionally does God send out help explicitly "from on high" to save the king (Pss 17:17; 56:4; 143:7 LXX).

6. Lastly, Solomon asks God to "send out" wisdom from heaven and from his glorious throne, "that, being present with me, she may labor with me and that I may learn what is well-pleasing before you, for she knows all things and understands them and will guide me prudently in my actions and guard me with her glory" (Wis 9:10). The relevance of this important passage for the interpretation of Gal 4:4 will be considered in a moment.

The Sending Out of Moses

Given the context in Galatians and several references to the "sending out" of Moses in the Septuagint, we should consider whether Paul's language is to be explained by a typological relationship between these two figures. Commentators often find here a reworking of the exodus motif, but the redemption of Gal 4:4 is not simply a repeat of the exodus.[17] In Paul's argument, deliverance from Egypt resulted in the imposition of the Law and a long period of enslavement or tutelage. The sending out of God's Son, therefore, *undoes the damage* done at the time of the exodus; it *brings to an end* the period of enslavement that began when the Law was imposed on Israel "because of the transgressions" (Gal 3:19*).[18] Nevertheless, there is a case for thinking that Moses has constituted for Paul a paradoxical *type* for Jesus in such a way as to account for the language of sending out to redeem. God sends out (*exapostellō*) Moses to bring the people out of Egypt (Exod 3:12); he "sent out (*exapesteilen*) Moses, his slave, and Aaron, whom he chose; he placed in them the words of his signs and of the wonders in the land of Ham" (Ps 104:26–27*

---

17. Wright confidently avers that anyone familiar with the literature of second temple Judaism will recognize that Gal 4:1–11 is a "compact exodus-story" (*Faithfulness*, 656); cf. Scott, *Adoption*, 162–65; Rastoin, "Freedom," 259–60.

18. Cf. Lee, *Preexistent Son*, 309.

LXX); he "sent out" (*exapesteila*) Moses when he redeemed (*elytrōsamēn*) the people from a house of slavery (Mic 6:4).[19]

Stephen's speech before the Council in Acts 7 provides an interesting perspective on an implicit correspondence between Jesus and Moses. Stephen makes the point that Israel at first rejected Moses as "ruler and judge," just as, implicitly, they had recently rejected Jesus. Nevertheless, God "sent (*apestalken*) him as both ruler and redeemer (*lytrōtēn*) by the hand of the angel who appeared to him in the bush" (Acts 7:34–35*). This is not quite Paul's language in Gal 4:4–5, but it is close, and the parallel can be developed further. Jesus, obviously, is the prophet like Moses whom God would raise up (7:37). More importantly, Moses spoke with the angel on Mount Sinai and took the "living oracles"—the Law "in ordinances (*diatagas*) of angels"; but the people refused to obey him, demanding instead that Aaron should make gods to go before them (7:35–41, 53*).

Whether or not Paul heard this diatribe (Acts 8:1; 22:20) or something like it, there are a number of points of contact with his argument in Galatians. In particular, he says that the Law was "added because of the transgressions"; it was "ordained through angels by the hand of an intermediary" (*diatageis di' angelōn en cheiri mesitou*), to function as a guardian "until the seed should come to whom it has been promised" (Gal 3:19*). The "transgressions" are usually understood in general terms, and there has been much debate over whether *charin* is to be understood to denote cause or purpose.[20] But the article may suggest that Paul has in mind *the* transgressions of Israel in the wilderness and particularly the worship of the golden calf (cf. 1 Cor 10:1–10). This gives sharper narrative focus to the idea of mediation. Philo says that Moses, having heard that the people had turned to "lawlessness" and had fashioned a god in the form of a bull, hurried down from the mountain to act as an "intermediary and mediator" (*mesitēs kai diallaktēs*) (*Moses* 2 165–66). In the account of the episode in Exod 32 God tells Moses that his people have acted *lawlessly*, that they have "quickly transgressed from the way which I commanded them," therefore God will destroy them and make a great nation of Moses instead (Exod 32:7–10* LXX). Moses mediates and intercedes on behalf of the people,

19. See Scott, *Adoption*, 165–69; Lee, *Preexistent Son*, 308–9. Scott draws attention to *Frg. Tg.* Exod 12:42, according to which, when the time for the redemption of the world has come, "Moses will go out from the midst of the wilderness to heaven and King Messiah from the midst of Rome," and both will lead the flock, suggesting that the royal messiah functions as a "Second Moses" (165).

20. See Martyn, *Galatians*, 354: "Because the basic meaning of transgression is the breaking of an established and recognized command, Paul surely thinks of the Law as antedating these transgressions and, indeed, very probably as producing them"; cf. Bruce, *Galatians*, 175; Fung, *Galatians*, 159–60; Longenecker, *Galatians*, 138–39.

asking God to remember his promise to the patriarchs. As a result the Lord is "propitiated (*hilasthē*) concerning the evil that he said he would do to his people," and Moses sets off down the mountain with the two tablets of witness (Exod 32:14* LXX). Conceivably, then, Paul thought of Moses as an intermediary (*mesitēs*) in the more complex sense that he mediated between Israel and YHWH at a time of existential crisis, and that the addition of the Law to deal with this stand-out expression of the disobedience of the exodus generation was an element in the mediation.

Jesus, therefore, the prophet like Moses (Acts 3:22; 7:37), the "seed" to come (Gal 3:19), was "sent out" from the theophanic event of his baptism both to redeem those under the Law and to become their ruler. Moses negotiated the beginning of the period of the Law, propitiating the anger of YHWH against the people of Israel. Jesus negotiated an exit from the Law, his death serving as a "propitiation" (*hilastērion*) (Rom 3:25) for the transgressions which again threatened a disobedient generation of Israel with annihilation in the present evil age. There is indeed a correspondence here, but it is a *reversal* of the exodus narrative, not a simple parallel. The argument is not that a new exodus is needed but that the regrettable state of affairs which the exodus *produced*—Israel under the custodianship of the Law—has come to an end. Israel's subjection to the Law is *like* slavery (the child is no better off than a slave), but it is a natural legal arrangement with a fixed term.

The Apocalyptic Revelation of the One Sent Into the World

In an extended comment on the sending of the Son in Gal 4:4, Martyn puts forward a developmental hypothesis: an early Christian sending formula, rooted in traditions about the sending of Moses and the prophets, first acquired connotations of the sending of an angel, Wisdom, or the Spirit, and then gained a distinctively "apocalyptic" sense in Paul's writings.[21] The ground for the apocalyptic extension is presented with some equivocation. Paul says that it pleased God "apocalyptically to reveal his Son to me" (Gal 1:16), which is taken to mean that the sending or revealing of the Son was an invasion of the cosmos by God in the person of Christ. The language, however, does not necessarily imply personal pre-existence. The more useful question is "whether Paul understands Christ to be a this-worldly figure or an other-worldly one." The answer, Martyn says, is both. Christ was "born of a woman," enslaved to cosmic powers, sent at one level in much the same way that the prophet-apostle Paul was sent (cf. 1:10), finally dying on the cross. But as an other-worldly character, his being sent into the whole cosmos to

21. Martyn, *Galatians*, 406–7.

"redeem from slavery all human beings" is unparalleled.[22] "In this sense the Son is a distinctly other-worldly figure who has his origin in God."

The argument appears to hang on two assumptions. The first is that in Galatians Paul conceived of the plight in cosmic terms. Martyn has already made the point that Paul has adapted the simpler "Jewish-Christian sending tradition" to the "issues at stake in Galatia."[23] Because sin is a matter of enslavement to cosmic powers, redemption must come from outside the cosmos. Campbell clarifies the soteriological rationale for the apocalyptic incursion: Christ can deal with humanity's bondage to sin only by entering it from outside, "then to carry it on to a point of utter extinction or termination on the cross." If the journey had begun in the world, under the conditions of bondage, it would appear to be a "story of self-help." Rather, "Paul seems to suggest at times that God has deigned to send his Son *into* this state from outside it . . . in order to rescue and liberate those trapped in it."[24] The second assumption is that in Galatians the "content of God's revelation proves to be in the first instance the Son whom God has sent invasively into the world."[25] Martyn takes it that in this letter *apokalypsis* signifies not "revelation" or "unveiling" but "an invasive act on God's part"—the sending of Christ and Christ's Spirit into the world.[26]

Neither assumption is tenable. First, it is not humanity subject to cosmic powers that is redeemed by the sending of the Son but Israel under the Law, struggling to deal with the turmoil of the present evil age.[27] Jewish obligation to the Law has turned out to be an instance of the larger enslavement of humanity to the *stoicheia* of the cosmos, which is why the whole arrangement needs to be brought to an end; but the narrative at this point centers on Israel. There is no logic of redemption in the Jewish Scriptures which says that the redeemer must *come from outside*; and in the New Testament the logic is that Jesus, who far from being an outsider was born under the Law, is *thrown out*, suffers "outside the gate in order to sanctify the people through his own blood" (Mark 12:8; Heb 13:12). Redemption is by expulsion rather than incursion. Secondly, there is no good reason not to think that the decisive *apokalypsis* of the Son to Paul (Gal 1:16) was the revelation of the "righteous one," who suffered and was

22. Martyn, *Galatians*, 407–8.

23. Martyn, *Galatians*, 166.

24. Campbell, "Story of Jesus," 108.

25. Martyn, *Galatians*, 158.

26. Martyn, *Galatians*, 144.

27. Against also Longenecker, *Galatians*, 170: "Set in the context of a fulfillment motif, the statement tells us that Jesus, God's Son par excellence, is the culmination and focus of all of God's redemptive activity on behalf of humanity."

vindicated, along the lines of Luke's account (Acts 9:4–5, 15; 22:7–8, 14, 21; 26:14–18).[28] The Son preached by Paul to the nations was from David according to the flesh and "appointed Son of God in power according to the Spirit of holiness from resurrection from the dead" (Rom 1:4*). It is an exaltation, not an invasion, that is *revealed*.

Conclusion

Most commonly in the Greek Old Testament and literature of second temple Judaism when *people* are "sent out," it is to fulfil a task, and the emphasis, accordingly, is not on the place *from which* they are sent but on the place *to which* they are sent. In a small number of cases the sending out is a banishment or liberation, and then the place *from which* they depart figures more prominently in the narrative: they are sent *from* their home, *from* their captivity. For example, Philo says that God sent out Adam from the "Paradise of happiness, to till the ground from which he had been taken" (*Alleg. Interp.* 1 96; cf. *Cherubim* 1).

On the basis of the literary evidence that we have, there is little reason to think that Paul's usage fits an established Hellenistic-Jewish type of the sending out (with *exapostellō*) of a heavenly person. There is nothing remotely suggestive of the literary character of the angelic missions in Testament of Abraham A and Joseph and Asenath. The sending out of Jesus, therefore, conforms most naturally to the pattern of a human person sent somewhere to carry out a divine commission—either a leader to deliver Israel from a predicament or a prophet to call Israel to obedience in the hope of averting catastrophe.[29] Besides, Paul has already said that it is a "seed" of Abraham who would come, not a heavenly figure (Gal 3:19). James Dunn says that the usage "underlines the heavenly origin of his *commissioning* but not of the one commissioned."[30] We notice, in par-

---

28. See, e.g., Betz, *Galatians*, 70–71; Bruce, *Galatians*, 92–93; Longenecker, *Galatians*, 31–32.

29. The close connection with the theme of the redemption of Israel from captivity to the Law makes it unlikely that the sending of Augustus (Horace, *Carm.* 1.2.29–52) or Romulus (Plutarch, *Rom.* 28.2.7–9) by the gods has had a bearing on Paul's language. Hengel notes that Horace is saying only that "he regards Augustus as a ruler sent by the gods," and that Plutarch draws on his Middle-Platonic doctrine of the migration of souls (*Cross*, 35–37).

30. Dunn, *Christology*, 39, his italics. See also Yarbro Collins and Collins, *King and Messiah*, 107 and n28, for the view that the sending out does not necessarily imply the pre-existence of the Son; Longenecker, *Galatians*, 170: "When considered part of a pre-Pauline confession, all that need be seen is a functional stress on God's commissioning of Christ to bring about the redemption of humanity"; and Tuckett, *Christology*, 51.

ticular, that the verb is used in accounts of the ineffectual sending out of the prophets as "slaves" to summon rebellious Israel to repentance (2 Chr 36:15–16; Jer 7:25–26; Ezek 2:3–4; 3:4–7).

The Sending Out of Wisdom

Solomon's prayer is that God will "send out" (*exaposteilon*) wisdom from his glorious throne "that, being present with me, she may labor with me and that I may learn what is well-pleasing before you." But he also asks the question a few lines later: "Who has learned your counsel unless you gave wisdom and sent (*epempsas*) your holy spirit from on high?" (Wis 9:10, 17). Does this account for the sequence in Gal 4:4–6*, as Eduard Schweizer and others have argued: "God sent out (*exapesteilen*) his Son . . . . God sent out (*exapesteilen*) the Spirit of his Son into our hearts . . . "?[31] Does it support the conclusion that the Son as embodied wisdom was sent from the same place as the Spirit?[32]

When Wisdom Comes Into the World

Solomon's request for wisdom and the spirit of wisdom to be sent out from the throne of God to labor with him and guide his actions (Wis 9:9–18) stands out against a two-part mythopoetic background. In the tradition Wisdom is, first, the enthusiastic agent of creation which—or who—subsequently sustains the cosmos (Prov 8:22–31). She is a radiant presence beside the throne of God (Wis 7:26; 9:4); she was in attendance at creation, and by her God "formed human beings to rule over the creatures that were

31. See Schweizer, "υἱός," 375–376: "Sending by God and the Son of God title are combined only in the realm of the logos and wisdom speculations of Egyptian Judaism. In fact the sending of the Son of God and the Spirit (Gl. 4:4–6) corresponds exactly to that of wisdom and the Spirit (Wis. 9:10, 17), while the interrelating of Son and sons (Gl. 4:6) may also be found in Philo . . . . Here, then, is the root of a very different idea of the Son of God in which the heavenly closeness of the pre-existent Son to God is decisive and constitutes His significance as the One sent down from heaven to earth." Kim says: "Once Jesus Christ, like Wisdom in Jewish speculation, is conceived of as having existed in heaven from the beginning, his appearance on earth—again like Wisdom—is naturally regarded as God's sending him or his descent from heaven" (*Origin*, 119). See also Chester, *Messiah*, 389–90; Wright, *Faithfulness*, 656–58, 671–72, 700–701, 877–78; Scott, "Comparison," 206; and the extensive discussion in Longenecker, *Galatians*, 167–70; and Longenecker, *Romans*, 694–95.

32. So Bruce, *Galatians*, 195: "If the Spirit was the Spirit before God sent him, the Son was presumably the Son before God sent him"; and Bowman and Komoszewski, *Putting Jesus*, 89.

made by you and to manage the world in holiness and righteousness and to pronounce judgment in uprightness of soul" (9:2–3, 9). But, secondly, God "poured her out upon all his works, among all flesh according to his giving, and he furnished her abundantly to those who love him" (Sir 1:9–10). She has descended from heaven, less as a principle of rationality than as practical moral and political wisdom, in search of a dwelling place on earth, with mixed success.[33] It is this second stage in the Wisdom myth that is of interest to us here.

Wisdom, in the view of the author of Baruch, is an undervalued commodity. The rulers of the earth have vanished, leaving no trace of their works, because they did not find wisdom (Bar 3:15–19). People of old did not understand the paths of wisdom—the Canaanites, the sons of Hagar, the merchants of Merran and Thaiman, the story-tellers and "seekers for intelligence" (3:20–23). God did not choose the giants, the mighty warriors, and "give them the way of knowledge"; therefore, they perished for lack of insight (3:24–28). Who has ascended into the sky, the author asks, to bring wisdom down or crossed the sea to trade gold for wisdom? "There is no one who is familiar with her way, nor one who thinks much about her path." Even Israel is in exile because the people have "forsaken the spring of wisdom" (3:9–12). But the creator God is familiar with wisdom; he "discovered her by his intelligence" and gave her to his servant Jacob; and after this, wisdom "appeared on earth and associated among humans" (3:29–38). Thus wisdom, or the "way of knowledge," is the "book of the commands of God and the Law which exists for the age" (4:1*). The author exhorts exiled Israel to turn and take hold of wisdom, to "pass through toward the shining in the presence of her light." What is pleasing to God has been made known to them; there is no need to give their glory and advantages to a foreign nation (4:2–4).

In a similar vein Ben Sirach has Wisdom declare in the divine assembly that she "came forth from the mouth of the Most High" and searched among the nations for a place to take lodging. The creator of all—including of wisdom—commanded her to encamp in Israel. So Wisdom "ministered before him in a holy tent" and subsequently was established in Jerusalem, where she "took root among a glorified people" (Sir 24:4–8*). The benefits of wisdom are also closely associated with Torah, which supplies abundant wisdom, understanding, and instruction (24:23, 25–27).

Similitudes of Enoch, however, tells a more pessimistic story. Wisdom "went out to dwell with the children of the people" but could find no dwelling place and was obliged to return and establish herself "among the angels."

---

33. See Hengel, *Cross*, 46–49.

Iniquity, on the other hand, "went out of her rooms, and found whom she did not expect," and dwelt with them (1 En. 42:1–3). This may be a misplaced passage,[34] but it appears to presuppose an expected judgment against the "sinners," against "those who deny the name of the Lord of the Spirits" (41:1–2; cf. 38:2). The reference is probably to foreign forces, in the first place, whose "devotion is to the gods which they have fashioned with their own hands," but may also include the rich and powerful in Israel, who will be given into the hand of God's elect on a future "day of burden and tribulation" (45:1–2; 46:7; 48:8–10). Under such troubled eschatological circumstances wisdom regains a purchase in the world. The prayers of the righteous "on behalf of the blood of the righteous ones which has been shed" will reach the Lord of Spirits, and judgment will be executed for them (47:1–4). The Son of Man or Chosen One, who was "concealed in the presence of (the Lord of the Spirits) prior to the creation of the world," will reveal the wisdom of God to the elect (48:6–7). "In him dwells the spirit of wisdom, the spirit which gives thoughtfulness, the spirit of knowledge and strength, and the spirit of those who have fallen asleep in righteousness" (49:3). The close association between spirit and wisdom is again worth noting, as is the reference to the spirit of the righteous whose blood was shed.

Wisdom is, therefore, appropriated by Israel in different ways, in keeping with the divergent perspectives of the traditions. It is embodied in the Law as the expression of a good way of life, without any suggestion that the Law pre-existed. The point has been made by Boccaccini, Murphy, and Collins, for example, that the identification of wisdom and Torah is asymmetrical: the fact that wisdom is concretized as Torah does not entail the eternal pre-existence of Torah. So John Collins notes that Torah does not become a cosmic principle in Sirach. "There are no poems describing how Torah came forth from the mouth of God or circled the heavens before creation. The point of the identification is to accredit the Torah as a valid concretization . . . of universal wisdom, not to attribute a cosmic role to Torah itself."[35] In the Enochic tradition personified Wisdom has been rebuffed by Israel but is revealed to the persecuted elect through a heavenly mediator at a time of eschatological upheaval. This is a wisdom—and

34. Nickelsburg and VanderKam, 1 Enoch, 55nb, locate 41:9—42:3 after 41:2.

35. Collins, Jewish Wisdom, 61; cf. Dunn, Colossians and Philemon, 89; Dunn, Theology of Paul, 274: "it was not so much that the law was preexistent as that preexistent Wisdom was now to be recognized as the law"; McGrath, Only True God, 45–46; Waddell, Messiah, 64–65. Waddell, Messiah, 131–32, summarizes Boccaccini's thesis that Hellenistic Judaism added to the Sapiential tradition, which understood wisdom as a creation of God and agent of creation, the idea that, in Boccaccini's words, Torah is "the historical embodiment of the heavenly wisdom."

spirit—therefore, that makes sense of the suffering of the righteous, in-
spires perseverance, and gives some insight into the eventual resolution
of the crisis. The relevance of this tradition for Christology will become
apparent later. The question to be considered here is whether Solomon's
request for wisdom to be "sent out" has any bearing on the interpretation
of the sending out of the Son in Gal 4:4.

The Sending Out of Wisdom and Spirit

There are a number of observations that I think we can make here. First,
wisdom is imagined as a woman present in the world, easily found by
those who judge and rule, "sitting at their gates" or along the path, if they
take the trouble to look for her (Wis 6:14–16). The wisdom that is sent out
from heaven, therefore, is manifested in human activity and expressed in
good governance in particular. It is an aspect of human intellection and
endeavour: wisdom begins with the desire for instruction (6:17), it is an
attribute of good kingship (6:20–21, 24), it is an "unfailing treasure for human beings," and those who get it are "commended for the gifts that come
from instruction" (7:14); God guides wisdom and instructs the wise, and
has given to Solomon "unerring knowledge" of the world (7:15–22). In
every generation wisdom "passes into holy souls and makes them friends
of God and prophets; for God loves nothing except the person who lives
with wisdom" (7:27–28). Wisdom is the "fashioner of all things that exist" because "understanding is productive" (8:6). Wisdom is exhibited in
self-control, intelligence, courage, the "subtleties of speech and the solu-
tions of riddles," understanding of the seasons, quick judgment, and the
accumulation of wealth (8:7–21).

Secondly, the writer has already spoken of wisdom as a "philanthrop-
ic spirit" (*philanthrōpon . . . pneuma*) and has received a "spirit of wisdom"
(Wis 1:6; 7:7; cf. Pss. Sol. 18:7; Isa 11:2). A good scribe will be filled with
"a spirit of understanding" and will "pour forth words of his wisdom"
(Sir 39:6). Wisdom is a prerequisite for understanding the mind of God.
Solomon asks: "Who has learned your counsel unless you gave wisdom
and sent (*epempsas*) your holy spirit from on high?" (Wis 9:17). This, he
explains, is how "the ways of those on earth were set right" (9:18), and he
goes on to give some examples: wisdom delivered Adam from his own
transgression, and six righteous individuals, along with examples of what
happens when people depart from wisdom (10:1–21). In other words,
God has intervened *on a number of occasions*, by giving wisdom and sending his Spirit, to teach people how to act rightly and so be delivered from

their predicaments. Spirit and wisdom are two sides of the same coin: they are concretely and practically experienced; they are expressed in speech and action, in the resolution of crises.

Thirdly, Wisdom of Solomon is explicit about the provenance of both wisdom and spirit ("from the holy heavens . . . from on high"); Paul expresses no interest in the place *from where* the Son and the Spirit are sent. Having been redeemed from the Law, the Galatian believers have acquired "adoption" and have received the Spirit of the Son who cried out, "Abba! Father!" in Gethsemane, meaning that they are no longer slaves to the *stoicheia* of the world but are heirs of God, who will *inherit*—by way of their own experience of anguish and doubt prior to suffering—the future rule of God, through his Son, over the nations (Gal 4:7; 5:21). In this context sonship has nothing to do with origin or with being "far closer to God than the others."[36] It has to do with inheritance, as in the parable: the son is sent from the same place as the servants to do the same work; he differs from the servants in that he is "beloved," which takes us back only as far as Jesus' baptism, and has an inheritance, which the wicked tenants think they may grab for themselves.

Fourthly, the parallelism of "sending out" the Son and "sending out" the Spirit of the Son is presumably not accidental, but what are we to infer from it? It may seem obvious that the Spirit is sent out from heaven (cf. Acts 2:33) and that this connotation should be read back into the sending out of the Son. But this is not a necessary inference, and arguably the reverse is the case: the sending out of the Spirit *is like* the sending out of the Son, because those who have been supplied with the Spirit (Gal 3:5) are bound to replicate the experience of the Son by crying, "Abba! Father!" The close association of the sending of the Spirit and the sending of the prophets in the face of Jewish obstinacy is evident in Zech 7:12* LXX: "they made their heart disobedient in order not to listen to my Law and my words, which the Lord Almighty sent out (*exapesteilen*) by his Spirit and by the hands of the prophets before, and there was great wrath from the Lord Almighty." This would go a long way towards accounting for Paul's language: the Spirit has been *sent out* to empower not only the prophet-like witness of the Son against Israel but also the witness of those who come to share in his sonship.

We remind ourselves that Paul is thinking *backwards* from the experience of the Galatians to the earthly life of Jesus. The gospel he preached to them came "through a revelation of Jesus Christ"—the exalted Son revealed to him as he went about his zealous persecution of the church of God (Gal 1:11–17). When they heard this message about a heavenly Son,

36. Martyn, *Galatians*, 406.

they believed it and *began with the Spirit* (3:2–3). The problem that this created for Paul was that the Galatians lacked an adequate back-story, and it was too easy for Jewish teachers, with all the authority of tradition, to come and persuade them that their faith needed to be merged with the existence of Israel under the Law. So Paul has to convince them both that Christ crucified has put an end to the Law and that their own experience must be grounded in the story of Christ crucified—to the extent that the Spirit of the crucified Son in them cries out, "Abba! Father!" when they share in his suffering (cf. 6:14). But the general point to make is that Paul only needs to bring to mind what happened *before the preaching of the heavenly Son and the sending of the Spirit.* The sending of the Son to Israel, born of woman, born under the Law, stands in contrast not with his dis-embodied, pre-Jewish existence in heaven but with the pneumatic, post-Jewish experience of converted gentiles. It is this dynamic which accounts for the parallelism between the sending out of the Son and the sending out of the Spirit of the Son.

Conclusion

In a study comparing the apocalyptic elements that Galatians and the Epistle of Enoch have in common, James Scott affirms Schweizer's argument about the sending of wisdom and concludes that "the incarnate Son of God him-self is the *embodiment* of the divine revelation of wisdom that is universal-ized and becomes the source of righteousness of the whole human race."[37] In fact, neither analogy supports such a universalization of the motif. On the one hand, the wisdom that Solomon seeks is a practical competence, a prerequisite of good government, which seems the least likely antecedent for the sending of the Son to redeem Israel. On the other, in Similitudes of Enoch an eschatological wisdom of faithful resistance dwells in the Son of Man figure and is given to the righteous because the normal wisdom em-bodied in Torah—the wisdom of good government—has departed, iniquity has found a place in Israel instead, and crisis has ensued. This is arguably more relevant for a reading of Paul, but then what we would have is not the incarnation of a pre-existent person but the actualization in the coming of Jesus of the *particular and peculiar* wisdom needed for Israel to be delivered from the present evil age. At this point in the story, therefore, we are some distance from the Hellenistic idea of the sending of "divine propagators of civilization, philosophers or other important people" or of a ruler such as

37. Scott, "Comparison," 206.

Alexander or Augustus.[38] The sending out of the *spirit of the Son*, then, ensures that the wisdom oddly exhibited in the catastrophic course of Jesus' career is now also actualized in those who believe in him, who are likewise sons, who will share both in his sufferings and in his inheritance. But this thought is barely perceptible in the text.

His Own Son

Does the fact that in Rom 8:3 God sends "his *own* Son" (*ton heautou huion*), rather than simply "his Son," involve a distinction between God's own pre-existent Son and his "son" Israel, as Fee maintains?[39] There is conceivably an implied contrast with the "sonship-giving" (*huiothesia*) that was Israel's (Rom 9:4), but this seems rather remote and does not, in any case, clearly require pre-existence. Contextually more appropriate would be the idea that God *took ownership* of Jesus in his suffering even though he appeared to his opponents to be a "sinner." Later in the chapter Jesus is "his own Son" (*tou idiou huiou*) who is not spared but is given up for all (8:32). Or the expression may anticipate the extreme circumstances under which the Son would cry out, "Abba! Father!" Perhaps more to the point, "his own Son" indicates the priority of Jesus in relation to those who are his brothers because they have received a "spirit of adoption (*huiothesia*)." To be "his own Son" rather than simply one of many "sons of God" is not to have pre-existed but to be the prototype for the suffering and vindication of others, the "firstborn among many brothers" (8:14, 28–29).[40]

The tradition may also have distinguished between the prophets sent to Israel as slaves of YHWH and the Son sent to Israel *from the same household* to do the work of a slave. The Chaldean historian Berosus, according to Josephus, describes how Nabolasar "sent his own son (*pempsas . . . ton huion heautou*) Nebuchadnezzar against Egypt, and against our land, with a great army" (*Ag. Ap.* 1:132*). The contrast here, presumably, is with other

38. See Zeller, "Christology," 324; Hengel, *Cross*, 33–36. Lee defines the distinction between the sending of wisdom to guide individuals and the sending of the Son to "die as a human actor" as one between inspiration and incarnation (*Preexistent Son*, 303). But the embodiment of an *eschatological* wisdom in a human actor who dies constitutes a third option, one which does not require the pre-existence of the Son.

39. Fee, *Christology*, 246–47; also Fitzmyer, *Romans*, 484–85.

40. Yarbro Collins thinks that "his own Son" could be "explained in terms of election, as God chose Israel" (Yarbro Collins and Collins, *King and Messiah*, 120), but the focus is eschatological and redemptive. According to Philo, Abraham was said "to have had many children, but did not see fit to call any of the others his own son (*huion autou*), except one" (*Rewards* 61*). The reflexive pronoun distinguishes the worthy from the unworthy.

military leaders who might have been sent, so Paul may only be emphasizing the fact (along the lines of Jesus' parable of the vineyard, which we will come to shortly) that this time God sent "his own Son" rather than one of his "servants" the prophets.

The Participle Genomenos

The participle *genomenos*, which occurs twice in Gal 4:4, has usually been understood as a straightforward reference to Jesus' "birth"—*born* of a woman, *born* under the Law. This interpretation has been questioned in support of the argument for Christ's pre-existence. Matthew Bates makes the case, in the first place, for *tou genomenou* in Rom 1:4, arguing that the participle from *ginomai* should be translated not "who was born" or "who was descended" but "who came into existence," directly signifying pre-existence.[41] Although *ginomai* can mean simply "be born," this is rare in the New Testament; the thought is usually of a "change in status or mode of existence" (emphasis removed). Two examples in Paul are thought especially to bear this out. That God sent his Son once the fullness of time had arrived (Gal 4:4) suggests to Bates that "for Paul, the Son already existed prior to the arrival of this fullness of time . . . , that is, during the time when humanity *en masse* was enslaved to 'the principles of the world.'" Also the phrase "having come into being under the law" is reckoned to imply that "the Son's true origin is outside the era of the Mosaic law." The second example is the expression *en homoiōmati anthrōpōn genomenos* in Phil 2:7, which Bates translates "coming into being in the likeness of humankind" (emphasis removed). In both these passages, it is argued, the participle signifies not the simple human birth of Jesus, for which *gennaō* would have been the more appropriate verb, but the change from a heavenly to an earthly existence.[42]

Several considerations seem to me to count against this line of thought. First, there are numerous examples in Hellenistic Jewish writings of the unremarkable use of *ginomai* with reference to the birth or coming into being of a person. In Gen 4:18* LXX *ginomai* and *gennaō* are used to translate the niphal and qal forms of the Hebrew *yalad* respectively: "to Enoch was born (*egenēthē*) Gaidad, and Gaidad fathered (*egennēsen*) Maiel . . . ." The language of Gen 21:3* is very close to Rom 1:3: "Abraham called the name of his son who was born (*genomenou*) to him, whom Sarah bore him, Isaac." Joshua "circumcised the sons of Israel born (*genomenous*) on the way in the

41. Bates, "Christology of Incarnation," 115; Bates, *Gospel Allegiance*, 51–53; see also Fee, *Christology*, 215–16.

42. Bates, "Christology of Incarnation," 116–17.

wilderness" (Josh 21:42). Solomon says of his own birth: "And I, having come into existence (*genomenos*), I drew in the common air . . . " (Wis 7:3*). Tobit says that God made Adam and gave Eve to him, and "from these came into being (*egenēthē*) the seed of humans" (Tob 8:6*). It is also common for the mother or lineage to be designated by the preposition *ek*: Shecaniah proposes to cast out the foreign women "and those born from (*ta genomena ex*) them" (Ezra 10:3* LXX); the third-century BC writer Demetrius the Chronographer makes reference to "those born from (*tōn genomenōn ek*) Keturah," of the family of Abraham, and to Jokshan, a son of Abraham "born from (*genomenou . . . ek*) Keturah" (Dem. 3:1; cf. Josephus, *Ant.* 2:257); Ishmael was "born to Abraham from (*genomenos ek*) the concubine" (Josephus, *Ant.* 1:214); the name Issachar signifies "one born from hire" (*ton ek misthou genomenon*) (*Ant.* 1:308); a slave may have "children born from (*genomenōn ek*) a slave woman" (*Ant.* 4:273); David was "born from" (*ek . . . genomenon*) such modest lineage as Ruth, Obed, and Jesse (*Ant.* 5:337); the Hyksos and "those born from them" (*tous ex autōn genomenous*) had possession of Egypt for more than five hundred years (*Ag. Ap.* 1:84).[43]

Bates is aware of this background but is more impressed by the sheer preponderance of instances in the New Testament where *ginomai* signifies not a person's birth but his or her *becoming something else*. But the question is how many of these *ginomai* statements might be understood to refer to a change of status *at the time of a person's birth*. The answer is not very many. There is a small number of instances where Paul uses *gennaō* clearly with reference to physical birth (Rom 9:11; Gal 4:23, 24, 29),[44] and perhaps two cases where he uses *ginomai* in contexts that could suggest that a person's birth is in view (Rom 1:3; Gal 4:4).[45] Given this parity and the well attested use of *ginomai (ek)* in Jewish-Hellenistic Greek to refer to the normal coming into being of a child there seems no reason to dismiss the traditional interpretation of *tou genomenou ek* as "born of" or "descended from." What is characteristically at issue in these statements with *ginomai* and *ek* is not the physical circumstances of the birth but the distinctive historical or genealogical relationship.[46] The construction is exactly right for locating Jesus' historical existence vis-à-vis David or Israel.

43. These examples contradict the claim made by Bates that *genomenon ek gynaikos* is exceptional "but explicable if the virgin birth is latent in the background" ("Christology of Incarnation," 117).

44. In three passages *gennaō* is used metaphorically (1 Cor 4:15; 2 Tim 2:23; Phlm 10).

45. Bates rightly discounts 1 Cor 15:47 ("Christology of Incarnation," 115–16n26), but there is also nothing in Phil 2:6–7 that elicits the thought of Jesus' birth.

46. Cf. Dunn, *Christology*, 40: "*Genomenon* (born) refers to Jesus as one who had

We have seen that it is not an argument for pre-existence that the Son came in the fullness of the time—that the temporal expression rather determines the troubled historical conditions under which the Son was "sent out" to redeem those under the Law. In neither Rom 1:3 nor in Gal 4:4 is there any indication of a change in status or mode of existence. Bates maintains that "according to the flesh" highlights "the Son's *transition* to the weak, frail, decaying state of fully embodied human existence within the messianic line of David."[47] But *kata sarka* qualifies not the coming into being directly but the whole idea that Jesus was from the seed of David in anticipation of the contrasting "according to the Spirit" in Rom 1:4. It does not signal an incarnational Christology; it denotes the original royal Jewish humanity of the one who would rule over the nations on the strength of a resurrected "spiritual" life (Rom 15:12; 1 Cor 15:44–46).

Paul later writes in Romans that "Christ has become (*gegenēsthai*) a servant of the circumcision for the sake of the truthfulness of God" (Rom 15:8*), but the template for this *becoming* is Ps 68:9–10 LXX: Christ made the conscious decision not to please himself but to suffer alienation and reproach for the sake of the God of Israel (Rom 15:3). In this case, *gegenēsthai* signifies a change of status *in the course of life*, again in response to a historical crisis. This is grammatically different from the *genomenos ek* construction of Rom 1:3 and Gal 4:4 and more like the "*genomenos* in the likeness of humans" clause in Phil 2:7, where the genealogical aspect is missing but the thought of a change of status is very much to the fore. Finally, in the context of Galatians, *genomenon hypo nomon* implies not that "the Son's true origin is outside the era of the Mosaic law," but that he lived as a Jew *before the era of gentile participation in redeemed Israel on the basis of Spirit rather than of Law.*

Born of a Woman in the Likeness of Sinful Flesh

If *genomenon* gives us no particular reason to highlight the birth of Jesus and even less some change of status, we still have to ask why Paul insists on the normal humanity of Jesus at this point. That Jesus was a "seed" of Abraham has been a significant part of the preceding argument (Gal 3:16, 19), but "born of a woman" does not connect him with Abraham's lineage in the way that "born under the Law" associates him with the Israel of Moses. Bart Ehrman takes it as evidence that Paul regarded Jesus as a pre-existent

been born, not necessarily to his birth as such."

47. Bates, "Christology of Incarnation," 117, 122.

angel: "What other option is there, exactly?"[48] Bates jumps on this: "why not the obvious, the incarnation of the *Son*?"[49]

Dunn also notes the problem: "If the natural implication of Paul's language was that he was referring to the man Jesus, whose ministry in Palestine was sufficiently well known to his readers, why bother to say that he was a man?" His solution is to highlight the soteriological aspect of Paul's argument. On the one hand, Jesus was sent to experience "the condition of man in all its inferiority and bondage" in order that humanity might be delivered from that condition. A Qumran text gives an idea of the likely force of the expression: "As what can he, born of a woman, be reckoned before You? Kneaded from dust, his body is but the bread of worms; he is so much spit, mere nipped-off clay—and for clay his longing" (1QS 11:21–22).[50] On the other hand, "born of a woman" is a reference not to the moment of Jesus' birth but to "a *state* prior to the decisive act of redemption."[51] But this still does not explain why Paul felt it necessary to stress the fact that Jesus was born of a woman under the Law. What is the alternative state of affairs that this is meant to counter? Even if the thrust of the argument is soteriological, it seems difficult to avoid the christological *implication* that he may otherwise be perceived not to have existed as one born of woman under the Law. I have argued that neither the sending out nor the participle *genomenon* introduces the thought of pre-existence, but from the broader perspective of Paul's mission to the gentile Galatians there may have been good reason for him to remind them that the *now* heavenly Christ, experienced through the Spirit which cries, "Abba! Father!" was once a player in Israel's story. The exalted Jesus *pre-existed* as an ordinary mortal Jewish male and as such was sent out to redeem those under the Law. Dunn may assume too much when he says that Jesus' ministry in Palestine was well known to Paul's readers.

In the parallel argument in Rom 8:3–4 the sending motif is again introduced at the point of transition between Law and Spirit. The Law was unable

48. Ehrman, *How Jesus*, 252–54, 267–69; page 267 for the quotation. Cf. Betz, *Galatians*, 207; Longenecker, *Galatians*, 166: "only the second of the participial clauses, 'born under the law,' is really germane to the argument of Galatians; the first, 'born of a woman,' is never discussed in the letter."

49. Bates, "Christology of Incarnation," 116n27.

50. Cf. Job 14:1; 15:14; 25:4; 1QHa 5:31–32; 21:2; 4Q428 f14:2; 4Q501 f1:5. In Matt 11:11 "those born of women" (*gennētois gynaikōn*) translates the Hebrew idiom (Hagner, *Matthew 1–13*, 306); LXX has *gennētos gynaikos* for the Hebrew *yelud 'ishah* in the Job texts. See Dunn, *Christology*, 40; Longenecker, *Galatians*, 171. This rather than a "latent" reference to the virgin birth explains the fact that only the female role is mentioned (against Bates, "Christology of Incarnation," 117). In the Qumran texts the thought of physical *formation* is more prominent.

51. Dunn, *Christology*, 40–42.

to give life to Israel because it was always frustrated by the flesh. So God did what the Law could not do: "having sent (*pempsas*) his own Son in the likeness of sinful flesh and for sin, he condemned the sin in the flesh . . . " (Rom 8:3*). Subsequently, the "requirement of the Law" is fulfilled by those who walk according to the Spirit. Does "in the likeness of sinful flesh" signify incarnation as traditionally assumed?[52] Is this a sending *from heaven*?

This is still part of an argument about Israel and the Law, addressed more or less expressly to Jews (cf. Rom 2:17; 3:1; 4:1; 7:1)—no doubt as a précis of countless synagogue debates—not about humanity and some abstract principle of existential bondage.[53] The "sin," therefore, to which Paul refers is the sin that in this "present evil age" has put Israel at enmity with God and subject to wrath (5:9–10). Although death reigned from Adam to Moses, it was only Israel which had the Law and whose sin, therefore, was counted (5:13–14; cf. 3:19). But if the narrative context may be narrowed in this way, then "in the likeness of sinful flesh" stands in contrast not to a non-fleshly pre-existent condition but to a less controversial, Torah-compliant messianic agency. What underpins Paul's argument here would be the concrete idea that Jesus *appeared to be a sinner* in the eyes of those whose responsibility it was to uphold Torah.[54] God sent his Son to Israel not as a blameless adherent of Torah but as an *outlaw*, a renegade, who in the end suffered the shocking humiliation of rejection by the Jewish authorities and execution on a Roman cross—indeed, he became a curse for the Jews because he was hung on a tree (Gal 3:13).[55] This is another way of talking

52. Byrne says that the motif "does not necessarily carry the implication that Christ had some form of personal existence ('preexistence') in the divine sphere 'prior' to his human history" but thinks that it is required by Gal 4:4 and 2 Cor 8:9 (*Romans*, 243).

53. See Perriman, *Future of the People of God*, 114. Jewett and Kotansky argue, against Hamerton-Kelly's claim that "flesh" equates to Jewish religious legalism or exclusionism, that while the Pauline doctrine emerged in the controversy about circumcision, it now "functions as a universal symbol for the crippling competition for honor that distorts every human endeavor" (*Romans*, 483). Byrne speaks of the goal of the divine sending "in terms of benefits for the human race" (*Romans*, 242–43).

54. This renders moot debate over whether *homoiōma* signifies identification or mere likeness with sinful flesh (see Branick, "Sinful Flesh," 248–50; Gillman, "Another Look"; Fitzmyer, *Romans*, 485). It is not ontology that is at issue but the perception of concrete behavior. The "likeness (*homoiōmati*) of the transgression of Adam, who is a type of the one to come," is the concrete expression of sinning as Law-breaking, which did not happen until the Law was instituted (Rom 5:14). In the same way, Jesus was a concrete instance—at least in appearance—of sinning as Law-breaking, condemned by the Law.

55. See Perriman, *Future of the People of God*, 113–14. That God "made him to be sin who knew no sin" (2 Cor 5:21) may presuppose this realistic background, as indeed the statement in the same passage that Christ was once known to Jews like Paul "according to the flesh" (5:16).

about the redemptive solution that was "apart from the Law"—the scandalous acceptance by God of the death of this seeming sinner as a "propitiation" for the sins of Israel (Rom 3:21–25).

There is a compelling precedent for this reading, I think, in the Wisdom of Solomon, in the account of the righteous man who calls himself a "child (*paida*) of the Lord," who boasts that God is his Father, who is a "son of God," but who is condemned to a "shameful death" by the wicked leadership of Israel (Wis 2:12–24). As a result, "in the sight of human beings they were punished" as wrongdoers, but "their hope is full of immortality, and having been disciplined a little, they will be greatly benefited, because God tested them and found them worthy of himself" (3:4–5). They will shine out, they will run like sparks through straw; they will "judge nations and take possession of peoples" (3:7–8*). Read against this highly pertinent background, the "likeness of sinful flesh" appears not as a subtle definition of the ontology of incarnation but as a precise and realistic acknowledgement of the fact that in the eyes of most Jews, and especially of the leadership of Israel, among them Paul himself, Jesus had been justly punished as an offender against the Law and against YHWH. Paul has constructed his compressed reasoning in more abstract terms in keeping with the polarizing rhetoric of the passage, but there are numerous points of contact, both linguistically and conceptually, between Romans and Wisdom of Solomon;[56] and historically the sharply focused Jewish-political narrative constitutes a more plausible background to his thought than supposed early Christian speculation on the incarnation.

Christ's controversial engagement with Israel "in the likeness of sinful flesh" then becomes the fitting archetype for the experience of those who are *in him*, in whom the Spirit of Christ is active (Rom 8:9–11), who share in his sonship, who cry, "Abba, Father," in their distressing Gethsemane moments (8:15), who suffer with him in the expectation of sharing in his resurrection glory (8:17, 30), who are being conformed to the image of the persecuted Son "in order that he might be the firstborn among many brothers" (8:29), who must endure ostracism, harassment, and punishment even to the point of death (8:35–36), judged to be sinners both by Jews and gentiles, but not ultimately liable to accusation and condemnation (8:1, 33–34). The "likeness (*homoiōmati*) of his death," in which believers have been "grown together," is represented symbolically by baptism but it is also the likeness of a *sinful and disgraceful* death and therefore entails the *crucifixion* of the old person with him (6:5–6).

56. See Linebaugh, *God, Grace, and Righteousness*, 13–20, citing Gaventa's judgment that the two works "might profitably be read together" (20).

The Order of Events

Finally, can anything be determined from an implied order of events in Gal 4:4? Does the sending out necessarily precede the being "from a woman"? Fee maintains that the *genomenon* clauses are "most likely intended to be posterior to the main verb," since otherwise the participles would have to be "expressed as antecedent to the main verb."[57] Grammatically, however, these clauses describe the condition or status of the "Son" who is the object of the sending out. If Paul had meant that the sending preceded the action of *genomenon*, we would expect a different construction: "having been sent, the Son became human . . . " or "God sent his Son to be born of a woman . . . ." We have a comparable construction in Josh 21:42 LXX: Joshua "took the flint knives with which he circumcised the sons of Israel born (*genomenous*) on the way in the wilderness." The action of the participle logically *precedes* the action of the aorist main verb ("circumcised").[58] Josephus speaks of the dignity and splendor to which God "brought David being (*genomenon*) from" humble lineage (*Ant.* 5:337). Against the sentence order, David's existence or birth *precedes* the action of the aorist main verb (*anēgage*). Fee's argument, therefore, carries little weight.

The Son Sent to the Dysfunctional Vineyard of Israel

There is no reason to think that Paul's use of the sending formula in Gal 4:4 and Rom 8:3 draws purposefully on Jesus' parable of the son sent to the vineyard (Matt 21:33–46; Mark 12:1–12; Luke 20:9–18). The son in the parable comes not in the likeness of sinful flesh but in the likeness of a slave; he does the work of the slaves sent out before him. He is a prophet not a savior; he is sent not to redeem but to get the fruit owed by the tenants. His death is not a propitiation for the sins of Israel but an outrage that provokes the anger of the vineyard owner and severe punishment. Paul makes no reference in these texts to the prophets sent before the Son,

---

57. Fee, *Christology*, 216. Longenecker suggests that the sending out "coincides with the Son's human birth, which is a notion comparable to the theme of God's call, commission, and sending of his prophetic servants from their birth that appears elsewhere in Scripture" (*Galatians*, 171); so too Fung, *Galatians*, 182.

58. Cf. "God convicted Cain being (*genomenon*) the murderer of his brother" (Josephus, *Ant.* 1:57*); perhaps also 2 Macc 10:10*: "Now we will declare the things concerning Antiochus Eupator, born (*genomenon*) the son of that impious man . . . ." Here *genomenon* follows the reference to things that happened during the reign of Antiochus Eupator, but the aorist either looks back to his birth as the son of Antiochus Epiphanes or more simply establishes his identity.

nor does he make any use of the rejected stone saying (Ps 118:22–23), with which Jesus concludes the parable.

Nevertheless, there is a case to be made in support of Dunn's contention that the parable provides "probably the closest parallel, with its thought of Jesus as 'beloved son' being sent as the eschatological climax of God's dealings with Israel and being killed for his inheritance as a consequence of his mission."[59] We have seen that there is a strong Old Testament tradition of the sending out of prophets in vain to avert the wrath of God against his people (e.g., 2 Chr 36:15–16; Jer 7:25–26; Ezek 2:3–4; 3:4–7). The slaves are sent out "at the season" (tōi kairōi) or "when the fruit season (ho kairos tōn karpōn) drew near" (Mark 12:2; Matt 21:34; Luke 20:10), whereas the Son was sent to redeem Israel "when the fullness of the time came" (Gal 4:4), and Christ died for the ungodly "at the right time" (kata kairon) (Rom 5:6). The chronologies are not exactly the same—the parable requires the slaves and the son to be sent at the same season; but it seems reasonable enough to detect an echo of a sending to Israel at a critical moment. Also, as Dunn points out, in both the parable and in the Galatians passage we have "a close conjunction of the ideas of sonship and inheritance" (Mark 12:6–7; Gal 4:7).[60]

Finally, in 1 Thess 2:14–16 Paul makes reference to the Jews in Judea who "killed both the Lord Jesus and the prophets," who "fill up the measure of their sins" by opposing the preaching of the gospel to gentiles, and who since have been subjected to the wrath of God (1 Thess 2:15–16; cf. Matt 23:34; Luke 11:49; 13:34; Acts 7:52). Fee may be right to insist that the reference is to such *Christian* prophets as Stephen and James, but this must still be regarded as a continuation of the historic behavior of Israel.[61] By killing Jesus and the prophets whom he would send to them they proved themselves to be "sons of those who murdered the prophets" (Matt 23:31–34). Paul's "fill up their sins" reproduces quite closely the thought of Matthew's Jesus: "Fill up the measure of your fathers" (Matt 23:32). The exceptional designation of the Christian martyrs as "prophets" may in fact

---

59. Dunn, *Galatians*, 215; cf. Dunn, *Christology*, 40; Dunn, *Theology of Paul*, 278. Cerfaux says that Paul "was provided by Christian tradition with the theme of the sending of the Son of God," notably the parable of the vineyard (*Christ*, 447). Kuschel notes the view of van Iersel that Paul's statement presupposes the sending of the prophets and that, in contrast to Wis 9:10, nothing is said about a prior existence of the Son in heaven: "What Paul writes about the sending of the son can in no way be understood of a situation preceding the beginning of history, but rather of an event following Jesus' birth and preceding his resurrection" (*Before All Time*, 274–75).

60. Dunn, *Christology*, 40.

61. Fee, *Thessalonians*, 97–98; for the older opinion that the Old Testament prophets are in view see Bruce, *Thessalonians*, 47; Richard, *Thessalonians*, 120–21.

be a deliberate reminiscence of the Synoptic tradition. So it appears that an argument about the killing of the prophets *both before and after* the killing of Jesus was known to Paul, which makes it likely that the narrative of the son sent to the vineyard was also available in some form, at whatever remove, as an interpretive frame for the sending of Jesus to redeem those under the Law.

Conclusion

The sending out of the Son, as Paul has presented it, happens not in cosmic space and universal time but in Jewish space and historical time. The purpose is correspondingly restricted: it is not to redeem humanity but to redeem those under the Law, whom the Law could not save from the impending destruction that would be the wrath of God (cf. Rom 9:22). Such a narrative immediately suggests the relevance of Jesus' parable of the sending of the Son to uncooperative Israel to do the work of a prophet-servant. But the "sending out" of the Son is probably, in Paul's mind, most like the sending out of Moses not only to lead the people out of slavery but also, as things turned out, to negotiate the imposition of the Law in response to the transgression in the wilderness. Paradoxically, though, Jesus "negotiated" an end to the custodianship of the Law for Israel and deliverance from the long history of transgression that now threatened the very survival of the nation. The language of being or becoming or being born from a woman, under the Law, in the likeness of sinful flesh, may reflect a retrospective contrast with the current heavenly existence of the exalted Lord, but in the first place it evokes the central controversy of Jesus' vocation. If the idea of the sending of wisdom has had any bearing on Paul's argument, it is in the sense that the eschatological wisdom of God has finally found traction *in his people*, not only in the controversial death of the Son but also in the painful witness of the apostles and the churches insofar as they are inspired by the characteristic Spirit of the Son.

3

The Eschatological Wisdom of God

THE SENDING FORMULA, SCHWEIZER says, does not intrinsically entail the thought of pre-existence—any more than it is entailed in Old Testament references to the sending of the prophets or in the "full parallel of the sending of servants and the son" in the vineyard parable.[1] He maintains, however, that pre-existence is likely to have been *presupposed* here since it is evident elsewhere in Paul in the form of a Logos or Wisdom Christology. Thomas Söding, likewise, admits that the sending statements are, as a matter of tradition, independent of any pre-existence Christology but argues that they are naturally read as complementary to the incarnational motifs of renunciation, self-emptying, and self-humbling that appear in 2 Cor 8:9 and Phil 2:6–8: Christ was "wealthy" in heaven but he became "poor"; he was "in the form of God" but he emptied himself and appeared as a human person.[2]

The more substantive argument for the pre-existence of Christ, therefore, rests on two thematic types: the *materialization* of primordial wisdom and the *self-abasement* of a glorious divine figure. In practice, no sharp interpretive boundary can be drawn between the two categories, either because traditions intersect or because interpreters disagree. In this chapter we will look at two passages in which the thought of Christ's pre-existence has been found and explained—at least in part, at least by some interpreters—as a reworking of well-known Jewish Wisdom themes: the purported inclusion of Christ as an agent of creation ("through whom are all things") in the Shema in 1 Cor 8:6; and the identification of him with the "spiritual following rock" in the wilderness in 1 Cor 10:4. But we will also consider—by way of transition to a lengthy examination of the renunciation described in Phil 2:6–8—the suggestion that Paul sometimes spoke of Christ as a "man from heaven," who temporarily surrendered his heavenly "wealth" and embraced the poverty of incarnation (2 Cor 8:9; 1 Cor 15:47; Rom 10:6–7).

1. Schweizer, "υἱός," 375.
2. Söding, "Gottes Sohn," 66.

One God and One Lord

It is the view of many proponents of an early high Christology that in 1 Cor
8:6 Paul has taken the extraordinary step of including Jesus in the Shema and
therefore in the divine identity. In Greek the Shema begins: *Akoue, Israēl;
kyrios ho theos hēmōn kyrios heis estin*: "Hear, Israel, the Lord our God is one
Lord" (Deut 6:4* LXX). The affirmation is less ambiguous than it is in Hebrew: the positioning of the verb at the end seems to make it a singular statement about the oneness of the god who is about to give them the land (6:1–3).
The god YHWH-*Kyrios* is "one," therefore they are not to "go after other gods
from the gods of the nations around you" (6:14*).[3] The high christological
argument is that Paul has taken the traditional confession and has assigned
the main terms separately to the Father and the Son: "for us (there is) one
God, the Father, from whom all things and we for him, and one Lord, Jesus
Christ, through whom all things and we through him" (1 Cor 8:5–6*). "What
Paul has done seems plain enough," Fee writes. "He has kept the 'one' intact,
but he has divided the Shema into two parts, with *theos* (God) now referring
to the Father, and *kyrios* (Lord) referring to Jesus Christ the Son."[4] Since the
"all things" of creation came into being through him, the statement amounts
to a "plain, undeniable expression of Paul's presuppositional conviction about
Christ's preexistence as the Son of God."[5]

   We may wonder, however, whether Paul does, in fact, keep the "one"
intact. He has already asserted that "an idol is nothing in the world and
there is no god but one" (1 Cor 8:4*).[6] This looks like a generalized appeal
to Old Testament affirmations of the *oneness of God* in opposition to the
polytheism of the nations (cf. Deut 4:35, 39; Isa 44:6, 8; 45:5; Mal 2:10, 15),
without drawing attention to the Shema in particular. "Lord" occurs twice in
the Shema but is absent here.[7] This seems odd if Paul had intended to divide

---

3. Cf. Weinfeld with regard to the Hebrew: "the connotation of 'one' here is not
solely unity but also aloneness" (*Deuteronomy 1–11*, 337).

4. Fee, *Christology*, 90. Cf. Wright, *Climax*, 129: "Paul has placed Jesus within an
explicit statement . . . of the doctrine that Israel's God is the one and only God, the
creator of the world." Paul has thus redefined the Shema christologically to give "a sort
of christological monotheism." See also Witherington, *Conflict*, 198; Dunn, *Theology of
Paul*, 267–68; Bauckham, *God Crucified*, 36–39; Bauckham, *Jesus and the God of Israel*,
101–2; Waddell, *Messiah*, 123–24, 143–44; Tilling, *Christology*, 83, 90–92; Huijgen and
Versluis, "Unity," 219–22; Loke, *Origin*, 26–32; Fletcher-Louis, *Christological Origins*,
32–39; Capes, *Divine Christ*, 77.

5. Fee, *Christology*, 91.

6. The close relation between the two parts is apparent from the grammatical structure: *ouden eidōlon . . . oudeis theos . . . .*

7. See Fitzmyer, *First Corinthians*, 341.

the Shema between "one God, the Father" and "one Lord, Jesus Christ"—all the more so if this is or echoes a familiar confessional statement, as is widely supposed.[8] It then appears to be on the basis of the presence of many gods *and many lords* in the pagan world that he constructs the two part confession regarding the "one God, the Father" and the "one Lord, Jesus Christ."[9] It is sometimes thought that the "many gods" are the traditional deities, which are not often designated as *kyrioi*, while the "many lords" are the deities of the newer mystery cults, such as the *kyrios Sarapis*.[10] Murphy-O'Connor has argued that the verse has the form of "many pagan *heis*-acclamations addressed particularly to Serapis." He cites as a pertinent example: *heis Zeus Sarapis / megalē Isis hē kyria* ("One [are] Zeus [and] Sarapis / Great [is] Isis the 'Mistress'").[11] A "rather crude instance" is the cry of the Ephesian silversmiths: "Great is Artemis of the Ephesians" (Acts 19:28).[12] Weiss, on the other hand, distinguished between the Olympian "gods" and the *kyrioi* who were deified men;[13] and there may be some force to James McGrath's suggestion that the "many gods" are the "so-called gods" in heaven and the "many lords" are those on earth.[14] But the distinction appears to be introduced, in the first place, because Paul is about to speak quite emphatically both of *one* God and of *one* Lord in order to preclude all conflicting loyalties.[15] This is

8. See Thiselton, *First Corinthians*, 628–29.

9. Gaston and Perry argue that "lords" preempts the statement in verse 6 and has been introduced for that purpose; "gods" and "lords" are not the same thing ("Monotheism," 193–94). Paul is acknowledging that for the pagan "there are many who would claim reverence, not just those strictly identifiable as gods."

10. Fee, *First Corinthians*, 412; cf. Foerster, "κύριος," 1047; Kuschel, *Before All Time*, 287–88; and Zeller, "Christology," 318–19: the "lords" in competition with Christ—Egyptian, Syrian and Thracian gods—are "propagated by a strong and impressive minority in a henotheistic manner with εἷς [*heis*] or μέγας [*megas*] acclamations. Therefore it is tempting to see these competing deities in the background of 1 Cor 8.5–6." Thiselton retains Bousset's association of "many lords" with the *kyrios*-cults (*First Corinthians*, 633).

11. Murphy-O'Connor, "Cosmology," 256. He finds a similar acclamation in 1 Tim 2:5*: "For one God, and one mediator of God and people!"

12. Zeller thinks that "Paul or his tradition clothed their monotheistic confession in a Hellenistic form moulded not on Deut 6.4 but on Xenophanes, as is often the case in Hellenistic Judaism": "One god, greatest among gods and men, not like mortals in body or thought" (Xenophanes fr. 23) ("Christology," 320).

13. Conzelmann, *1 Corinthians*, 308n35; see also Talbert's discussion of the "ancient Mediterranean distinction between two types of deities" (Talbert, *Christology*, 7–8).

14. McGrath, *Only True God*, 41. According to Fantin, Paul's statement is an implicit polemic against the "one lord" Caesar ("Lord of the Entire World," 206–11); against this see Fee, *First Corinthian*, 412n65.

15. So Conzelmann, *1 Corinthians*, 143: the "conjunction is due simply to the Christian confession which is to be quoted immediately afterwards."

pointedly *unlike* the Shema with its single *heis*. The effect is not to fuse two identities in one but to *dissociate*, to create two distinct affirmations, anticipated in the preceding acknowledgement of many gods and many lords: not only is God the Father one but the Lord, Jesus Christ, also is one—two separate unities. McGrath makes the point well: "The fact of the matter is that Paul does not say that there is one God who is both Father and Son; he says rather that there is one God and also one Lord."[16]

Here we may usefully consider a rather curious and ingenious supplement to the mainstream case for a "Christological monotheism" reading of 1 Cor 8:6. Fletcher-Louis has argued that a numerical-critical analysis of the verse lends support to the idea that Paul has included Jesus in the Shema—evidence all the more compelling for being covert and cryptic.[17] Very simply, excluding the *alla* ("but") at the start of the verse, the two "one" statements have 13 words each in Greek, adding up to 26, which is the numerical value of YHWH: *yod* (10) + *he* (5) + *waw* (6) + *he* (5) = 26. Moreover, the numerical value of the Hebrew word *'ehad* ("one"), which stands emphatically at the opening of each line, is thirteen. "So the numerical structure of the reworked Shema encodes both the name of God, *Yhwh*, and the key, climactic word at the end of the Shema ('. . . *Yhwh-Kyrios* your God, is *one!*')."[18]

The numerical analysis may be correct. Let us suppose that it is. But has its significance *in context* been correctly expounded? Fletcher-Louis assumes that the equation moves *from* the two thirteen word "one" statements *to* the answer, which is the one YHWH-*Kyrios*. But this *logic* is not reflected in the actual reasoning of 1 Cor 8:6. We have 13 and 13, but Paul does not say that this adds up to 26. In fact, the argument of the passage moves in the opposite direction: *from* the given Jewish datum that there is "no God but one" (8:4) *to* the recognition that "for us" the two *functions* must be spoken of apart from each other in order to explain how things now stand: yes, there is one God, the Father, who is creator of what we are; but there is also—independently—one Lord, Jesus Christ, who is the agent by which this new state of affairs has come about. If there is any validity in the numerical analysis, the point is not that Jesus has been assimilated into the Shema but that what would formerly have been done by God alone has become a joint undertaking. It is that 26 has been *divided*—by God himself, by the delegation of authority—to create two separate thirteens.

16. McGrath, *Only True God*, 39.

17. Fletcher-Louis, *Christological Origins*, 39–49.

18. Fletcher-Louis, *Christological Origins*, 47.

We have run ahead of ourselves, however. We need to give some thought to what is happening with these two modes of engagement in the creative process.

Father and Lord

The phrase "God our Father and the Lord Jesus Christ" occurs frequently in the Pauline corpus, occasionally with sufficient explanatory context to shed light on the nature or function of the relationship. God is the Father of our Lord Jesus Christ when believers are urged to live in a Christ-like manner (Rom 15:5–6; cf. Col 1:3). God the Father comforts the apostles, who share in the afflictions of their Lord Jesus Christ (2 Cor 1:3–5). The Lord Jesus Christ gave himself to deliver his people from the present evil age "according to the will of our God and Father," who is the one who should be glorified throughout the coming ages (Gal 1:3–4). The "God of our Lord Jesus Christ," who is the "Father of glory," raised Jesus from the dead and seated him at his right hand (Eph 1:17, 20). Believers give thanks to "God the Father in the name of our Lord Jesus Christ" or "through him" (Eph 5:20; Col 3:17). The confession that Jesus Christ is Lord will bring glory to God the Father (Phil 2:11). The apostles pray to their "God and Father" that the Thessalonians will remain steadfast in their hope in the future intervention of "our Lord Jesus Christ" to deliver them from the wrath to come (1 Thess 1:2–3, 10; cf. 3:11–13). Both "our Lord Jesus Christ himself" and "God the Father" comfort and establish the believers, but the emphatic "himself" (*Autos*) makes Christ an independent comforter; and "our Lord Jesus Christ" is the model of glory to which the brothers have been called by God (2 Thess 2:13–17). In these more or less formulaic expressions the relationship is functionally asymmetrical.[19] Jesus as Lord is the object or agent of the Father's actions, the means to a divine end; he determines the relational context and pattern for behavior that eventually will bring empire-wide glory to Israel's God. Paul's assertion in 1 Cor 8:6 that there is "one Lord, Jesus Christ, through whom" God has brought about "all things" would appear to be an expression of just this asymmetry.

There may be better ways to account biblically for this dynamic distinction between the "one God" and the "one Lord" than the simple appeal to the Shema. First, God is sometimes described as "God of gods and

---

19. Against Capes who says that the two figures are "linked closely and act as one" (*Divine Christ*, 75), obscuring the eschatological narrative that frames the formula. The phrase "Father of our Lord Jesus Christ" may well suggest an intimate relationship, but it is never in these contexts one of shared "divine identity."

Lord of lords" (Deut 10:17; cf. Ps 136:2–3). In Daniel the "Lord of lords" part of the formula begins to take on a political aspect. Nebuchadnezzar declares that the Most High is "God of gods and Lord of lords and Lord of kings, because he does signs and wonders and changes seasons and times, removing the reign of kings and setting others in their place" (Dan 4:37 LXX; cf. 2:47). God is creator and therefore sovereign over the natural order, but he also intervenes in the affairs of nations. By contrast, the "gods of the nations do not have power in them to give away the kingdom of a king to another king." When the pre-flood generation cries out against the bloodshed and oppression being wrought upon the earth, the angels declare of God that he is "the Lord of lords, and the God of gods, and the King of kings, and the seat of his glory (stands) throughout all the generations of the world" (1 En. 9:4). Potentially, therefore, the "Lord of lords" has an eschatological sphere of activity, which is brought into rather sharp focus in Revelation. The Lamb who will conquer the hostile kings of Rome is "Lord of lords and King of kings, and those with him are called and chosen and faithful" (Rev 17:14); and the rider who will strike down the nations and rule them with a rod of iron is "King of kings and Lord of lords" (19:15–16). It is not the "God of gods" who acts at this moment but the one who is Lord among many lords.

A passage in Malachi, secondly, addressing the problem of Jewish idolatry also gestures towards a functional distinction between "God" and "Lord":

> Did not one God create us? Is there not one father of us all? For why did each forsake his brother in order to profane the covenant of our fathers? Judah was forsaken, and an abomination occurred in Israel and in Jerusalem, for Judah profaned the holy things of the Lord with which he loved and sought after foreign gods. The Lord will utterly destroy the person doing these things until indeed he has been humiliated from the tents of Jacob and from those bringing sacrifice to the Lord Almighty. (Mal 2:10–12* LXX)

It is the "one God . . . one father" who created Israel (not the whole world here); but it is the "Lord" who will destroy those of God's people who busy themselves with foreign gods. Paul, remember, is writing about believers who eat food sacrificed to idols and who risk provoking the Lord to jealousy (1 Cor 8:4; 10:20–22). It is the same God in Malachi, of course, but the rhetorical shift from God as Father to Lord as judge is arguably more relevant for understanding Paul's statement than the identification of YHWH-*kyrios* as one God in the Shema. The distinction cannot be developed systematically, but Philo introduces a degree of theological clarity into our reflections by differentiating rather formally between the God who *creates* and the Lord who *governs*.[20] The two cherubim mounted on the ark of the covenant, he argues, represent "the two most ancient and supreme powers of the divine God, namely, his creative and his kingly power; and his creative power is called God; according to which he arranged, and created, and adorned this universe, and his kingly power is called Lord, by which he rules over the beings whom he has created, and governs them with justice and firmness" (*Moses* 2 99; cf. *Planting* 86–87; *Abraham* 121). Here the government of God is expressed in general terms, as we would expect from Philo the rationalizer, but if the distinction is translated into the more discordant voice of a prophetic-apocalyptic program, the rule of the *Kyrios* over his people in the midst of hostile nations takes on sharply historical and political dimensions.

Thirdly, Zechariah foresees "days of the Lord" when he will gather the nations against Jerusalem to plunder the city; half the population will go into captivity; but then the Lord will go out to fight against the nations and to secure the safety of the remaining population. Living waters will flow out from Jerusalem, and "the Lord will become king over all the earth; on that day the Lord will be one and his name one" (Zech 14:1–9 LXX). Finally, the people who remain from the nations which fought against Jerusalem will "also go up year after year to do obeisance to the King, the Lord Almighty, and to keep the feast of tent pitching" (14:16). Dean McBride takes the "one Lord" statement to be an early development of the Shema tradition, affirming the "universal eschatological rule of God over the nations," a theme taken up by Paul in Rom 3:29–30.[21] This may account for the "one God . . . one Lord . . . " pattern in 1 Cor 8:6, but the eschatological context for the extension needs to be taken into account: YHWH becomes "king," "one Lord," and *kyrios pantokratōr* when he judges and comes to rule over the nations.

Function and Identity

Richard Bauckham asserts the importance of "identity" over against the old distinction between "functional" and "ontological" categories.[22] He

20. Barker maps Philo's distinction on to her "second God" thesis (*Angel*, 222).

21. McBride, "Yoke of the Kingdom," 278n10; see also Smith, *Micah-Malachi*, 289; Rowe, "Name of the Lord," 148–49.

22. Yarbro Collins differentiates between two kinds of divinity, functional and ontological ("but not in a later creedal sense") ("How on Earth," 57). Daniel's "one like a son of man," the Son of Man in Similitudes, and Jesus in some Synoptic passages are functionally divine when they "exercise (or are anticipated as exercising) divine

says that this is a misleading approach because the categories "do not reflect an adequate understanding of the way Jewish monotheism understood God." Specifically, in his view, in Jewish understanding the unique sovereignty of God was not simply a "function" that could be delegated to someone else. Sovereignty or lordship was a definitive characteristic by which the one God was distinguished from "all other reality" and therefore could not be reassigned. "The unique divine sovereignty is a matter of *who God is*. Jesus' participation in the unique divine sovereignty is therefore also not just a matter of what Jesus does, but of *who Jesus is* in relation to God."[23] The point is that if God had transferred his *essential* sovereignty to Jesus, he would have transferred a fundamental aspect of his *being*. This would create a second god—"outright ditheism," as Bauckham calls it.[24] I struggle to see the force of this.

First, the relevant distinction in the present case is not between function and ontology but between *two different functions*. The Shema affirms the god YHWH-*kyrios* as Israel's exclusive god prior to the entry into the land. They are not to go after the gods of the neighboring peoples, "for the LORD your God in your midst is a jealous God—lest the anger of the LORD your God be kindled against you, and he destroy you from off the face of the earth" (Deut 6:14–15). The basis for the commandment is that "the LORD brought us out of Egypt with a mighty hand" with the intention of giving the land to them (Deut 6:20–23). This creator function, including rescue and fatherhood, gives way to an eschatological function in the later texts.

Secondly, if God delegates even a core function to another, it is not clear how that compromises his divine identity or results in the existence of another god. It means only that, rather than exercising his sovereignty directly in relation to the world, God exercises it *indirectly*, through an agent who has been appointed for that purpose.[25] Even if we allow that

---

activities like ruling a universal kingdom, sitting on a heavenly throne, judging human beings . . . ." The description of Christ as being "in the form of God," on the other hand, is to be understood ontologically: "he was god-like in appearance or nature, that is, a heavenly being as opposed to a human being."

23. Bauckham, *God Crucified*, 41 (original emphasis).

24. Bauckham, *Jesus and the God of Israel*, 101.

25. 1 Tim 2:5* constitutes an instructive parallel: "For (there is) one God, and one mediator (*mesitēs*) of God and people, the person Christ Jesus." Cf. McGrath, who also notes the significance of 1 Thess 1:9–10: "The Thessalonians had abandoned idol worship in order to serve the God whom Jews and Christians believe is the only true God, and as Christians, they further understand Jesus to be God's unique son and agent of salvation" (*Only True God*, 42). Note also his discussion of Abel and the Son of Man as exalted judges in T. Ab. A 12–13; B 10–11, and 1 En. 61–62 (43–44). Whether or not the statement is Pauline, it is not far from the description of Moses as a "mediator"

sovereignty or lordship is definitive of the identity of God, it is only the *function*, not the identity, that is granted to another. This, after all, was the essence of biblical kingship. At a basic level Israel's king was a *proxy* for the direct rule of YHWH over his people (cf. 1 Sam 8:7). Bauckham recognizes the importance of Ps 110 for the development of New Testament Christology, but what the psalm describes is precisely a transferred or delegated rule: the king has a mighty scepter, he rules in the midst of his enemies, but it is YHWH who subdues his enemies, who sends forth the king's scepter, who will shatter kings on the day of his wrath, who will execute judgment among the nations.[26]

The relevance of this for understanding the eschatological purpose of Jesus' lordship can hardly be overstated. It is not only a person who has been added to, or included in, the operation of divine sovereignty but also a *program*. Christ became a servant to the circumcised, Paul writes in Romans, so that the nations might glorify Israel's God for his spectacular mercy towards his people; but the final outcome would be the rule of this descendant of David, this "root of Jesse," over the nations (Rom 15:8–12).[27] The saints in Corinth call on the name of the Lord Jesus Christ now in the confidence that on a future "day of our Lord Jesus Christ" he will be revealed to the world (1 Cor 1:2, 7–8). As Lord he is the eschatological judge who will bring to light the intentions of the apostles and commend them accordingly (4:5; cf. 5:4–5). He is provoked to jealousy by believers who "partake of the table of the Lord and the table of demons" (10:21); they are judged by the Lord now so that they will not be condemned along with the rest of the world when he comes (11:32). He has been given authority to reign at the right hand of the Father "until he has put all his enemies under his feet" (15:25; cf. Phil 2:9–11). This coherent eschatological narrative about the Lord Jesus, which entirely frames Paul's argument in the letter, presents him not as an integral part of the divine identity but as a uniquely authorized instrument of the political or governmental purposes of God in the coming ages.[28] This is the

---

in Gal 3:19–20*: "the mediator (*mesitēs*) is not of one, but God is one." The one God, therefore, is confessed as savior (1 Tim 2:3), but there is "one mediator" alongside the one God who, like Moses, intervened at a time when the existence of God's people was under threat, giving himself as a ransom for many in Israel. God is Israel's savior but there is one mediator or agent of that salvation. This is the "testimony" and content of the apostle's teaching to the nations (1 Tim 2:6–7).

26. Bauckham, *God Crucified*, 29–31.

27. For the interpretation see Perriman, *Future of the People of God*, 13.

28. Zeller rejects the view that 1 Cor 8:6 is a reworking of Deut 6:4 ("Christology," 320–21). The transference of LXX phrases with *kyrios* to Jesus is "due to the fact that Christ assumed the divine functions of judge and saviour"; but in Paul's statement Christ as Lord is compared not to YHWH but to the many *kyrioi*.

answer to the objection of Fletcher-Louis, aimed at McGrath's analysis, that if the YHWH-*Kyrios* of the Shema is not identified with Jesus, "then it is not at all clear what the word *kyrios* is doing as part of Jesus' name or title."[29] The eschatological task associated with the word *kyrios* is the devolved one of judging the nations which hitherto have sacrificed food to idols.

The other key narrative of kingship used by the early church to shape the proclamation about Jesus is found in Ps 2. This is usually understood as an enthronement psalm, but this may not be quite accurate.[30] On the face of it, YHWH has already set his king on his holy hill, but the nations are up in arms, and the kings of the earth are conspiring against him (Ps 2:1–6). Under these particularly dangerous conditions, the novel decree is issued as an assurance of victory: the hostile nations will be given over to YHWH's Son as his possession, and he will "break them with a rod of iron and dash them in pieces like a potter's vessel." The sense of the metaphor "today I have begotten you" is not that the king is enthroned at this moment but that he is now entitled to ask for an inheritance. The future domination over the nations, contrary to current appearances, is the critical point.

In Luke's narrative in Acts, the disciples draw out the significance of Ps 2 after the interrogation of Peter and John by the Jewish council (Acts 4:5–22). They pray to God, the "master" (*despota*), who "made the heaven and the earth and the sea and everything in them," and then quote the lines about the hostility of the kings and rulers of the earth towards YHWH and his Anointed (4:24–26). This is what had recently happened in Jerusalem: Herod and Pilate, along with the gentiles and the peoples of Israel, had conspired to put an end to Jesus' mission. But they were only doing "whatever your hand and your plan had predestined to take place" (4:28). So the kings and rulers of this age plotted to thwart God's plans, but his response—in effect, though it is not explicitly stated—is to declare to his king: "You are my Son; today I have begotten you. Ask of me, and I will make the nations your heritage, and the ends of the earth your possession" (Ps 2:7–9). The same *functional* distinction is operative: the God who made the heaven and the earth is confronted with a political crisis, and his response is framed in the drama of the Psalm: the one who has been seated at the right hand of God as both Lord and Christ (Acts 2:34–36) *has been authorized* to judge and rule over the many "lords," Jewish and gentile, who conspired "against YHWH and against his anointed."

The same concrete perspective may be discerned in Paul, not least in 1 Corinthians. The rulers of this age, he says, are doomed to pass away (1

29. Fletcher-Louis, *Christological Origins*, 37.

30. See Craigie, *Psalms 1–50*, 64–65.

Cor 2:6–8). He is thinking not of universal and perennial power structures but of the leadership in Jerusalem, in league with Roman provincial power, who "crucified the Lord of glory."[31] Indeed, the present form of the world, as the Corinthians know it, is passing away (7:31). A day of the Lord Jesus Christ will come, when he will be revealed to all people—and when, we may add, he will be confessed by the nations and will rule over them (1:7–8; Phil 2:11; Rom 15:12). This is a *political* narrative, and it gives us a *political* understanding of Jesus' function as Lord.

The assertion that "for us there is one God, the Father . . . , and one Lord, Jesus Christ," certainly looks back to seminal Old Testament affirmations that Israel's God YHWH-*kyrios*, the creator of heaven and earth, is "one" to the exclusion of all other gods. But more importantly, it reflects a development within the Old Testament that begins to differentiate between the generative function of God and the eschatological function, albeit falling somewhat short of the terminological precision of Philo's statement.[32] To this extent, appeals to the Shema as the interpretive context for 1 Cor 8:6 are misplaced because by this stage another narrative has been taken up to express convictions about how the unfolding eschatological crisis would be resolved. The "one Lord, Jesus Christ" has played a role in relation to God the Father, culminating in his exaltation to the right hand of God to rule in the midst of his enemies, with the prospect eventually of gaining the nations which had provoked the crisis as his inheritance, to rule with a rod of iron. In other words, Jesus has been included not in the divine *identity* expressed in the Shema but in the divine *purpose* expressed in an intensifying narrative of conflict, judgment, and rule.

The Psalms make this a simple matter of delegation. A situation has arisen in which the one God has seen fit to bestow on the crucified Jesus a function that hitherto was reserved as his own prerogative. The risk of ditheism hardly arises and in any case is obviated specifically by Paul's development of the apocalyptic narrative in 1 Cor 15:24–28. Christ must reign as the king at YHWH's right hand, in accordance with the terms of Ps 110, until the last enemy of his people, death, is destroyed. But then the Son will deliver the kingdom to God the Father and become subject to him, so that "God may be all in all."[33] The oneness of God is not compromised because the

---

31. Cf. Kuschel, *Before All Time*, 280.

32. Cf. Gaston and Perry, "Monotheism," 194.

33. Hays says that "It is impossible to avoid the impression that Paul is operating with what would later come to be called a subordinationist christology" (*First Corinthians*, 266); cf. Wanamaker, "Philippians 2:6–11," 187–88; Thiselton, *First Corinthians*, 1236–37; and see further Perriman, *Son of Man*, 239. Fee, *Christology*, 113–14 maintains, quite unconvincingly, that it is not the Son's *person* that is subordinated in the

authorization of Jesus to act as Lord, in the political sphere of kingdom, as long as there are enemies, is conditional and subsidiary. Once the last enemy has been destroyed, this novel arrangement will no longer be needed, and the exclusive and undivided status of the one God will be restored.

Through Whom Are All Things

If the statement "(there is) one Lord, Jesus Christ" affirms the current status of Jesus as Lord above many lords, seated at the right hand of God, future ruler of the nations, what is the scope of the qualification "through whom all things and we through him"? This evidently parallels the description of God in the preceding line: "from whom all things and we for him." The common understanding, then, is that "all things" (ta panta) is a reference to the original creation, therefore the one Lord must be the agent through whom that creation came about. The whole passage, Fee argues, "typically for Paul, encloses the work of the Son within that of the Father."[34] Both creation (all things "from" the Father and "through" the Son) and redemption (we "for" the Father and "through" the Son) are encompassed.

The statements can obviously be read against a background of both Stoic and Hellenistic-Jewish thought. It is an ancient and widely held belief, according to the author of the Pseudo-Aristotelian De mundo, that "all things are from God and are constituted for us by God, and nothing is self-sufficient if deprived of his preserving influence" ([Mundo] 6 397b). In an apostrophe to the Cosmos or Nature, Marcus Aurelius declares, "From you all things, in you all things, for you all things" (Med. 4.23*). So too Philo says that many things must come together for something to come into being: "the by what, the from what, the through what, the because of what"—corresponding to the cause, the material, the instrument, and the purpose (Cherubim 125*). So it may be said that God is the cause "by whom" the world came to be, that the four elements are the material "from which" it was made, that the word of God was the instrument "by which" it was made, for the purpose of the goodness of the builder.[35]

There are two similar statements in the Pauline corpus. The description of the Son as the one by whom, through whom, and for whom all things were created in Col 1:15 will be considered in chapter 9. In Rom 11:36 we have a wholly theocentric version of the formula: "For from

---

end but his role: autos ho huios is emphatically "the Son himself" who is subordinated.

34. Fee, Christology, 91; cf. Bauckham, Jesus and the God of Israel, 101–2.

35. For the background in Stoicism and Middle Platonism, see Sterling, "Wisdom," 245–47.

him and through him and to him are all things." In formal terms this is a straightforward Hellenistic-Jewish affirmation about God,[36] but is it meant as a statement about creation? It comes as the climax to an argument about the prospects for Israel. A hardening in part has come upon them, gentiles are being incorporated unnaturally into the root of the promises made to the patriarchs, but if Israel repents—if not before then after the calamity of divine judgment—they will be grafted back in, and, in this way, all Israel will be saved.[37] God does not regret bestowing the gifts and calling listed in Rom 9:1–5. He has consigned all Israel to disobedience but in order that he "may have mercy on all" (Rom 11:28–32). Paul then expresses wonder at the wisdom and workings of God in language that notably invokes the narrative of Israel's redemption from exile (11:34; cf. Isa 40:13).

At this point it is difficult to see why the "all things" statement in Rom 11:36 should be a reference to creation and not to the dense "eschatological" narrative about Israel, to which it comes as a doxological climax.[38] Similarly, "all things from God" in 1 Cor 11:12 is asserted as part of an argument that has no interest in cosmology and explicitly ranks Christ below God (11:3). "Might that then also be the case here, in 1 Cor. 8.6?" Karl-Josef Kuschel asks. "There is no compelling reason to suppose otherwise."[39] If "from him and through him and to him are all things" in Rom 11:36 is to be heard as a wisdom statement, it has nevertheless been adapted to express the highly irregular, innovative wisdom by which God has seen fit to deal with Israel's trespass. The eschatological perspective is underlined by the closing words: "To him be the glory for the ages, amen" (Rom 11:36*); and at the end of the letter Paul encapsulates the overarching purpose of his mission—that "the only *wise* God" should be glorified throughout the ages "through Jesus Christ" (16:27). It is all an outworking of the wisdom of God *through the agency of Jesus Christ*. While in Rom 11:36 agency ("through whom") is attributed to God alone, it is the *confession of Jesus as the one Lord* of both Jews and Greeks that lies at the heart of the creative process: "for the same Lord is Lord of all . . . . For 'everyone who calls on the name of the Lord will be saved'" (Rom 10:8–13). This is not quite the argument of 1 Corinthians 8:6, but it

36. See Byrne, *Romans*, 361; Moo, *Romans*, 743–44; Jewett and Kotansky, *Romans*, 721.

37. For the detailed argument see Perriman, *Future of the People of God*, 135–38.

38. Dunn suggests that the statement is closer to 1 Cor 15:27–28 than to 1 Cor 8:6 (*Romans 9–16*, 704). Bauckham maintains that in 1 Cor 8:6 Paul further includes Christ in the creator's relationship to creation by transferring the "through whom" attribute to him (*Jesus and the God of Israel*, 103). See also Loke, *Origin*, 28–29.

39. Kuschel, *Before All Time*, 287.

establishes a solid conceptual frame for reading the earlier text as a statement about the novel process of salvation rather than about creation.

Fee insists that there is nothing in the context of 1 Cor 8:6 to "remotely suggest that Jewish Wisdom lies behind Paul's formulation."[40] That may be questionable.[41] In any case, we appear to find in the wider context of the letter a pattern of thought that accounts very well for the intersection of apocalyptic-lordship and creation-wisdom themes. Paul is convinced that the cross is the wisdom of God, by which God is bringing "to nothing things that are" and causing the "rulers of this age" to pass away (1 Cor 1:21–24, 28; 2:6; cf. 7:31). Because the weak and foolish Corinthians are "in Christ Jesus," they will be instrumental in this eschatological process and will inherit the age to come (cf. 6:9). In the background, therefore, is the controlling idea that one world or age is being brought to nothing and a new world or age is being brought into existence by the foolish wisdom of God. A civilization which honors many gods and many lords will be replaced, sooner or later, by a civilization for which there is one God *and* one Lord.

There is both a "from" God part to this argument and implicitly a "through" Christ part. God clearly takes the initiative in the re-creative action, but it is "from him" (*ex autou*) that the Corinthians are "in Christ Jesus" (1 Cor 1:30). At the same time Christ is the agent of the transformation as "power of God and wisdom of God" (1:24; cf. 1:30). In a different context, but still with reference to the foolishness of the wisdom of this age, Paul asserts that "all things are yours, whether Paul or Apollos or Cephas or the world or life or death or things present or things to come—all are yours, and you are Christ's, and Christ is God's" (3:18–23). In other words, the "all things" of this new reality, which are quasi-cosmic in scope, are theirs *through* Jesus. Indeed, those "called to be saints" in Corinth owe their very existence as such to him. This means that at least the second part of 1 Cor 8:6, but probably the whole verse, is a statement not about creation but about "new creation."[42] If we read 1 Cor 8:6 not with reference to a general Jewish

40. Fee, *Christology*, 93; cf. Lee, *Preexistent Son*, 287–88; Bauckham, *Jesus and the God of Israel*, 101–4.

41. See Dunn, *Theology of Paul*, 272–75; Hurtado, *Lord Jesus Christ*, 125; Dunn, *Beginning*, 805n272.

42. Murphy-O'Connor says that the "unified thrust of the verse . . . is exclusively soteriological" ("Cosmology," 265). Kuschel argues that if we take into account the likely usage of the acclamation "one God, the Father—one Lord Jesus Christ" in the context of baptism or as an ecstatic cry in the liturgical assembly, "there is much to be said for the conclusion that the christological content of this formula is the new creation of those who rely on Christ" (*Before All Time*, 288–89). And: "the theological *ta panta* might refer to the very first creation of the world; by contrast, the christological *ta panta* refers (as is usual in Paul) to the prevailing circumstances in the present"

Wisdom theology but in the light of the specific argument about wisdom in this letter, which is an eschatological argument, then it appears that the "one God, the Father" is—as in Mal 2:11–12—the creator of a new people by means of a foolish wisdom, and Jesus, on whom the name of "Lord" has been bestowed, is the one *through* whose suffering the "all things" of the new age have come about and *through* whom the eschatological community exists.[43] The hypothesis of his eternal pre-existence is not required.

The Rock Was the Christ

The statement that the rock that followed the Israelites in the wilderness was "the Christ" belongs to Paul's overtly typological reworking of the exodus narrative (1 Cor 10:1–4*).[44] The journey "under the cloud" and "through the sea" was equivalent to baptism, the "spiritual" food and drink miraculously provided were the bread and cup of the Lord's supper, and "the rock was the Christ." The parallel narrative structure sets up the specific warning. The Israelites all participated in the redemptive events of the exodus; nevertheless, "with most of them God was not pleased, for they were overthrown in the wilderness" (10:5). The story has been retold in such a way that the actions serve expressly as instructive "types" for Paul and his readers (10:6). The Corinthian believers have all participated in baptism and the Lord's supper, but if they engage in idolatry and sexual immorality, if they put Christ to the test, if they grumble, they will likewise be overthrown.

An argument for pre-existence is often drawn from the past tense of the verb: "the rock was (ēn) the Christ." Joseph Fitzmyer, for example, says

(290). He also makes the point that in Paul the Kyrios is "never a protological figure . . . but is always already an eschatological figure" (289). Yarbro Collins allows for the possibility that "Paul is taking the idea of a new creation seriously here and implying that the resurrection and exaltation of Christ made him equivalent to God's wisdom" (Yarbro Collins and Collins, *King and Messiah*, 111–12; discussed also in Loke, *Origin*, 28; Waddell, *Messiah*, 130). This is less helpful. The point is rather that through the folly and failure of the cross the creative wisdom of God has brought something wonderfully new into existence.

43. Dunn suggests that 1 Cor 8:6 should be seen as an "extension of the thought" of the earlier discussion of the wisdom of God: "Christ who because he is now Lord now shares in God's rule over creation and believers, and therefore his Lordship is the continuation and fullest expression of God's own creative power" (*Christology*, 182, italics removed; cf. Dunn, *Theology of Paul*, 274). This is essentially correct but too broadly conceived: I argue at a number of points that Paul's focus is more narrowly on Israel and its relation to the nations.

44. The belief that the rock followed them seems to have its origins in a Jewish tradition, first attested in L.A.B. 10.7 (late first century AD), based on Num 20–21 (Fitzmyer, *First Corinthians*, 382–83; Fee, *First Corinthians*, 494–96; Thiessen, "Rock," 104).

that it "implies that he is thinking of the preexistent Christ as that rock."[45] He notes that in a "parallel predication" in Gal 3:16 we have the present tense: "It does not say, 'And to offsprings,' referring to many, but referring to one, 'And to your offspring,' who is (*estin*) Christ." In this case, however, Paul means literally that Abraham's offspring is Christ. We also have the present tense in Acts 4:11: "This Jesus is (*estin*) the stone that was rejected by you, the builders, which has become the cornerstone"; and in Paul's "allegorical" interpretation of Hagar and Sarah: "these women are (*eisin*) two covenants" (Gal 4:24–25).[46] But the appeal to these texts overlooks the peculiar manner in which Paul has constructed the typology in 1 Cor 10:1–4*. He does not say, interpreting allegorically, that the passage through the sea *is* baptism or that the food and water consumed by the Israelites in the desert *are* the bread and the cup. Rather the language of solidarity with Christ has been impressed upon the exodus narrative. That the rock "was the Christ" corresponds to the other past tense (aorist and imperfect) statements: the fathers "were baptized into Moses," they "ate the same spiritual food," they "drank the same spiritual drink," they "were drinking from the spiritual rock that followed them." Paul is reading the Christ story back into the Moses story; the past tense signifies the meaning of the rock to the Israelites *according to the terms of the eucharistic analogy*. As Kuschel says, "what we have here is a new 'look' at the history of Israel from the perspective of Christ, the exalted Lord, a perspective of the Spirit."[47] The details do not stand independently; the whole narrative, including the statement about the rock, is the typology.

Another parallel is the interpretation of Num 21:18 at Qumran, with reference to the founding of the Damascus community: "'the well the princes dug, the nobility of the people dug it with a rod' . . . . The Well is the Law, and its 'diggers' are the repentant of Israel who went out of the land of Judah and dwelt in the land of Damascus" (CD 6:2–5). Fitzmyer says that the implied verbs here are also in the present tense (the well *is* the Law, the diggers *are* repentant Israel).[48] But the point is that Num 21:18 is being read

---

45. Fitzmyer, *First Corinthians*, 383; so too Conzelmann, *1 Corinthians*, 167: "The 'was' of the typological statement, of the interpretation of the rock as being Christ, means real preexistence, not merely symbolic significance"; Witherington, *Conflict*, 218; Dunn, *Theology of Paul*, 279–80; Thiselton, *First Corinthians*, 729–30; Lee, *Preexistent Son*, 290; Fee, *Christology*, 95; Thiessen, "Rock," 120; Fee, *First Corinthians*, 496.

46. Fitzmyer misreads the account of the water from the rock in Wis 11:1–4 (*First Corinthians*, 383). The water is just water, not wisdom; it is a "remedy for their thirst out of hard stone." But wisdom "prospered their actions by the hand of a holy prophet." Fee is quite exercised about this point (Fee, *Christology*, 96n33).

47. Kuschel, *Before All Time*, 283; cf. Hurtado, "Pre-existence," 745: the aim is "to 'Christianize' the wilderness events for ethical exhortation."

48. Fitzmyer, *First Corinthians*, 383.

allegorically *in order to say something about an event in recent Jewish history*, when the covenanters went out into the desert. This is the opposite of what Paul is doing. He is not "reading Exodus as metaphor for early Christian experience," as Richard Hays puts it.[49] Rather he reimagines the Old Testament narrative through the lens of the Christ-oriented analogue in order to bring out the *literal* relevance of the exodus events. The story is not an allegorical prefiguring of baptism and the Lord's supper; it is a *realistic* example of spiritual complacency and catastrophic judgment, the force of which is elicited by superimposing the new situation on the old.

The later exhortation not to "test Christ (*ekpeirazōmen*), as some of them tested (*epeirasan*) and were destroyed by the snakes" (1 Cor 10:9*) should not lead us to conclude that the Israelites tested the pre-existent Christ in the wilderness.[50] If we translate "as some of them did" (ESV), this may seem a reasonable inference. But the repetition of the verb without the prefix *ek-* suggests that the *implied object* is "God," remembered from verse 5: the Israelites tested God, who was not pleased with them, and they were overthrown in the wilderness.[51]

Rock and Wisdom

Given the prominence of the association between Christ and wisdom already in the letter (1 Cor 1:18–30; 2:6–16; 8:6), it seems likely that the identification of the rock with Christ owes something to Jewish Wisdom traditions.[52] Wisdom of Solomon makes wisdom the provider of water

49. Hays, *Echoes*, 91.

50. Against Gathercole, *Preexistent Son*, 30. Gieschen leans towards the view that Christ is identified as the "Destroyer" (1 Cor 10:10), the "angelomorphic figure who carried out the 10th Plague . . . and destruction in Jerusalem at time [sic] of David" (Exod 12:23; 1 Chr 21:12, 15) (*Angelomorphic Christology*, 325–28). The link with the wilderness story is found in Wis 18:14–25: the angelomorphic "word" of God brings the tenth plague to Egypt; the "destroyer" inflicts a plague on the Israelites in the wilderness. This identification seems unlikely, however, given the close association of the "destroying angel" (1 Chr 21:15 LXX) with plague. In the Wisdom narrative the "anger" does not last long because a "blameless man" intervenes, "bringing the weapon of his own ministry" (Wis 18:20–23; cf. Num 16:47–48). When the Destroyer sees Aaron's insignia, he withdraws in fear (Wis 18:24–25). Gieschen finds further support in the more difficult reading of Jude 5: "Jesus, who saved a people out of the land of Egypt, afterward destroyed those who did not believe" (328–29).

51. Note also the repetition of "grumbled" in verse 10.

52. See, e.g., Thiselton who also outlines the broader role attributed to wisdom in the exodus journey in Wisdom of Solomon (*First Corinthians*, 728–29). Waddell assumes a midrashic interpretation of the Old Testament story, in which the "pre-human" form of the messiah figure appears, in order to press the parallel with Philo's speculation

from the rock, though not the rock itself (Wis 11:1–4). The rationale is quite straightforward: wisdom prospered the works of the people "by the hand of a holy prophet"; therefore, they overcame their enemies and had the good sense to call on wisdom when they were thirsty. Philo, on the other hand, reads the story as an out-and-out allegory of the life of the soul. The thirst in the wilderness is that of the passions; it seizes upon the soul "until God sends forth upon it the stream of his own accurate wisdom." The "abrupt rock is (*estin*) the wisdom of God, which being both sublime and the first of things he quarried out of his own powers"; and the water is "a most beautiful draught to drink, namely, wisdom, from the fountain which He himself has brought forth out of his own wisdom" (*Alleg. Interp.* 2 86–87).[53] Conceivably, the identification of Christ with the following rock by way of wisdom preceded—and was even the catalyst for—the quasi-midrashic composition of the typology. But then it is precisely the introduction of wisdom into the equation that makes a realistic or literal identification of the rock with a pre-existent Christ so improbable. The rock *was* Christ in the same way that passing through the sea *was* baptism into Christ and eating and drinking in the wilderness *were* participation in the Lord's supper. In both situations the wisdom of God was dynamically engaged, and the relevant lessons had to be learned.

God Is the Rock, the Rock Is Christ, Therefore Christ Is God?

There is a further dimension to the argument about pre-existence that needs to be considered. Matthew Thiessen has suggested that Paul's identification of the rock with Christ also presupposes the description of God as a rock in the Song of Moses (Deut 32:1–43) and Pss 78 and 95. In this case, the "startlingly high Christological claim" would be not only that Christ pre-existed but that he pre-existed as God.[54]

---

regarding the "middle position" of the Logos (*Messiah*, 136–40). The Logos, according to Philo, stands on the boundary between the creator and the created, and declares: "'And I had stood in the middle of the Lord and of you,' being neither unbegotten as God nor begotten as you, but being in the middle of the extremes, being a hostage to both" (*Heir* 205–6*). Roon however, argues that Paul's language derives entirely from Old Testament passages ("Relation," 228–31).

53. When Philo discusses the passage, the assimilation works the other way: "the abrupt rock is (*estin*) the wisdom of God, which being both sublime and the first of things he quarried out of his own powers, and of it he gives drink to the souls that love God" (*Alleg. Interp.* 2 86). The biblical narrative serves a philosophical argument about the journey of the soul.

54. Thiessen, "Rock," 104. See also Roon, "Relation," 230; Ciampa and Rosner, *First Corinthians*, 451; Fee, *First Corinthians*, 496; Thiselton, *First Corinthians*, 729;

That Paul had the Song of Moses in mind when he was writing 1 Cor 10 seems likely—note the reference to sacrifices made to demons in Deut 32:17 (cf. 1 Cor 10:20) and to provoking the Lord to jealousy in 32:21 (cf. 1 Cor 10:22). Perhaps, too, Paul's insistence that there are lessons to be learned from the experience of the fathers echoes the exhortation to "Remember the days of old; consider the years of many generations; ask your father, and he will show you, your elders, and they will tell you" (Deut 32:7). The Song of Moses, however, looks ahead to Israel's experience in the land. The exodus events *prefigure* the later apostasy and rebellion. God found Jacob in the desert, but then he "made him ride on the high places of the land, and he ate the produce of the field" (32:13). We are now in Canaan. What Jeshurun got from the flinty rock was not water but honey and oil; he grew fat on the produce of large herds of sheep and goats, he ate the finest wheat, and drank foaming wine.[55] Then, following the Greek text, the people abandoned God; they sacrificed to demons, went after foreign gods which "their fathers did not know," and provoked the Lord to jealousy with their idols (32:15–21 LXX). The point is that the mistakes made in the wilderness would be—as Moses saw it—reproduced in the land on a larger scale and with far more severe consequences (32:21–27). Hence the lesson: remember the days of old. The rhetorical method is remarkably similar to Paul's, except that Paul is still hopeful that the Corinthians will learn the lesson in time. But there is no warrant for Thiessen's conclusion that the wilderness rock, which was the Christ, may be identified with God on the basis of the several references to God as the "Rock" in the Song of Moses. The description of God as the "Rock," the "Rock of his salvation," and the "Rock that bore you" (32:4, 15, 18, 30–31) belongs to the experience of Israel in the land and is not at any point connected interpretively with the wilderness rock, which is developed in its own way in the typology.

A similar case is made for the references to the wilderness rock in Pss 78 and 95.[56] It is again quite conceivable that Paul drew inspiration from these texts, but nothing in either psalm points to the identification of God as Rock with the rock struck in the wilderness. God is not that rock; he is the one who splits the rock and causes water to flow from it, just as he opened the doors of heaven and rained down manna for the Israelites (Ps 78:15–16, 20, 23–24). When God is described as "their rock . . . their redeemer" (78:35), a different narrative is evoked, one of battle and

---

Bauckham, *Jesus and the God of Israel*, 100.

55. Thiessen thinks that the reference to honey and oil in Deut 32:13 alludes to the fact that manna tasted like honey and oil (Exod 16:31; Num 11:8; cf. Philo, *Worse* 115) ("Rock," 109n17). More likely the manna is a *foretaste* of provision in the land.

56. Thiessen, "Rock," 108–10.

slaughter, and a different imagery. They remember—or fail to remember—
that God is their rock when they are killed, or when he redeems them from
their enemies (78:34, 42). This rock is a fortress, a place of refuge (e.g., Pss
18:31–42, 46–48; 42:9; 62:2, 6–7; 89:22–26; 94:20–23). It is no more than
a coincidence that in the lengthy accounts of the wilderness experience in
the Song of Moses and Ps 78 God is also described as the rock who safe-
guards his people when they are threatened with violence—or who delivers his people to their enemies when they are unfaithful (Deut 32:30–31).
Ps 95 opens with a celebration of the Lord as "the rock of our salvation"
and includes the exhortation, "do not harden your hearts, as at Meribah,
as on the day at Massah in the wilderness, when your fathers put me to the
test and put me to the proof, though they had seen my work" (Ps 95:8–9).
Thiessen thinks it "conceivable that readers/hearers could have identified
the wilderness rock . . . with God the rock," but this seems a stretch.[57] On
the one hand, the reference is not to the striking of the rock but to Israel's
intransigence, the fact that the fathers put God to the test. On the other,
the saving acts of YHWH are his "work," meaning that YHWH is not the
rock but the one who causes water to flow from the rock.

Finally, if Paul's account of the exodus events in other respects echoes
the language of the Septuagint, as Thiessen repeatedly suggests, we have
then to reckon with the remarkable fact that the translators have removed
all references to God as "Rock" from the Old Testament texts. Thiessen
attempts to compensate for this deficiency by invoking Benjamin Som-
mer's thesis that God was sometimes understood to indwell physical objects such as the stone set up by Jacob at Bethel (Gen 28:11–22).[58] He also
argues that Philo regarded the rock as the source of God's wisdom and
thus as a "hypostasis of the divine," and could state that "God dwells not
merely upon the rock, but even in it."[59] The conclusion is that if Paul could
speak of Christ taking upon himself "a single human flesh-and-blood
body" (Rom 1:3; Gal 4:4) and then being transformed into a resurrected
"pneumatic body" (1 Cor 15:42–50), we may suppose that he entertained
a Stoic conception of the "bodily fluidity of Christ" as the basis for the
identification with the wilderness rock.[60]

The reading of Philo, however, is flawed. Referring to Exod 17:6, Philo
takes God standing "on the rock in Horeb" *before the arrival of the Israelites*
as a figure for his ubiquity and permanence "before you or any one of the

57. Thiessen, "Rock," 110.

58. Thiessen, "Rock," 116–19; see also the discussion in Hays, *Echoes*, 94.

59. Thiessen, "Rock," 119.

60. Thiessen, "Rock," 121–22.

objects of creation had any existence" (*Dreams* 2 221). The rock on which God is established is interpreted as "the highest and most ancient authority of power," from which wisdom flowed. God is not the rock; he is the one who "brought the stream of water out of the solid rock." Philo then likens this tableau to Moses' vision of the God of Israel standing on Mount Sinai: "I saw the place where the God of Israel stood" (222; cf. Exod 24:9–11). In both cases, God is seen standing on, not in, the physical object; he is not identified with the rock any more than he is identified with the mountain. We have seen reason to doubt, moreover, the incarnational reading of Rom 1:3 and Gal 4:4; and the "pneumatic" resurrection body is not unique to Christ (1 Cor 15:46–49). There is no basis here for the notion of a "bodily fluidity" that would encourage us to let "the rock was the Christ" stand as a statement of pre-existence.

He Was Rich But Became Poor

Fee takes it to be more or less self-evident that Jesus' self-impoverishment in 2 Cor 8:9 is a metaphorical reference to the incarnation.[61] He seems to recognize that the statement would work perfectly well without the pre-sumption of pre-existence, but he argues, on the one hand, that Paul has already told the Corinthians that Jesus is the one "through whom all things" were created (1 Cor 8:6), and on the other, that the same riches-to-rags story is told in Philippians 2:6–8: "the plain sense of the metaphor in this case carries all the freight in a presuppositional way of the normal sense of the language and theology of Phil 2:6–7."[62]

Nothing in the passage, however, directly or obviously requires pre-existence. It seems to me that Dunn is right to warn against bringing the assumption of an "established christology of incarnation" to its interpre-tation.[63] The Macedonians are presented as a model for the Corinthians because they *abounded* in joy—and presumably in faith, word, knowledge,

61. Fee, *Christology*, 162–65; also Harris, *Second Epistle to the Corinthians*, 579; Waddell, *Messiah*, 128–29.

62. Fee, *Christology*, 165. Cf. Söding, "Gottes Sohn," 62: the wealth which Christ renounced consisted crucially "in the belonging to God of the pre-existent one, which the Philippians hymn identifies as being determined by God's form and equality with God"; and Martin, *2 Corinthians*, 440–41: "Christ's pretemporal life is here expressed as 'being rich' . . . . The riches of Christ, then, are 'His pre-existent status,' tantamount to his 'being in the form of God' . . . ." Hurtado also makes pre-existence in 2 Cor 8:9 dependent on interpretation of 1 Cor 8:6 and Phil 2:6–7: "among the ideas he expected his converts to be acquainted with and to appreciate was the belief that Jesus had really come from God" (*Lord Jesus Christ*, 123–24).

63. Dunn, *Christology*, 121; see also Kuschel, *Before All Time*, 296.

earnestness, and love—and, despite their extreme material poverty and the great affliction that they were enduring, they had also *abounded* in generosity as an expression of the grace of God. The Corinthians are urged to follow their example. They too *abound* in faith, word, knowledge, earnestness, and love (2 Cor 8:7) and they now have the opportunity to prove the genuineness of this *abundance* (8:8) by practicing the same radical generosity. So in the case of the churches what we have to call a "spiritual" abundance or wealth *is given deeper expression* in the sacrificial giving of their limited material means.

This argument about the concrete demonstration of "grace" is then reinforced by an appeal to what they know about "the grace of our Lord Jesus Christ." The construction in verse 9 does not suggest an exchange of mutually exclusive states, which is often implied in English translation: "he was rich . . . he became poor" (ESV). Rather, the present participle (*ōn*) after the aorist verb (*eptōcheusen*) signifies a continuing condition: "he became poor, being rich . . . ." The construction is put to similar use in Josephus's account of the attempted seduction of Joseph by the wife of Potiphar, a passage which we will come back to at a dramatic moment in the development of our thesis. The woman speaks of the vehement passion "by which she was forced, though being mistress (*biasthein despoina ousa*), to be humbled in respect of her dignity" (*Ant.* 2:46*). She did not cease to be (present participle) his slave-owner when she was driven (aorist) to demean herself. This effectively rules out any thought of incarnation.

The logic is replicated in the letter to the church in Smyrna (Rev 2:8–11). Like the Macedonians they currently suffer "affliction" and "poverty," but, the "one like a son of man" says, "you are rich." They are about to suffer more severely—some of them will be thrown into prison. But if they are "faithful unto death," they will receive the crown of life. Given that the suffering and hope of the recipients of these letters is so clearly patterned after Christ's own experience, we may reasonably suppose that the paradox of Christ's poverty as suffering while being at the same time rich became a compelling trope for the persecuted churches. The gain that comes through suffering is a pervasive theme in 2 Corinthians (1:5; 2:14–17; 4:7; 5:18–19; 11:16—12:10).[64] The catalogue of apostolic hardships culminates in the words "as poor, yet making many rich; as having nothing, yet possessing everything" (6:10). All this points to the conclusion that the metaphor of becoming poor refers not to incarnation but to the acceptance of suffering

---

64. Cf. Dunn, *Christology*, 121. Elsewhere wealth becomes an ironic attribute because it is incompatible with the path of suffering (1 Cor 4:8; Rev 3:17–18).

and death.[65] Gathercole's contention that Paul has "telescoped" incarnation and cross into a single action merely underlines the implausibility of the argument: if the incarnation can be so easily equated with Jesus' death, it no longer stands as a distinct ontological event.[66]

The Man from Heaven

Gathercole is of the opinion that "he was rich" in 2 Cor 8:9 is "clear evidence of preexistence."[67] Perhaps Paul has in mind apocalyptic notions of a heaven "built of gold and other precious metals and jewels"; or perhaps the thought is of the "glorious union of the Father and the Son in eternity" (cf. John 17:5). He then suggests that reference is made to the prior heavenly existence of Jesus in two other passages. We have in 1 Cor 15:47 a "fairly clear reference" to Christ as "the second man from heaven" in contrast to Adam as "the first man from the earth, of dust." Less certainly, the sequence of Christ's descent and ascent in Rom 10:6–7 may have been determined by the order of incarnation and ascension, with the implication that Christ pre-existed in heaven.[68] We can understand why people might want to bring Christ down *now* from heaven, but what would it mean to bring him up from the abyss or from the dead?

A case for the heavenly origin of the second Adam has also been mounted on *history-of-religions* grounds by Charles Gieschen. He maintains that Paul understood Christ to be "the visible appearance of God in heaven as an angelomorphic Man."[69] This is the "heavenly man" (*ho epouranios*) of 1 Cor 15:44–49, a passage which locates Paul in an "*Anthrōpos* tradition" that goes back through Philo, *Corpus hermeticum*, and gnostic literature to Ezekiel's theophanic vision of "a likeness with a human appearance" (Ezek 1:26). Further support for this provenance is to be found, Gieschen suggests, in Paul's identification of Christ as the "Glory," notably in 2 Cor 3:4—4:6.[70] He cites Philo's theory that two *anthrōpoi* were created,

---

65. Cf. Dunn, *Theology of Paul*, 291. Hurtado objects that the single metaphor of self-impoverishment is "hardly a basis for restricting the reference to a single act, Jesus' death" (*Lord Jesus Christ*, 120), but the most that he can do is keep the question open and appeal to other texts, notably Phil 2:6–8, in support of a pre-existence reading.

66. Gathercole, *Preexistent Son*, 26.

67. Gathercole, *Preexistent Son*, 26.

68. Gathercole, *Preexistent Son*, 26–27; also Cullman, *Christology*, 167–71; Martin, *Spirit*, 137; Moo, *Romans*, 654–55; Capes, "Exegesis," 139–48; Fee, *First Corinthians*, 876n347.

69. Gieschen, *Angelomorphic Christology*, 329.

70. Gieschen, *Angelomorphic Christology*, 331, 333–37.

one heavenly, one earthly, as an example of "contemporary exegesis on the subject" that could have influenced Paul.[71] Philo's argument in *Allegorical Interpretation* 1 31–32 and *On the Creation of the World* 134–39 is that the human being was first made according to the "image of God"—"an idea, or a genus, or a seal, perceptible only by the intellect, incorporeal, neither male nor female, imperishable by nature" (*Creation* 134). The incorporeal first *anthrōpos* or soul was then breathed into the second *anthrōpos* made of clay. The human person, therefore, is "Mortal as to his body, but immortal as to his intellect" (135).

We will have more to say about Gieschen's angelomorphic Christology when we get to the Philippians encomium. For now, the question is only whether, when Paul speaks of a second man "from heaven," he means that Christ *originated* in heaven and then was born on earth. This seems doubtful. This is an argument about resurrection (1 Cor 15:42). The perishable precedes the imperishable, the weak precedes the powerful, the "natural (*psychikon*) body" precedes the "spiritual (*pneumatikon*) body" (15:44*). The first man, Adam, *became* "a living *psyche*"; the last Adam presumably also *became* "life-giving spirit." In sum: first the *psychikon*, then the *pneumatikon* (15:46). Christ first existed as *sōma psychikon*, but he *became* life-giving *pneuma* at his resurrection and so now exists as *sōma pneumatikon*. The same point about the order of bodily existence will be made regarding those who will be raised at Christ's coming: first they bear the image of the one of dust, then they *will* bear the image of the heavenly one (15:23, 49).

Gieschen notes that in the *Anthropos* traditions the heavenly man usually precedes the earthly man and suggests that Paul has reversed the order for polemical reasons, "motivated by his eschatological concerns."[72] But this is contrived, surely. The passage gives us no reason to differentiate between a latent sequence of heavenly man followed by earthly man and a polemical adaptation of the tradition. The eschatological argument of 1 Cor 15 is primary, coherent, and sufficient. At no point does it require the premise of the pre-existence of the heavenly man. Christ died and was raised on the third day as "the firstfruits of those who have fallen asleep" (1 Cor 15:3–4, 20); as in Adam all die, so in Christ shall all be made alive, in the proper order (15:21–23); Christ will reign until the last enemy has been destroyed, at which point he will deliver the kingdom to the Father (15:24–25). The argument about the order of the two types of body and of the two Adams then comes simply as Paul's answer to the naïve question, "How are the dead raised? With what kind of body do they come?" (15:35).

71. Gieschen, *Angelomorphic Christology*, 330.
72. Gieschen, *Angelomorphic Christology*, 330.

Next, Paul includes larger groups in the somatic contrast. First, Adam is "from the earth, of dust"; therefore, all people are "of dust." They are not "from the earth" because only Adam was formed from the earth. Secondly, Christ is "from heaven" and "heavenly" (*epouranios*); therefore, those who die in Christ (cf. 1 Cor 15:20–23) *will* also have a heavenly *pneumatikos*-somatic existence. So the two *ek* phrases are not simply synonyms for the adjectives: "from the earth" is the basis for being "of dust," "from heaven" is the basis for being "heavenly."[73] But in the context of the argument, "from heaven" must be a reference to Christ's resurrection existence in heaven at the right hand of God (cf. 15:25). Clearly Paul is attributing the *pneumatikos* or heavenly existence of resurrected believers to the fact that Christ was raised from the dead, not to his supposed heavenly pre-existence, which has no causal relation to the future resurrected life of believers. Since he does not actually say that the second man is "from heaven, heavenly," corresponding to "from the earth, of dust," it may be that *pneumatikos* is assumed from the previous verse: it is his *pneumatikos*-somatic existence that is "from heaven" because it was God who raised him from the dead.[74]

Who Will Bring Christ Down?

Gathercole's tentative proposal regarding the sequence of descent and ascent in Rom 10:6–7 has been defended and developed by David Capes, who argues that Paul's application of Deut 30:12–13 to Christ presupposes use of the passage in the Wisdom tradition. "By identifying Christ as Torah-Wisdom that comes from heaven, he appears to attribute preexistence to him."[75] He then completes the story by applying the second phase to the resurrection of Christ from the dead. "Thus both the incarnation and resurrection of Messiah Jesus are celebrated in Paul's intertextual play."[76] Paul, however, is developing an argument about the "righteousness based on faith," which depends neither on ascending into heaven to bring Christ down nor on descending into the abyss to bring Christ up but simply on confessing that God raised Jesus from the dead and calling on the name of the risen Lord (Rom 10:8–13). Appeal to the pre-existence of Christ and his descent to earth is quite out of place here.[77] The thought is not of

73. Fee, *First Corinthians*, 876–77, who argues nevertheless that "from heaven" is not a reference to Christ's pre-existence.

74. 𝔓46 has completed the parallelism by adding *pneumatikos* to *anthrōpos*.

75. Capes, "Exegesis," 146.

76. Capes, "Exegesis," 145; for the argument see 142–45.

77. Roon thinks that "Paul undoubtedly regards Christ as the one who came down

what happened to Christ but of *what the Jew must now do* in order to be saved—and, more importantly for the present argument, of what he or she must *not* do. The commandment was near for Israel to hear and do but not because it had been brought down from heaven—any more than it had been brought from beyond the sea. So the analogy is only that Christ is likewise near to be confessed by the Jews.

For the Wisdom background Capes cites Bar 3:29–30, but here the Old Testament conceit is used rather differently.[78] The writer asks: "Who has gone up into the sky and taken her and brought her down from the clouds? Who has crossed over the sea and found her and will bring her in exchange for choice gold?" The questions are asked not about the Jews but about the magistrates, hunters of beasts and birds, merchants, storytellers, and philosophers of the nations. None of them found wisdom in the sky—perhaps alluding to those who "make sport among the birds of the sky and who store up silver and gold" (Bar 3:17)—or traded for it across the sea. Not even the giants of old were given "the way of knowledge" and, therefore, they perished because of their recklessness (3:15–28). But God "discovered the whole way of knowledge and gave it to Jacob his servant and to Israel beloved by him." There is no *descent* of wisdom corresponding to the quest to bring it down from the sky; it is merely given in the form of Torah (4:1). There is, therefore, no analogical basis for the view that Paul uses Deut 30:12–13 to speak of the descent of a pre-existent Christ from heaven.

Capes argues, finally, that interpreting bringing Christ down as a reference to the ascended Christ "violates the narrative structure of Paul's essential story," but I think that this misconstrues Paul's rhetoric.[79] The questions are hypothetical, more or less proverbial, as in the original text. Bringing Christ down from heaven or up from the dead are not sequential options, any more than fetching the commandment from the sky or from beyond the sea are sequential options. They are simultaneously open to the Jew seeking the righteousness of God at any moment—but figuratively, not really. Paul's phrasing of the questions reflects the fact that God raised Jesus from the dead and established him as Lord in heaven, but the *literary order* has been determined by the Deuteronomy passage.[80]

from heaven and was raised from the dead . . . . This thought, however, does not play any part in the argument of R. x" ("Relation," 227–28).

78. Philo makes the "good" the object of the quest to heaven or beyond the sea (*Posterity* 84–85).

79. Capes, "Exegesis," 146.

80. Cf. Dunn, *Christology*, 185; Dunn, *Theology of Paul*, 281.

Conclusion

The confession of 1 Cor 8:6 is not a reworking of the Shema but a very concise summary of the eschatological narrative that drives Paul's entire thought. With both Jewish and Greek incomprehension in mind (1 Cor 1:18–25), he affirms that the one God of Jewish tradition, who is Father to Israel, is the *source* of the new things that are happening—not least of the eschatological communities that must bear witness to the coming transformation—and that the one Lord Jesus Christ is the *means* by which these things are happening. Wisdom language is used but *paradoxically*, because both Jews and Greeks struggle to understand how such a re-creation of the world might be achieved through a crucified protagonist and the unprepossessing and often abject adherents of his cult.

There is a degree of contingency to the embodiment of pre-existent wisdom in the creative event of Jesus' death and resurrection. As Dunn sees it, Paul is making the astonishing claim that Jesus is "the clearest exposition and explanation of divine Wisdom, that the cross is the fullest embodiment of the wisdom which created the universe and which humans need if they are to live the good life."[81] The asymmetry is rightly grasped: wisdom is embodied in a sequence of events centered on Christ crucified; Paul is not saying that Christ pre-existed under the name or in the form of the primordial wisdom of God. But the asymmetry is funneled towards a narrower conception of the significance of Christ crucified. The cross is not the fullest embodiment of the wisdom by which the universe was created; rather it is the decisive manifestation of the creative wisdom of God *under these eschatological circumstances*, when the form of this world is passing away. Likewise, the purpose is not that humans should "live the good life" but that churches such as the one in Corinth should bear faithful witness, under difficult conditions, until they inherit the kingdom of God. Christ was the embodiment of the foolish but profoundly innovative wisdom through which God was transforming the status of his people in the world.

Different use is made of the wisdom motif in the extended comparison between the experience of Israel in the wilderness and the circumstances of believers in Corinth, but the effect is to reinforce the underlying representation of Christ as a decisive manifestation of the eschatological wisdom of God. The point in this case is not that the pre-existent Christ was present in the wilderness. It is that the rock, perhaps as a representation of divine wisdom in a time of difficult transition, was with the Israelites in the same way that Christ is present for the church—and lessons must be learned.

81. Dunn, *Theology of Paul*, 274.

The paradox is restated in the metaphor of Christ's self-impoverishment in 2 Cor 8:9. Remove the *presumption* of pre-existence and this reads quite naturally as an account of his earthly experience. The logic of the metaphor is reproduced in the experience of the Macedonians and of the church in Smyrna: they are wealthy in the Spirit—possessed of joy, faith, word, knowledge, earnestness, and love—but at the same time willingly accept the extreme impoverishment of affliction and material hardship. That this logic also anticipates the transition from *morphē theou* to "form of a slave" will become apparent later. Finally, it is evident that the two passages which have been thought to allude to the descent of Christ from heaven say no such thing. In both cases, though for different rhetorical purposes, it is Christ's resurrection and exaltation that account for his heavenly existence.

4

Being in the Form of God

Of the two or three texts in Paul that are routinely referenced in confident support of a doctrine of Christ's pre-existence the most important is the first paragraph of the summary of Christ's career in Phil 2:6–11.[1] The encomium states that Jesus was *en morphēi theou* and that he took the *morphē* of a slave. Traditionally, this change in "form" has been understood in incarnational terms: Jesus pre-existed in heaven "in the form of God" but he was "born in the likeness of men"; he was "found in human form"; and especially in the degrading circumstances of his execution he took on the "form of a slave" (Phil 2:6–8). The question to be addressed in this chapter is whether Paul is likely to have thought that the living God possessed a *morphē, in which* Jesus might have existed prior to his earthly life. The literary-linguistic evidence suggests that a first-century Greek-speaking Jew would have found the idea outlandish. J. Behm says, for example, that in the Old Testament "it is a fundamentally alien and impossible thought that God should have a form open to human perception, or that He should reveal Himself in sensual form."[2] But the argument has been made either that *morphē* equates to some more abstract quality such as "essence" or "glory,"

1. Whether the passage is *formally* hymnic or poetic remains an open question, but in my view it *functions* as an encomium and is probably best read as elevated prose. Cf. Fee, "Hymn," 39–43; Yarbro Collins, "Origins," 370–71; Tobin, "World of Thought," 92; Reumann, *Philippians*, 364–65; Holloway, *Philippians*, 116. I do not rule out the possibility that it has a measure of literary independence as a self-contained piece about Christ or as a digest of a lengthier composition, of which someone other than Paul was the author. Beyond noting the obvious two part structure I will not take into account considerations of stanzaic arrangement or meter (cf. Gordley, *Christological Hymns*, 51–52). I take the advice of Keown (*Philippians 1:1–2:18*, 370), and analyze verses 6–8 "based on the 'usual' grammatical clues"—notably, the aorist main verbs coordinated with *alla* and *kai* ("he did not consider . . . *but* he emptied himself . . . *and* . . . humbled himself . . . ") and aorist participle clauses. Hurtado says that three indicative verbs "form the syntactical backbone of the passage" (*How on Earth*, 95).

2. Behm, "μορφή," 749.

or that some manner of *humanlike form* is in view, whether of Christ himself as a heavenly pre-human, of God anthropomorphically conceived, of the first man or Adam (ch. 5), or of an angel or some other prominent heavenly figure (ch. 6). Before we get on to a review of the various theories, however, we will survey the incidence of *morphē* in the literature of Hellenistic Judaism to get a feel for the use of the term.

Morphē in Hellenistic Judaism

The word *morphē* is widely used in the major corpora in a variety of contexts but only rarely in relation to the one God of Jewish belief. The phrase *morphē theou* is nowhere found in this connection. Two Jewish texts, however, have been cited as positive evidence for the view that God may be said to have a *morphē* and may be considered separately: Philo's reference to a "certain very beautiful form" seen by Moses in the burning bush (*Moses* 1 66); and a comment made by Josephus about the propriety of attributing "form and magnitude" to God (*Ag. Ap.* 2:190).

Septuagint

The *morphē* of an object or person is the outward appearance. Gideon's brothers were like him: they had the "appearance, form (*eidos morphē*) of sons of kings" (Judg 8:18); their physical features—build, handsomeness of face, and such-like—identified them as being of superior or aristocratic birth. Nebuchadnezzar was filled with anger, and "the form (*morphē*) of his face was distorted" (Dan 3:19). Tobit says that when he was taken into exile in Nineveh, unlike his compatriots he refused to eat the bread of the nations "because I was mindful of God with my whole soul." However, God gave him "favor and *morphēn*" before Enemessaros, and he was made the king's buyer of provisions (Tob 1:12–13). Interpreters often give the word a more abstract sense here, such as "status"; but *morphē* is still a reference to the *appearance* of Tobit. Like Daniel and his friends, who refused to eat the king's food (Dan 1:15), he *looked no worse* for his abstemiousness and was rewarded with advancement.[3] Parents "impress upon the tender nature of a child a remarkable likeness both of soul and of form (*morphēs*)" (4 Macc 15:4). The children are not mistaken for their parents, but they have something of their "form" or outward appearance, as well as a psychological likeness. A piece of wood is given the "form" of a man by a craftsman (Isa 44:13). Sometimes the form cannot be seen. Describing the plague of

---

3. Cf. Moulton and Milligan, *Vocabulary*, s.v. μορφή, 417.

darkness that came upon the Egyptians, the author of Wisdom of Solomon says that the Egyptians could hear the voice of God's "holy ones" (that is, the Israelites), for whom there was great light, but could not see their "form" (*morphēn*) (Wis 18:1–2). Some things are *form*-less: Job's friend Eliphaz says that a "spirit" came upon his face at night, when things are difficult to see anyway, and his hair and flesh quivered; he heard a breeze and a voice, but the presence had no visible "form" (*morphē*) (Job 4:16).

Philo

In Philo, too, *morphē* signifies the physical or perceptible form of a person, creature, or object. God shaped the "human form" (*morphēn anthrōpinēn*) out of clay (*Creation* 135; cf. 76; *Migration* 3).[4] Adam rejoiced at the creation of the woman because she had a "cognate appearance" and a "form (*morphēn*) of the same kind" (*Creation* 151*). Subsequent generations, however, have been at all times inferior in "forms" (*morphas*)—that is, in appearance—and strength (*Creation* 140). Some men are "clothed with the form (*morphēn*) of a human body so as to give an appearance of gentleness," but behave as wild animals (*Moses* 1 43). Effeminate men "counterfeit the coinage of nature by adopting the passions and forms (*morphas*) of licentious women" (*Spec. Laws* 1 325*). Philo means that they dress, adorn, and paint themselves as female prostitutes. Lines from Euripides are quoted to the effect that when an organism—a plant or animal—dies and decays, "another form" (*morphēn heteran*) is produced (*Alleg. Interp.* 1 7*; cf. *Eternity* 5–6, 30, 144; Euripides, *Chrys.* 839). The "dispositions of the soul" are contrasted with the "forms (*morphas*) of bodies" (*Abraham* 147). The powers of God, which may be called "ideas," give "forms to formless things" (*morphas amorphois*) in the same way that a seal leaves a physical impression in wax (*Spec. Laws* 1 47*; cf. 329; *Eternity* 79). In this case, "form" is a metaphor for intellectual order but it presupposes a literal sense corresponding to the visible mark left in the wax. Likenesses of body with respect to "form (*morphēn*), posture and movement" are passed on from one generation to the next (*Embassy* 55*): the child *looks like* the parent. Caligula appropriated the demigods by "transforming and remodeling the essence of one body into multifarious forms (*morphas*), like

---

4. The precise point of Philo, *Creation* 76* is unclear: "Having called the species 'human,' most beautifully he distinguished the outward appearances (*eidē*), saying that they have been created 'male and female,' not yet of those having received a form (*morphēn*) individually, since the boundary characteristics of the outward appearances (*eidōn*) inhere in the species . . . ." Perhaps *eidē* is used for the general physical differentiation between male and female while *morphē* signifies variation of outward "form" from person to person.

the Egyptian Proteus" (*Embassy* 80*): the *morphē* is the outward appearance that the "essence" (*ousian*) of the body takes. Philo challenges the emperor to stop imitating the true Apollo, "for not as the counterfeited coin is the form of a god (*theou morphē*)" (*Embassy* 110*). The golden calf that the Israelites worshiped at Sinai was a "handmade bull-form (*tauromorphon*) god" (*Moses* 2 165*). Devout Jews behold the "visible types and forms (*morphas*)" of their sacred laws, but no "handmade form (*morphēn*)"—no idol—has ever been admitted into the temple (*Embassy* 211, 290*; cf. 299, 346). An actor changes into "another form" (*morphēn heteran*) for the benefit of the spectators (*QG* 4 204). A person is known by the distinctive "quality and form" (*poiotēta kai morphēn*) of the face (*QE* 2 3).

Philo insists repeatedly that God is not in human form: "neither is God anthropomorphic (*anthrōpomorphos*), nor the human body of divine appearance (*theoeides*)" (*Creation* 69*; cf. *Alleg. Interp.* 1 36; *Sacrifices* 95; *Posterity* 4; *Unchangeable* 59; *Planting* 35; *Confusion* 135; *Prelim. Studies* 115; *Names* 54). Sometimes, however, he shows himself to humans "in the resemblance of the angels," presenting to the minds of those imagining him his glory in "another form (*heteromorphon*), as image not copy"; but it is *taken to be* the actual "archetypal outward appearance" (*Dreams* 1 232). In other words, people *mistakenly* think that they have seen the true form of God. This perhaps suggests that what is seen is not a separate angelic creature but a representation of God himself, "only in another form." God has a *morphē* in this case but only when he makes himself visible to people in the world, and then only in some indirect and inessential sense as an *eikōn*. In the heavenly sphere he is seen by the angels as he is, without any "form."

The use of the verb *morphoō* agrees with this pattern, though there tends to be a higher level of abstraction involved. It is notable also that in most cases the emphasis is less on the *appearance* of what is formed than on the contrast with a prior *formless* condition—in other words, on the *process*. The "world-shaper" began to "form" (*morphoun*) the disorderly "substance" (*ousian*) of the world (*Planting* 3*; cf. *Dreams* 2 45). Earth and water were mixed and "formed" (*morphōthenta*) into the human-shaped body (*Dreams* 1 210*). It is "fitting for God to give form (*morphoun*) to formless things and to endow what is ugly with marvellous beauty" (*Eternity* 41*). The word of God is the "seal by which each of existing things is invested with form (*memorphōtai*)" (*Flight* 12). Rationality, wisdom, and Torah are the result of a process of *formation*, bringing order to human behavior. God "formed" (*emorphou*) the rational part of the soul in people (*Flight* 69; cf. *Spec. Laws* 1 171). He "formed (*emorphōsas*) the archetypal patterns of our instruction, which were indistinct, so that they might be visible"—he taught Abraham wisdom and brought about the birth of wise

Isaac (*Dreams* 1 173*). Central to the reasoning process is to "form form-less things (*amorpha morphōsai*) with types and patterns" (*Confusion* 87*). Artists and craftsmen give form to unformed matter. Impious men neglect divine things and have "fashioned (*morphōsantes*) an infinite variety of ap-pearances by the arts of painting and sculpture" (*Decalogue* 7). The makers of idols have "fashioned (*morphōsantōn*) stocks, and stones, and silver, and gold, and similar materials according to their own pleasure" (*Decalogue* 66, cf. 72; *Spec. Laws* 1 21; *Spec. Laws* 2 255). Conversely, people devoted to the "service of the soul," rather than of the body, are content with the "bare conception" (*phantasian monēn*) of God's existence and do not "at-tribute form" (*mē morphōsantes*) to him (*Unchangeable* 55*). The angels who dined with Abraham, though incorporeal, "presented the appearance (*memorphōsthai*) of a body in human form by reason of their favour to the virtuous man" (*Abraham* 118). In a rather obscure piece of argumenta-tion Philo asserts, first, that Moses was created according to the pattern of an "incorporeal being" no different from the divine "image" (*eikonos*); then secondly, that he imitated God by forming the "outward appearance" (*emorphou ta eidē*)—of the Law, the tabernacle?—according to "his arche-typal patterns" (*Confusion* 63).[5] Finally, a miscarried fetus is no longer "un-fashioned and unshapen" but "formed" (*memorphōmenon*) if its distinctive parts and qualities are apparent (*Spec. Laws* 3 108, cf. 117).

Philo consistently uses *morphē* for the concrete, perceptible, and dis-tinctive "form" that a thing has. The *morphē* is not the essence or substance or nature of something; it is how that thing appears to the observer. It means "shape," "physical character," or "outward appearance," a meaning that may then be used metaphorically to give definition to more abstract objects of thought. The verb, as we might expect, commonly denotes a process by which what was formless *acquires form* and becomes perceptible or appre-ciable. We will get to the passage about the bush in a moment, but we can say provisionally that for Philo *morphē* is emphatically not something that God has, other than in the very specific sense that a human form is some-times erroneously attributed to him by those to whom he appears.

Josephus

Josephus employs *morphē* frequently for a person's "face" or "countenance" or physical appearance more generally (*Ant.* 2:61, 98, 102; 5:125; 6:45, 162; 7:190; 15:51; 16:7; 17:324, 329; *J.W.* 2:101, 104). Pharaoh had the same dream "in two forms (*morphais*)," involving first cattle, then ears of corn.

5. Note the discussion in Horbury, *Jewish Messianism*, 94.

The meaning or substance of the dreams is the same, but the *imagery*—the manner of visualization—is different (*Ant.* 2:84). When the daughter of Pharaoh says that she has "brought up a child in form divine (*morphēi . . . theion*) and in mind noble," she differentiates between the *outward appearance* of Moses, which is godlike, and his inner character of mind (2:232*). The woman in Endor who raised Samuel described him as being "like a god in form (*morphēn*)" (6:333*). A phantasm appeared to Gideon in the "form of a young man" (5:213*). The cherubim on the ark of the covenant are "flying creatures, but in form (*morphēn*) resembling nothing seen by humans" (3:137*). The temple veil was embroidered with many and diverse figures but not with the "forms" (*morphas*) of animals (3:113, 126; cf. *Life* 65). The Jews are forbidden to "honor idols and images formed (*memorphōmenous*) after the Greek fashion" (*Ant.* 15:329*). In a lengthy polemic against idolatry Josephus says that some people have transformed the basest human passions "into the nature and form of a god (*theou . . . morphēn*)"—that is, abstract qualities have been given the quasi-physical *appearance* of the gods who appear in the myths and whose statues adorn the cities (*Ag. Ap.* 2:248*). Greek sculptors enjoyed the privilege of imagining a certain "form" (*morphēn*) for a god and then fashioning it from clay (*Ag. Ap.* 2:252). The Egyptians claim that they have never been subdued by the kings of Europe and Asia because the gods fled to their country and "were saved by turning into forms (*morphas*) of wild beasts" (*Ag. Ap.* 2:128*).

Old Testament Pseudepigrapha

In the Greek Old Testament Pseudepigrapha the *morphoō* word group is frequently used for the external form of humans (Sib. Or. Prolog. 99; Sib. Or. 3:7, 27; 4:182; 8:366) and other beings, including supernatural beings. Benjamin longed to see the "figure" (*idean*) of Joseph and the "form (*morphēn*) of his face," and through the prayers of Jacob his father he came to see "his entire figure (*idea*) just as he was" (T. Benj. 10:1*). On a visit to Tartarus Ezra heard the voices of sinners but "saw not their forms (*morphas*)" (Gk. Apoc. Ezra 4:14). Different "forms" (*morphas*) of beings will be led down into judgment: the "representations (*eidōlōn*) of Titans born long ago," the giants, and then the different classes of the dead, killed in the flood, eaten by wild animals, or consumed by fire (Sib. Or. 2:230–36). There are different "forms" (*morphas*) of wild creatures (Sib. Or. 5:135–36). On the day of judgment "the heavenly luminaries will crash together, also into an utterly desolate form (*morphēn panerēmon*)"—in other words, into *formlessness* (Sib. Or. 2:200–201). People give form (*morphōsantes*) to wooden idols and sing praises to them (Sib. Or. 8:379).

When Death was sent to summon Abraham, he first "put on a robe of brightness, and made his appearance sun-shaped (*hēliomorphon*), and became fair and beautiful beyond the sons of men, being wrapped in the form (*morphēn*) of an archangel, his cheeks flashing with fire." He then put off "all his comeliness and beauty, and all the glory and the sun-shaped form (*hēliomorphon morphēn*) with which he was wrapped," and put on instead a tyrant's robe, making his appearance "gloomy and fiercer than every kind of wild animal" (T. Ab. A 16:6; 17:12–13*; cf. 16:12; 18:1). Death is neither an archangel nor the sun, but he assumes the *morphē* of these things.

In Testament of Solomon (first to third century AD) *morphē* is used for the various forms that demons take: a pederast, a winged creature, a lion, a woman with the legs of a mule, a half-horse-half-fish, a giant (T. Sol. 2:3; 4:2; 16:1; 17:1). One demon, when "conjured by the wise," can take three different "forms" (*morphas*), including that of Kronos (15:5*).

The "Form of God"?

Markus Bockmuehl asks whether Jewish writers ever used the word *morphē* for God. He thinks that the answer is yes, though instances are rare.[6] In an account of the burning bush, Philo says that "in the middle of the flame there was a certain very beautiful form (*morphē*), unlike any of the things that are seen, a most godlike image (*agalma*), flashing forth with a light more brilliant than fire, which one might have surmised to be an image (*eikona*) of the Being" (*Moses* 1 66*). But he is careful to *correct* the impression given that this was a visual representation of the God who is. Philo commonly uses the verb translated here "surmised" (*hypotopeō*) to denote a false impression or wrong assumption.[7] This is patently not the form of God.[8] Therefore, since the figure merely conveys a message about future events, Philo decides that it should be "called an angel" (cf. Exod 3:2). In one passage, Josephus uses *morphē* with reference to God: he is "manifest in works and benefits, and more conspicuous than anything, but form (*morphēn*) and magnitude are

---

6. Bockmuehl, "Form of God," 15; cf. Fowl, *Philippians*, 92.

7. Philo, *Sacrifices* 134; *Unchangeable* 21; *Drunkenness* 183, 205; *Confusion* 162; *Migration* 179, 182; *Dreams* 1 118, 182; *Joseph* 184; *Decalogue* 109; *Spec. Laws* 1 16; *Good Person* 3.

8. In the biblical texts the statement that the people of Israel "saw no form" (*temunah, homoiōma*) in the fire on the mountain underlines the prohibition against making carved images in the "likeness" (*temunah, homoiōma*) of any living creature (Deut 4:12, 15–18).

unuttered (*aphatos*) by us" (*Ag. Ap.* 2:190*). Bockmuehl takes this to mean that God has a *morphē* but that it is not "accessible to humans."[9] The point more probably is that "form and magnitude" are not spoken about because they are improper attributes when the subject is God. Josephus goes on to explain what he means (2:191–92). Even the most costly materials are unworthy to be used for an image of him; no artistry is sufficient for the purpose of imitation; it is impious to suppose that we can see or conceive or "form an image of" (*eikazein*) his likeness. Form and size pertain to objects—not least to idols—in the created sphere, not to God. Importantly, Josephus says that God created the world "not with hands, not with labors"—means which might be thought to pertain to form and size—but simply "by his willing" (*autou thelēsantos*) things came into being. Neither of these texts, therefore, departs from the established usage.

Conclusions

All the evidence considered here points in the same direction: in the extant literature of Hellenistic Judaism, *morphē*, when it is not used metaphorically, signifies the outward visible shape and appearance of a being or object. This is in agreement with wider Greek usage.[10] There are certain characteristic emphases that may have a bearing on the interpretation of the word in a passage such as Phil 2:6–8. The "form" of a being may indicate status or physical condition, it may misrepresent his or her status or condition, but *morphē* still means only "outward appearance." The word is often used in contexts where the relation between underlying or prior reality and outward appearance is at issue, but it does not on that account also signify the essence of the thing. There is a pervasive interest in the visible form taken by things—gods, angels, spirits, demons, ideas—that might otherwise be hidden or obscure. But the notion that the one God of Jewish belief might have a *morphē* is never positively entertained; indeed, it is expressly denied.

New Testament Usage

We find *morphē* in the New Testament only in Phil 2:6 and in the longer ending to Mark's Gospel, where it is said that Jesus "was revealed to two of them in another form (*en heterai morphēi*) as they were walking into

9. Bockmuehl, "Form of God," 15; cf. Fowl, *Philippians*, 92.

10. See Jipp, *Christ is King*, 129n221: "One cannot escape the fact that μορφή [*morphē*] signifies visible appearance"; cf. Hellerman, "Μορφη Θεου," 786; Hellerman, *Philippians*, 109–10. See also the comprehensive study of Fabricatore, *Form of God*.

the countryside" (Mark 16:12*). The latter instance is consistent with the general pattern (cf. Philo, *Alleg. Interp.* 1 7; *QG* 4 204): the word signifies the distinctive external appearance of a person or object. The cognate *morphōsis* has much the same sense, though it happens to be used in the New Testament for the outward expression of more abstract realities. The Jews have in the Law, Paul says, the practical "form" or perhaps "formulation" (*morphōsin*) of knowledge and truth (Rom 2:20); and he—or an imitator—warns that in the last days there will be people who have an "outward appearance of piety" (*morphōsin eusebeias*) but deny its power (2 Tim 3:5).[11] The "form" is not the essence of the thing—knowledge, truth, piety—but how it appears and is engaged with.

The verb occurs only once, when Paul appeals to the Galatians: "my children, for whom again I suffer birth pains until Christ is formed (*morphōthēi*) in you . . . " (Gal 4:19*). The immediate context is the fraught tug-of-war with the Judaizing interlopers: for Christ to be formed in them means that they will be able to stand firm and resist the pressure to submit to "a yoke of slavery." But to be *formed* in the image of Christ, so to speak, inevitably means to replicate his experience in their own lives. Paul speaks of himself as having been "crucified with Christ," so that it is "no longer I who live, but Christ who lives in me"; he boasts only in "the cross of our Lord Jesus Christ, by which the world has been crucified to me, and I to the world" (2:20; 6:14); and he urges them to become as he is (4:12). They should cast out the slave woman and her son, but "just as at that time he who was born according to the flesh persecuted him who was born according to the Spirit, so also it is now" (4:29). The pastoral context is different, but for Christ to be formed in these believers is essentially the same as being "conformed to the image" (*symmorphous tēs eikonos*) of Christ or "conformed (*symmorphizomenos*) to his death," finally to be "conformed (*symmorphon*) to the body of his glory" (Rom 8:29; Phil 3:10, 21). What is in view here is not a general spiritual progress but the specific and realistic imitation of Christ in his suffering, death, and vindication. Paul means what he says when he makes participation in Christ's inheritance *conditional*: "heirs together with Christ, provided that we suffer together (with him) so that also we might be glorified together (with him)" (Rom 8:17*).[12] In this argument, therefore, the *eikōn* belongs to Christ, but the *morphē* belongs to the persecuted believer, who is being purposefully shaped or molded in the image of the Son, who thus will become "firstborn among many brothers"

11. In *Planting* 70* Philo speaks of people who "put on a show of piety" (*epimorphazontōn eusebeian*).

12. See Perriman, *Future of the People of God*, 116.

(8:29). The same idea is expressed in 2 Cor 3:18* by a different compound verb: the apostles are "being transformed (*metamorphoumetha*) into the same image from glory to glory as from the Lord, the Spirit." The complex analogical structure has rather got the better of the simple idea of *morphē* as outward appearance in these statements, but the emphasis is still very much on physical behavior, concrete representation.[13]

The Inward Reality of God

If, then, on the face of it, *morphē* is such an improbable term for a Hellenistic Jew such as Paul to have used with reference to the one God, how are we to make sense of the expression *morphē theou* in Phil 2:6? What *exceptional* linguistic, rhetorical, or conceptual circumstance would make this meaningful to Paul's readers in Philippi?

It has been suggested on various grounds that the word would have signified outward form *as an authentic expression of some inner character or reality*. J. B. Lightfoot's supposedly Aristotelian view can be placed at the head of this stream of thought: *morphē* is not *ousia* ("being"), but "possession of the μορφή [*morphē*] involves participation in the οὐσία [*ousia*] also: for μορφή implies not the external accidents but the essential attributes."[14] Paul could not have spoken of God having a form in the sense of having "a figure, a shape"; so *morphē* "must apply to the attributes of the Godhead. In other words, it is used in a sense substantially the same which it bears in Greek philosophy."[15]

The express appeal to a classical philosophical background (to be fair, Lightfoot also found the idea in Plutarch, the Neoplatonists, and Philo) hardly made it out of the nineteenth century. But the basic argument has persisted: the outward "form" points inwards; it reveals what is essential to or characteristic of the thing.[16] So Marvin Vincent acknowledged that *morphē* would normally mean "shape" or "sensible appearance," which cannot be applied to God, but argued, without offering any evidence, that in Phil 2:6 the word must mean "that expression of being which is identified

13. The argument of Keown that the compound verbs "refer to essential change and not merely external form" is unnecessary (*Philippians 1:1—2:18*, 388). The "form" is a pattern of socially visible behavior.

14. Lightfoot, *Philippians*, 110; see also Beare: *morphē* "is not a synonym for 'substance' (*ousia*); the ontological concern of later dogmatic theology is not relevant here" (*Philippians*, 78); Martin, *Hymn of Christ*, 100–102.

15. Lightfoot, *Philippians*, 132.

16. See Weymouth, "Christ-Story," 408n1, for a list of scholars supporting an "essence" view.

with the essential nature and character of God, and which reveals it."[17] Others circumvented the plain meaning of the word in much the same way. H. A. A. Kennedy: Paul "means, of course, in the strictest sense that the pre-existing Christ was Divine. For μ. always signifies a form which truly and fully expresses the being which underlies it."[18] Jacob Jervell: *morphē* "means the essence or substance of the deity. The classical Greek meaning 'shape, external form, etc.' has been stripped off."[19] Rudolf Bultmann: the form of God in which Christ pre-existed is "not mere form but the divine mode of being just as much as the 'form of a servant' is the mode of being of a servant."[20] Lucien Cerfaux's explanation seems patently incoherent: the word expresses the way that a thing "appears to our senses," but if it is applied to God, "his μορφή [*morphē*] will be his deepest being, which cannot be reached by our understanding or sight, precisely because God is ἀόρατος [*aoratos*]."[21] F. W. Beare took the view that *morphē* "does, or can, retain in the usage of the New Testament its proper sense of 'form which corresponds to the underlying reality', in contrast with *schēma* . . . which may mean 'a false appearance.'"[22] He concluded that the form of God is "not to be conceived as a mere appearance, but as a form of experience which in some sense exhibits Christ's true nature." This hardly works given the immediately following statement that Christ was "found in *schēmati* as a human person"—clearly, a contrast between a true and false appearance is not the issue here. Last but not least, Ernst Käsemann argued that in Hellenistic Greek *morphē* had lost the older sense of "form" as distinct from substance, as part of a "mythical-philosophical antithesis," and had acquired a new meaning—a "mode of being under particular circumstances" or "Daseinsweise."[23] In effect, form and substance have been collapsed into a single notion—*being* with a particular form. The force of the preposition *en* must then be reckoned with: "One has a shape, style, posture. One is not really spatially 'in it.'"[24] But in Hellenism the preposition may be thought to define the "area" in which you stand, which "determines you like a force field (Kraftfeld)."[25] The "form of

17. Vincent, *Philippians*, 57–58.

18. Kennedy, "Philippians," 436.

19. Jervell, *Imago Dei*, 228.

20. Bultmann, *Theology*, 1:193.

21. Cerfaux, *Christ*, 385.

22. Beare, *Philippians*, 79; cf. Lightfoot, *Philippians*, 130–31.

23. See O'Brien, *Philippians*, 209; also Hamerton-Kelly, *Pre-Existence*, 160–61; Hawthorne and Martin, *Philippians*, 112.

24. Käsemann, "Kritische Analyse," 331.

25. Hamerton-Kelly, *Pre-Existence*, 161: "The Hellenistic individual understood the shape and substance of his existence to be the result of a constellation of forces."

God," therefore, is not something that Christ *has*; it is a "sphere" or "mode of being" in which he stands.[26]

Support for the thesis has waned in the last few decades as interest has shifted towards more exotic anthropomorphic and angelomorphic accounts, but it still has its defenders. Either the *morphē theou* is an intrinsic *expression* of the divine being or of some aspect of it, or the term is a direct reference to divine being. Fee argues that *morphē theou* cannot be understood apart from the parallel phrase *morphē doulou*. *Morphē* was "precisely the right word": it could be used to "characterize both the reality (his being God) and the metaphor (his taking on the role of a slave), since it denotes 'form' or 'shape' not in terms of the external features by which something is recognized, but of those characteristics and qualities that are essential to it."[27] The word means "that which truly characterizes a given reality" (italics removed) and is equivalent to "in very nature God" (NIV).[28] Teresia Wong says that "typical for μορφή [*morphē*] is the correlation between substance and appearance"; it "pertains to his being, accessible through his appearance"; the verse is a "solemn declaration of Christ's pre-existent divinity."[29] For Söding *morphē* is the "Gestalt" that finds expression when a person acts in agreement with an "authentic status and original role." The *morphē theou*, therefore, is the form which "characterizes the God-being of God, with which God through his original action as God appears and makes communication possible."[30] Gerald Hawthorne argues that a reference to "external appearance" works neither for "form of God" nor for "form of a slave"; therefore, a "new meaning" must be found. In the end, he reverts to Lightfoot, Kennedy, and Vincent and suggests, quoting Cerfaux, that when applied to God *morphē* must refer to his "deepest being, to what he is in himself, to that 'which cannot be reached by our understanding or sight, precisely because God is *aoratos*: in fact the word has meaning here only as referring to the reality of God's being,'" with the qualification that it nevertheless has to do with "God in his manifestation."[31] Dennis Jowers gets from the philosophical usage the

---

26. Käsemann, "Kritische Analyse," 331; cf. Cerfaux, *Christ*, 387. See Martin, *Hymn of Christ*, 105n2, for a summary; also O'Brien, *Philippians*, 206; Hawthorne and Martin, *Philippians*, 110.

27. Fee, *Philippians*, 204; cf. Fee, *Christology*, 378.

28. Fee, *Philippians*, 205.

29. Wong, "Problem," 273, 278

30. Söding, "Gottes Sohn," 59.

31. Hawthorne and Martin, *Philippians*, 114; also Jowers, "ΜΟΡΦΗ," 764; Hansen agrees but grounds it in the biblical notion that the appearance of God consists in his glory (*Philippians*, 134–38).

sense "immaterial actuality" and presents this as evidence that *ousia* was a valid meaning for *morphē* around the time of Paul.[32] John Reumann, in the end, follows Käsemann: *morphē* means "sphere," in the sense of "realm, place and relationships."[33] Joseph Hellerman argues that *morphē* can have an ontological sense, approximating to *ousia*, in philosophical texts and in Rom 8:29; 12:2; Gal 4:19.[34] Bonnie Thurston and Judith Ryan render *en morphēi theou hyparchōn* as "being in essence God," reducing the clause to a more or less categorical assertion of Christ's divinity.[35]

Michael Martin and Bryan Nash note that "Jewish and other ancient Mediterranean language concerning the μορφή [*morphē*] of a god, and in contrast to a human μορφή, generally has in view the god's 'form' and not the other meanings associated with the word." They assert that Hellenistic Jews sometimes made reference to the *morphē* of God (Job 4:16 LXX; Josephus, *Ag. Ap.* 2:190; Philo, *Moses* 1 66). The Greeks also used *morphē* to speak of the "form or shape" of their gods (we will look at these texts in chapter 7), but in a manner that is "frequently external and does not correspond to inward reality, as it does in Jewish monism"—a distinction that is only weakly substantiated.[36] Sometimes it is said that a god takes a human *morphē* and is "in" that *morphē* "with reference to form or shape." They conclude that the encomium begins with the assertion that Christ pre-existed in divine form, with the qualification that in a Jewish religious context "form of God" must be understood to mean "an accurate reflection of inward reality."

Finally, we may note certain explanations of the "form of God" which take it to be a reference to the *kenotically* re-imagined essence or inner reality of God. Bockmuehl thinks that Paul is alluding to the "inconceivable size and beauty" of Christ's bodily appearance, as we shall see in the next chapter, but the beauty is not a static attribute; it is expressed in "the eternally present but historically realised act" of taking the form of a slave.[37] The "mind" and action of Jesus, which the Philippians are to emulate, are "the translation into time, space, and creation of the eternal heavenly form of God." Michael Gorman likewise argues that it was not *in spite of* being in the form of God that Jesus emptied himself but *because* he was in the form

---

32. Jowers, "ΜΟΡΦΗ," 750, and the extended discussion in 761–65.

33. Reumann, *Philippians*, 344; cf. Jowers, "ΜΟΡΦΗ," 753–57.

34. Hellerman, "Μορφη Θεου," 785–86; cf. Lightfoot, *Philippians*, 128–30; Jowers, "ΜΟΡΦΗ," 749–50.

35. Thurston and Ryan, *Philippians*, 80–81; also those cited by Jowers, "ΜΟΡΦΗ," 763.

36. Martin and Nash, "Hymnos," 116–17.

37. Bockmuehl, "Form of God," 20–21.

of God. "Cruciform kenosis is the counterintuitive 'truth about God.'"[38]
A robustly anti-imperialist version of the same thesis is propounded by
John Dominic Crossan and Jonathan Reed. The encomium, they maintain,
"subverts and even lampoons" the prevailing Roman imperial definition of
"form of God" as a projection of power to the extent that the comparison is
now "not between despotic and kenotic rule, but between divine normalcy
and divine kenosis."[39] The suggestion is that, since Jesus is in the form of
God and is "the image of God" (2 Cor 4:4), kenosis is "not a passing exercise in ultimate obedience, but a permanent revelation about the nature of
God."[40] Mark Keown's argument in his recent commentary is a little difficult
to follow but seems to take a similar line: "Paul might be speaking literally
and yet ironically of Jesus being in the 'form' of God in a Jewish sense of the
'appearance' of a 'formless God.'"[41] That is, the "form" of God that Jesus had
in heaven was actually and paradoxically the "formlessness" or "essence" of
the invisible God. This invisible divine form is then manifested externally in
the form of a human slave, who dies on a cross.[42]

There is precious little lexicological support for the view that the
morphē of God is really a reference to an abstract or invisible attribute of
God.[43] It has been noted already that when Tobit says that God gave him
"favor and morphēn" before Enemessaros, the reference is likely to be to
his physical appearance, either despite or because of his refusal to eat the
"bread of the nations" (Tob 1:10–13).[44] The one example offered by Peter

38. Gorman, "Form of God," 163.

39. Crossan and Reed, Search, 288–89; see also Gordley on the Philippians encomium as "resistance poetry" (Christological Hymns, 104–9).

40. Crossan and Reed, Search, 290.

41. Keown, Philippians 1:1–2:18, 391.

42. Keown, Philippians 1:1–2:18, 392.

43. Cf. Holloway, Philippians, 117n21; Müller, "Christushymnus," 23–24; Fowl,
Story of Christ, 53–54: "In its most common usage at the time of the NT the μορφή
[morphē] of God would designate the appearance of God. By 'appearance' we mean
something visible and perceptible, not appearance as opposed to reality or essence in
a platonic sense."

44. Cf. Hawthorne, "Form of God," 99. The phrase charin, morphēn pros ton basilea
may have been conventional (Moulton and Milligan, Vocabulary, 417). For comparison: "the rustic differs from the city-dweller not in form (morphē) of body but in a
certain fitting out and disposition of the form (morphēs)" (Dionysius of Halicarnassus,
Din. 8*). Jowers thinks that this suggests the meaning "bearing" for morphē, but the distinction is between the basic physical form of the body and the visual enhancement of
that form in the case of the sophisticated urbanite ("ΜΟΡΦΗ," 759). Morphē is not the
comportment; it is the thing that is comported. Jowers similarly argues (759–60) that
morphē in Dionysius of Halicarnassus, Ant. or. Preface 1.1 cannot mean that "the new
rhetors were more handsome than their predecessors." But it is personified Rhetoric,

O'Brien that *morphē* signifies both external appearance and "that which inwardly corresponds . . . to the outward" also falls short.[45] In Sophocles's play, Electra thinks that she has been given the ashes of her murdered brother in a casket rather than his dearest "form" (*morphēs*). What she laments is that she cannot *see* the physical features of the beloved person, even if only his corpse; his ashes are no more than a "useless shadow" (Sophocles, *El.* 1156–59). The outward appearance may well be incidentally associated with invisible qualities—no doubt the physical appearance of Electra's brother would have revealed something of his status and character, even in death; but that is not what *morphē means*.

Moulton and Milligan cite evidence from the papyri in support of Kennedy's view that *morphē* "always signifies a form which truly and fully expresses the being which underlies it."[46] But this is more than can be inferred from the texts. For example, a god is invoked who "changes himself into sacred forms (*morphais hagiais*)" (*P.Leid.* W.vii.9*). Or a supplicant demands to see the "true form (*morphē*)" of the self-begotten creator of all, whose "true form none of the gods can see" (*P.Leid.* W.viii.28). Another incantation calls on the "spirit that flies in the air" to enter a boy's soul, "that he may receive the immortal form in mighty and incorruptible light" (*P.Lond.* 121.563).[47] The purpose is that he may "see the gods, all who are present at the divination" (121.549–50). In all these instances *morphē* signifies the form or appearance of the god that becomes *perceptible* to the devotee, if only in a vision. Whatever may be indicated or implied in any particular passage about the relation between *morphē* and an inner reality, the word nevertheless denotes the *outward appearance* of the person or thing that has the "form." So if *theou* signifies the one God, *morphē theou* must refer to the *outward appearance* of God, even if that outward appearance accurately manifests the inner reality of God. We cannot say that *morphē* points to the inner reality of God and then quietly drop the problematic semantic husk of "outward appearance," leaving ourselves with the inner reality alone.

Even in the philosophical texts the *morphē* is strictly the particular and perceptible aspect of what is otherwise abstract, indeterminate,

---

"intolerably shameless and histrionic," who lives "in greater ease, luxuriousness, and form." This aspect is in fact *contrasted with* "civic honors and high office." *Morphē* is not "social status"; it is the outward appearance of the harlot Rhetoric who made herself the means of attaining social status.

45. O'Brien, *Philippians*, 207 and n10.

46. Moulton and Milligan, *Vocabulary*, 417; also for the texts Behm, "μορφή," 747; and note Martin, *Hymn of Christ*, 103.

47. Betz, *Greek Magical Papyri*, 133–34.

transcendent, or formless.[48] The discussion in Plato, *Republic* 2 381c has to do with whether a god is likely to adopt an *inferior* "form," specifically by appearing disguised as a stranger in a city, rather than keep his or her own divine *morphē*. In an abstruse dialogue about the relation between opposites Socrates uses *morphē* for the particular "form" that an abstract "idea" (*eidos*) may take—fire as a form of heat, ice as a form of coldness, the number three as a form of oddness (Plato, *Phaed.* 103e). Aristotle's interest, conversely, is in the relation not between form and idea but between "form" (*morphē* or *eidos*) and "matter" (*hylē*) (*Metaph.* 11.2.13 1060b). The identification of "form" and "nature" in *Physics* 2.1 193a–b is postulated in contrast to a definition of nature as the "underlying material of all things."[49] So the "form" of an object such as a bed is what distinguishes it from the unformed materials out of which it was made. Nature is a combination of substance and form. Plutarch likewise differentiates between "the formless matter" (*hē amorphos hylē*) and the "form" (*morphēn*) in which it is "fashioned" (*schēmatistheisa*) (Plutarch, *Quaest. plat.* 4 1003b). The "shape" (*eidos*) of a thing "is not the elimination of the substance (*hylēs*) but a form (*morphē*) and order of the underlying material" (Plutarch, *Def. orac.* 35 429a*).[50]

If we take this course, therefore, we are still stuck with the problem that "form of God" would be a *reference* not to anything inward or essential but to the visible or tangible outward appearance of God. The philosophical distinction between substance and form cannot be inverted simply because we otherwise have no good way of talking about the "form of God." We are left having to suppose, therefore, that "being in the form of God," Jesus *looked like what God looked like*. Of course, it may be argued, as we will see, that God was indeed conceived as being anthropomorphic or angelomorphic, humanlike or angel-like in outward appearance, but that gets us into a quite different ball game.

The interpretation of *morphē* as more or less equivalent to *ousia* is typically presented as a matter less of historical exegesis than of theological exigency: when applied to God, the word *must* mean "being" or "essence" or

48. These are the texts referenced by Hellerman as examples of the "substantial use of the μορφή [*morphē*] word group" ("Μορφη Θεου," 785).

49. Cf. Aristotle, *Phys.* 1.7 190b20–21: natural objects are composed of "the underlying subject and the 'form' (*morphēs*) which their defining properties give to it."

50. Hellerman, "Μορφη Θεου," 786. Jowers maintains that Plutarch agrees with Aristotle that *morphē* and *hylē* are the "fundamental constituents of every corporeal substance" ("ΜΟΡΦΗ," 749–50), but this is misleading. Plutarch distinguishes quite clearly between the "matter and substrate" (*hylēn kai hypokeimenon*) and the "form and shape" (*morphēn kai eidos*) by which matter becomes "tangible <and> visible" (Plutarch, *An. procr.* 1013c). *Morphē* signifies the *perceptible* aspect of the object; it is not merely another constituent of its substance.

"inner reality," even though it does not.[51] Hawthorne's reference to a "new meaning" comes close to admitting as much. The evidence that Käsemann offers for the new Hellenistic sense of *morphē* amounts to two marginal passages (Sib. Or. 8:458; *Corp. herm.* 1.13–14) which, as we shall see, barely depart from the standard usage; and the argument about the spatial sense of the preposition founders on the absence of evidence that *morphē* meant "mode of being."[52] Behm says that "Materially, if not linguistically, the apostle's paradoxical phrase *morphē theou* is wholly in the sphere of the biblical view of God."[53] But this is just another way of saying that Paul cannot possibly have meant what he said. "Linguistically" matters. The analogous expression "taking the form of slave" confirms the conclusion. Jesus did not take on the *inner reality* or essence or being of a slave in any sense; he had the *outward appearance* of a slave, because this conventionally was the extreme counterpart to being godlike and, no doubt too, because he suffered an utterly degrading death on a Roman cross. If we need in this case to qualify the statement as metaphorical, as Fee does, then the explanatory relationship between the two expressions breaks down. If Paul had said that Jesus appeared *morphēi anthrōpou*, "in the form of a man" (cf. T. Benj. 10:7), there would be more point to the argument, though we are then alerted to the fact that being in or having the form of something are not the same as being that thing. Otherwise, why should being in the form of God have ontological priority? Why not conclude that Jesus was no more literally in the form of God than he had the form of a slave? I will argue in due course that rhetorically these are very similar statements, and that in both cases *outward appearance*, public perception, is precisely the point at issue.

Finally, does Keown's "ironic" equation of form with formlessness help? Can we make "form" mean "essence" by way of a somewhat whimsical inversion of the normal meaning? Paul intends to say that Jesus will take the "form" of a slave, so then does he pre-empt the figure "ironically" in an incompatible context in order to elicit the startling theological implications of the transformation? It has the air of an interpretive rather than a compositional device. Would Paul, having urged his readers to have a mindset that is somehow represented by the example of Christ,

51. Holloway, *Philippians*, 117–18: "Commentators have balked at the plain meaning of μορφῇ θεοῦ [*morphēi theou*] ('form of God'), since μορφή denotes not 'essence' but 'outward appearance' or visible 'shape,' implying that Paul, a Jew, thought God could be 'perceived by the senses.'"

52. Käsemann, "Kritische Analyse," 331–33; and see Fowl, *Story of Christ*, 52–53. The prepositional construction is no different to *en homoiōmati anthrōpōn* ("in the likeness of human persons") (Phil 2:7).

53. Behm, "μορφή," 752.

have then immediately adopted such an oblique and cryptic manner of reference to Christ's pre-existent relationship to God? Why risk his Greek readers getting hold of the wrong end of the stick and concluding that the God of their Jewish apostles had an external form, just as had the pagan gods which they had recently renounced?

Image and Glory of God

One way that scholars have sought to preserve the visual aspect of *morphē* without allowing more graphic human and angelic representations to intrude is by associating the term with the "glory" of God. So, for example, O'Brien takes up the argument that the word signifies "something more profound" or "more substantial" than mere external appearance and proposes that it is equivalent to *doxa* as an expression of the "nature" or "essence" of God. The reasoning is straightforward: *morphē* denotes visible form; the glory of God is conceived in the Old Testament and Jewish literature as a "shining light"; therefore, the *morphē* of God must be that radiant glory, which at least is visible even if it does not have much shape to it. The pre-existent Christ was "in the form of God" in the sense that he was "clothed in the garments of divine majesty and splendour."[54]

O'Brien leaves the metaphor undeveloped, but Hellerman has suggested that it plays on the close identification of clothing with social status in the Roman world.[55] Jesus uses a similar grammatical construction, he suggests, when he says that "those being in glorious clothing (*en himatismōi endoxōi . . . hyparchontes*) and luxury are in the royal courts" (Luke 7:25*). The association of clothing and glory is common in the biblical literature (e.g., Job 40:10; Sir 50:11; Matt 6:29; Luke 12:27) and Pseudepigraphal texts (1 En. 14:20–22; 62:15–16; 2 En. 22:8–9; T. Jac. 7:25; Let. Aris. 96–99). In Luke's account of the transfiguration, moreover, we "encounter references to clothing and glory in a context in which visible appearance is markedly emphasized."[56] The "appearance" of Jesus' face is changed, his clothes become dazzling white, and the disciples see his glory (Luke 9:29, 32). Hellerman

---

54. O'Brien, *Philippians*, 206–7, 208, 210–11; also Fowl, *Story of Christ*, 54; Wanamaker, "Philippians 2:6–11," 179–83. According to Behm, Paul constructed *morphē theou* in antithesis to *morphē doulou* ("μορφή," 750–51). The contrast is between the "image of humiliation and obedient submission" and the "image of sovereign divine majesty." "The specific outward sign of the humanity of Jesus is the μορφὴ δούλου, and of His essential divine likeness . . . the μορφὴ θεοῦ." The theological rationale for speaking of the visible appearance of God is that the *morphē* of God is the divine *doxa*.

55. Hellerman, "Μορφη Θεου," 792–93, 795–96.

56. Hellerman, "Μορφη Θεου," 796; also Hellerman, *Philippians*, 110–11.

concludes: "The function of clothing as a status symbol in the Roman world thus converges with the association of glory, clothing, and visible appearance attested in the above passages to render quite viable a status-glory-clothing interpretation of μορφὴ θεοῦ [*morphē theou*]."

A more elaborate account of the semantic relationship between *morphē* and *doxa* is generated by introducing "image" (*eikōn*) into the equation. R. P. Martin suggests that Paul's meaning is that, "As the image and glory of God in His pre-existent state, our Lord uniquely shared in the divine splendour,"[57] for which he puts forward three lines of evidence. First, he argues that *morphē* and *eikōn* are "interchangeable terms" in the Septuagint and are synonyms in other contexts.[58] Secondly, *eikōn* and *doxa* are likewise "parallel and equivalent terms," as is evident from the fact that both are used to translate the Hebrew *tmunah* ("likeness"). Thirdly, in the New Testament Jesus is described as the "image and glory of God"—unequivocally in the case of 2 Cor 4:4 and Col 1:15, less certainly in a few other passages where we find the thought of Jesus as the glory of God (Eph 1:17; Col 1:27; Jas 2:1) or the association of "image" and "glory" (1 Cor 15:49 combined with Phil 3:21; 2 Cor 3:18; Rom 8:29).[59] Paul's "doctrine of the last Adam" is a special application of the presentation of Jesus as the "form of God" or the "image and glory of God."[60] The phrase, therefore, is to be explained entirely on Old Testament grounds, without recourse to Hellenistic parallels. Jesus revealed himself to Paul as the one who from eternity was the "image" of, and manifested the glory of, the invisible God. By reversing the effect of Adam's disobedience, he became the "last Adam," the "image of humanity as God intended it"; and the church is being conformed to this "image of true manhood"—or we might say today, "image of true humanity."[61]

Form and Image

There are problems, in the first place, with the linguistic evidence offered by Martin. He presents only a very brief and not entirely coherent summary of F.-W. Eltester's evidence for the semantic equivalence of *morphē*

57. Martin, *Hymn of Christ*, 108.

58. Cf. Cullman, *Christology*, 176, drawing on Héring; Dunn, *Christology*, 115. Hengel says that *eikōn theou* and *morphē theou* are mutually interpretive (*Cross*, 14). Gieschen is persuaded by the argument of Fossum that there is an "interchangeability and common semantic field" between the terms *doxa*, *eikōn*, *homoiōma*, and *morphē* (*Angelomorphic Christology*, 337–38).

59. See also Fowl, *Philippians*, 92–94.

60. Martin, *Hymn of Christ*, 108–20.

61. Martin, *Hymn of Christ*, 119.

and *eikōn*: "image" (*tselem*) and "likeness" (*demut*) are parallel and equivalent Hebrew terms in Gen 1:26; the LXX has *eikōn* for *demut* in Gen 1:26–27; 5:3; 9:6; *tselem* is rendered by *eikōn* several times in Dan 2–3 and by *morphē* once in Dan 3:19; therefore, *eikōn* and *morphē* are to all intents and purposes interchangeable terms.[62] In fact, *eikōn* translates *tselem* in the Genesis texts cited, not *demut*, and it is unclear to me why it is necessary to assert the equivalence of *tselem* and *demut*. In Gen 5:1 we have *kat' eikona theou* for the Hebrew *bidmut 'elohim*, but it seems likely that the translator simply used "image" to stand for the couplet rather than "likeness," which is what we have in the Hebrew. In verse 3 *demut* is translated by *idea* and *tselem* by *eikōn*. In any case, the argument from the translation of *tselem* in Daniel fails. Whereas *eikōn* is used when *tselem* refers to idolatrous images, in Dan 3:19 *tselem* is the "image" of Nebuchadnezzar's face twisted with fury against the men in the furnace. *Morphē* is used rather than *eikōn* because the sense is quite different.[63] We have seen several examples in Hellenistic-Jewish writings of *morphē* referring to a person's face or countenance. It is also worth pointing out here that an image is an *object*, made of gold, set up to be worshiped (Dan 3:1–18), whereas the object *has a form*: "the form of his face was altered."[64]

In addition, a few non-biblical texts have been cited by Martin and others in support of the view that *morphē* and *eikōn* are roughly synonymous.[65] In the gnostic *Corpus hermeticum* 1.12, which gets a lot of attention in these discussions, God creates man co-equal to himself. The man is incomparably beautiful, the *eikōn* of his Father, and God falls in love with his own *morphē*. In the narrative *morphē* conveys, as *eikōn* would not, the beautiful appearance of the man, probably as a reflection of God's own supposed "physical" appearance. It is precisely because in the myth God is thought to have his own perceptible *morphē* that this becomes a more appropriate term for the created nature of man than the biblical *eikōn*. Dave Steenburg concludes that

62. Martin, *Hymn of Christ*, 108 and n3; cf. Howard, "Human Christ," 377n26.

63. Cf. Steenburg, "Case Against," 79, who also notes that Theodotion has *opsis* for Hebrew *tselem* in Dan 3:19. Also Fowl, *Story of Christ*, 51; Fee, *Philippians*, 204n49; Bockmuehl, "Form of God," 8; Jowers, "ΜΟΡΦΗ," 743.

64. The Syriac Peshitta has *dĕmûthâ* for *morphē* in Phil 2:6 (and in Mark 16:12), and it has been argued, e.g., by Feuillet, that this establishes the equivalence of *morphē* and *eikōn* by way of the juxtaposition of *tselem* and *demut* in Gen 1:26; *dĕmûthâ*, moreover, is used for *eikōn* in Rom 8:29; 1 Cor 11:7; 15:49; 2 Cor 3:18; Col 1:15; 3:10 (see Jowers, "ΜΟΡΦΗ," 743–44, who is unpersuaded by the argument). The use of *dĕmûthâ* for *morphē* more likely reflects the predominant use of *demut* in the Old Testament to mean "likeness" in the sense of visual appearance, typically translated by *homoiōma*, than any semantic agreement between *morphē* and *eikōn*.

65. See Jervell, *Imago Dei*, 228–29; Martin, *Hymn of Christ*, 109.

morphē "connotes the visible manifestation of divine beauty either directly or indirectly."[66] Similarly, in *The Clementine Homilies* 17.7 it is said that God molded the human person "in his form" (*Tēi . . . autou morphēi*) because God himself has a "most beautiful form" (*kallistēn morphēn*) and "body," which may be seen by the pure in heart. The texts will be considered in more detail in connection with the argument of interpreters such as Steenburg that "form of God" presupposes a *macranthropos* mythology.

In a lengthy late second-century Christian passage in Sibylline Oracles 8 *morphē* is used for both the created and re-created "form" of humanity.[67] Christ will "come to creation, not in glory but as a mortal, pitiable, without honor, without form (*amorphos*), in order that he may give hope to the pitiable; and he will give form (*morphēn*) to perishable flesh and heavenly faith to the faithless, and he will form (*morphōsei*) the primordial human fashioned by the holy hands of God . . . " (Sib. Or. 8:256–60*; cf. 8:285). The language is different, but that Christ is "without form" himself is likely to be an allusion to Isa 53:2–3 LXX: "he has no form (*eidos*) or glory, and we saw him, and he had no form (*eidos*) or beauty; but his form (*eidos*) was without honor . . . , he was dishonored and not esteemed." The *re-forming* of wretched humanity is an act of new creation, but it is conceived in antithesis to the outward appearance of the Isaianic servant, who had no form or beauty. No doubt, the *formation* entailed is spiritual, but it is a matter of *morphē* because it is thought of in visual terms.

There is a sense, however, in which God also owns this *morphē*. In the beginning God invited his "child" (*teknon*) to collaborate with him in the creation of humanity as an impression of "our image" (*eikonos*) *in two stages*. God creates *now* with his hands, in reference presumably to the shaping (*eplasen*) of the man from the dust of the earth in Gen 2:7 (cf. Sib. Or. 8:402); and *then* the Son "will heal our form (*morphēn*) by a word, so that we may give a common majesty" (8:265–68*). In other words, redeemed humanity is the work of both God and the Son, and it seems likely that "our form" is the "image" of God *insofar as* it is the outcome of this two-stage process: it refers to the outward appearance of humanity re-formed by the word of the Son. In a later passage, however, it is said that God, as the fashioner (*plastēs*) of humans, proposed to the Son, "let us make a man in all likeness to our form (*panomoiion . . . morphēi hēmeterēi*)" (8:442–43*). Steenburg notes the statement that "everything in the world will worship" the man who has been made like the "form" of God (8:442–44*), and

66. Steenburg, "Case Against," 84. Hawthorne and Martin claim, with reference to Steenburg, that "subsequent discussion has not supported this denial of synonymity" (*Philippians*, 111).

67. See also the discussion in Steenburg, "Case Against," 81–83.

suggests that this worship is grounded in the *physical* resemblance, connoted by *morphē*, between Adam and God (cf. L.A.E. 13).[68] Then, in the last times the Son came from heaven and put on "mortal form" (*broteēn . . . morphēn*); a word was "fashioned in mortal appearance (*ideēn*) and happened to become (*etychthē*) a boy by virgin birth" (Sib. Or. 8:458, 471–72*). This is the language of pagan metamorphoses, and the anti-pagan thrust of the passage is highlighted in the immediately following lines (8:487–95). But we also cannot rule out the possibility, given the explicit involvement of the Son in the creation process, that the passage has been influenced, albeit perhaps at some distance, by Phil 2:6: "our form" is the form shared by the Father and the Son, who was "in the form of God," but who, coming from heaven, took on the mortal form of a slave.

A passage in Sibylline Oracles 3 may shed some further light on the relation between *morphē* and *eikōn*. A characteristic denunciation of idolatry begins by asking why people "having a God-shaped form in (his) image" (*theoplaston echontes en eikoni morphēn*) wander in vain, not mindful of the creator (Sib. Or. 3:8–45*). The polemical point is that whereas humans have a form shaped by God in his image, they have wrongly thought that the "one God, sole ruler, ineffable, who lives in the sky, self-begotten, invisible" is revealed by the work of a sculptor's hand. On the contrary, God must reveal himself, for no mortal "is able to see God with eyes." He "created everything by a word." Indeed, it is God himself who "shaped" (*plasas*) Adam, the "first-shaped" (*prōton plasthenta*), and established the "pattern of the form of humans" (*typon morphēs meropōn*).[69] The collocation of the two terms may point to a subtle but coherent distinction between them: "image" belongs to God, "form" belongs to humanity; God *formed* men and women in his own *image*.[70] Arguably, "image" in this case is a dynamic concept. It speaks of God's creative engagement with the earth, which is

68. Steenburg, "Case Against," 83.

69. Likewise, Sib. Or. Prolog. 99. Sib. Or. 4:181–82 speaks of a resurrection when "God himself will form (*morphōsei*) again the bones and ashes of men."

70. A similar point was made earlier with respect to Rom 8:29: the *image* belongs to Christ, and the person who likewise suffers is *formed* in that image. A passage in the Talmud states that to be made "in the image of God" means "in the image (*tselem*) of the likeness (*demut*) of his form (*tavnit*)" (*Ketub.* 8a). Bockmuehl says that this "confirms the balance of Scripture, where human beings are in God's צלם [*tslm*] and in his דמות [*dmut*]; both of these terms can mean either an image or likeness in either two or three dimensions. But humanity is never said to be in God's תבנית [*tvnit*]—or, in the LXX, in his μορφή" ("Form of God," 16–17). The "form," in fact, is the "design" of the "building" which is Adam because God "out of His very self formed a building for eternity." The Poimandres text may diverge from the pattern inasmuch as it is said that the human being was the *eikōn* of his father and it is the beautiful *morphē* of God that is revealed to nature (*Corp. herm.* 1.12).

transferred to humanity as the responsibility to exercise dominion over it (Gen 1:26–28; cf. Wis 14:17), while "form" denotes the bodily shape and distinctive appearance that humanity has been given.

Further support comes from Philo, who argues that it was all downhill for humanity after the first man, Adam, the "prime of our entire race." Subsequent generations were ever more diminished in "forms" (*morphas*) and "powers" (*Creation* 140). In other words, no one has since matched Adam in physical appearance and ability.[71] This means, however, that "form of God" in Phil 2:6 cannot refer to something that is intrinsic to God, such as his nature or his glory. *Morphē* is what humanity has had since Adam because God *shaped* Adam's physicality, from the dust of the earth (Gen 2:7 LXX; cf. Philo, *Creation* 134), so that he might work in the garden. To say that a person is in the "form of God," on this basis, therefore, is incoherent.

Form and Glory

Martin's second argument is that *morphē* and *doxa* are equivalent because both are used to translate the Hebrew word *temunah* ("likeness").[72] *Temunah* is usually translated by *homoiōma* and always so in statements which entail the *denial* that God has a visible "likeness" (Exod 20:4; Deut 4:12, 15–16, 23, 25; 5:8). When the reference is to God in a positive sense, *doxa* is used (Num 12:8; Ps 17:15 = Ps 16:15 LXX). Only once in the Septuagint do we have *morphē*, for the "likeness" (*temunah*) that either was or was not before the eyes of Eliphaz (Job 4:16). Symmachus has *morphē* for *temunah* instead of *homoiōma* in Deut 4:12 because the absence of any "form" or "likeness" in the burning bush vision accounts for the prohibition against carved images a few verses later (Deut 4:15–18).[73] The implication is that *morphē* connotes the forms of pagan divinities. This strongly suggests that *morphē* was considered an *unsuitable term for speaking about God*. *Temunah* is never translated by *eikōn*.[74] The evidence leads, therefore, to the contrary conclusion: *morphē* and *eikōn* are not equivalent terms, and if anything, *morphē* is deliberately avoided in contexts where it might be applied to God, most likely because of its association with pagan idolatry and mythologizing.

71. In his discussion of the degeneration of humanity since Adam, Philo goes on to say that there are exceptions to the rule—people who "consider the attaining a likeness (*exomoiōsin*) to God who made them as the proper end of their existence" (*Creation* 144; cf. *Decalogue* 73; *Virtues* 8).

72. Martin, *Hymn of Christ*, 109–10.

73. Talbert, "Problem," 147n18, 151; Steenburg, "Case Against," 80.

74. Cf. Steenburg, "Case Against," 80.

Fossum notes that the *to'ar* ("form," "appearance") of the servant in Isa 52:14 is translated with *morphē* by Aquila but with *doxa* in the LXX.[75] But since the LXX translator has rendered "his appearance (*mar'eh*) was so marred" as "your appearance shall be without glory" (*adoxēsei . . . to eidos sou*), it is likely that the use of *doxa* for *to'ar* has been influenced by the preceding *adoxēsei*. The resulting parallelism is striking: *adoxēsei apo anthrōpōn // hē doxa . . . apo tōn anthrōpōn*. It would be hazardous to infer from this that *doxa* was a valid translation of *to'ar* or synonymous with *morphē*.[76]

The counterargument has been made that *morphē* and *doxa* need not be regarded as synonyms for the thesis to hold. Robert Strimple agrees that there is insufficient evidence for the view that *morphē*, *eikōn*, and *doxa* are synonymous but argues that the passage speaks of Christ's eternal "glory" not because *morphē means* "glory" but because the "form of God" is his glory.[77] We do not need to suppose, therefore, that *morphēn doulou* means "the glory of a slave." But this does not explain why Paul has the incongruous word *morphē* here and not *eikōn*—neither John 17:5 nor Heb 1:3 accounts for the usage; and we still have to find a corresponding translation of *morphēn doulou*. Is the expression likely to have been read as a reference to some such abstract quality as servility or wretchedness?

A rather ingenious variant of the "form of God" equals "glory of God" interpretation has been proposed by C. A. Wanamaker. Noting, on the one hand, the use of *morphē* to speak of the similarity between a child and a parent (4 Macc 15:4; Philo, *Embassy* 55) and, on the other, the view of some scholars that the encomium evinces the influence of the "Son of God" motif, he suggests that Jesus is presented as the eternal Son of God who reflects the visible appearance of the divine glory *as a son presents to the world the outward form of a parent*.[78] The difficulties with this view can be noted briefly. First, in the context of the parent-child relationship *morphē* is contrasted with the inner *psychē* of the person, which would entail an odd intensification of the visual and external aspect of being *en morphē theou*.

75. Fossum, "Christology," 263. See also Behm, "μορφή," 751n47, referring the point to Bertram.

76. Theodotion has *hē morphē mou* in Dan 4:33 (= 4:36 ET) where LXX has *hē doxa mou*, but since the Aramaic reads "my majesty and splendour," it seems likely that *doxa* translates "majesty" (*hadr*) and *morphē* "splendour" (*ziw*). The latter word is particularly associated with the appearance of the face and is also translated with *morphē* by Theodotion in Dan 5:6, where LXX has *horasis* (also Dan 5:9, 10; 7:28).

77. Strimple, "Philippians 2:5–11," 260–61; cf. O'Brien, *Philippians*, 209; Hellerman, *Honor*, 132.

78. Wanamaker, "Philippians 2:6–11," 183–87.

It is doubtful, secondly, that the theme of Christ's sonship has influenced the language of Phil 2:6–8, not least because it more naturally relates to his exaltation and enthronement (cf. Rom 1:4). The first paragraph of the encomium is not "redolent" of the sending of the Son passages (Gal 4:4; Rom 8:3) in a way that would encourage us to import the motif; and if Paul sometimes speaks specifically of the death of the Son (Rom 5:8–11; 8:32; Gal 2:19–20; cf. Col 1:13–20), I would argue—in keeping with a minor thesis of this study—that this reflects the temporal perspective of the apostolic mission, namely that the one who is *now* encountered as the exalted Son of God, heir to the future rule over the nations, died in a previous earthly existence. Thirdly, the biblical antecedents for the humanlike appearance of the glory of God are *theophanic* (Exod 24:17; Ezek 1:26–28; 10:4): the glory appears in an earthly setting, and *morphē* is not used, in all likelihood because of its association with pagan idolatry.

The contention of O'Brien and Hellerman, finally, that a clothing metaphor links "form" and "glory" fails for want of any evidence that being in the *morphē* of something might have been understood as a reference to dress. The idea that Christ was *clothed* in the glory of God is reasonable enough, but *morphē* seems never to have been used with reference to clothing. In fact, *schēma* would have been the more fitting term in this regard.[79]

The Glory of the Christ

The failure to establish any clear equivalence or semantic overlap between *morphē* ("form") and either *eikōn* ("image") or *doxa* ("glory") immediately weakens Martin's third body of evidence—Paul's description of Christ Jesus as the "image and glory of God." But the intrinsic difficulty here is that Martin treats glory as a general theological category without reference to the *eschatological* dimension which so thoroughly controls Paul's thought. It is the risen, not the pre-existent, Christ who has a glorious image in these passages.[80] Paul's *gospel* of "the glory of the Christ, who is the image (*eikōn*) of God" (2 Cor 4:4) is the announcement that the crucified Jesus has been raised from the dead and seated at the right hand of God (cf. Rom 1:1–4). It is to this "image" that the Jewish apostles are being conformed through

79. Lightfoot says that *morphē* "has not and cannot have any of those secondary senses which attach to σχῆμα [*schēma*], as gesture or dress or parade or pretext" (*Philippians*, 127); and LSJ s.v. σχῆμα 4.b "*dress, equipment*"; CGL s.v. σχῆμα: "manner, style" of dress, "dress, clothes" of an individual.

80. Cf. Kuschel, *Before All Time*, 294; and Reumann, *Philippians*, 344: "Anyone for 'divine glory' . . . overlooks the fact that in the hymn 'the obedient one only received this status after the humbling and not before.'"

suffering, from the transient glory of the Mosaic covenant to the enduring glory of the risen Lord (2 Cor 3:18; 4:17), which will eventually be made manifest to the world. Likewise, it is the beloved Son, who has inherited the kingdom, who is the "image (*eikōn*) of the invisible God, the firstborn of every creature" (Col 1:12–15*). Paul then goes on to say that through his current sufferings he is filling up what he has not yet experienced of the sufferings of Christ (Col 1:24).[81] The argument about "image" and "glory" is an argument about the participation of the apostles in the sufferings of Christ in the hope that they will share also in his resurrection glory. That this participation is described using compounds of *morphoō* (*metamorphoō*, *symmorphoō*) is not an argument against the view that *morphē* signifies external appearance or *Erscheinungsform*, as Jowers maintains.[82] The transformation is not internal but behavioral, visible, and public. The apostles are *seen* to suffer as Christ suffered: "God appointed us apostles last, as sentenced to death, because we became a spectacle (*theatron*) to the world, both to angels and to men" (1 Cor 4:9); and as those who are being in this way "conformed (*symmorphous*) to the image of his Son," they will be revealed to the world as "sons of God" (Rom 8:19, 29; cf. Col 3:4). They are being "transformed" (*metamorphoumetha*) into the image of the Lord by virtue of the fact that they are "afflicted . . . perplexed . . . persecuted . . . struck down . . .; always carrying in the body the death of Jesus . . . " (2 Cor 4:8–10).

The other passages cited by Martin fall smartly into line here. James exhorts his brothers not to "hold the faith of the glory of our Lord Jesus Christ in acts of favoritism" because they are "heirs of the kingdom," meaning that they will share in the glory that Christ now has on account of his suffering, resurrection, and exaltation (Jas 2:1–5*). Martin himself notes that if we connect the "image" of 1 Cor 15:49 with the "glory" of Philippians 3:21, we find that the *morphē* of the new "spiritual body" will be that which "belongs to the body of the glory which is His in His Exaltation."[83] Finally, it is through suffering that believers are "conformed" (*symmorphous*) to the image (*eikonos*) of the glorified Son, "in order that he might be the firstborn among many brothers" (Rom 8:29–30). There is some justification for

---

81. See Perriman, "Pattern," 62–68.

82. Jowers, "ΜΟΡΦΗ," 748–49; cf. Wong, "Problem," 271: "Μεταμορφόομαι [*metamorphoomai*] . . . far from being simply external, must be understood as implying the essential transformation of Christians into a new life."

83. Martin, *Hymn of Christ*, 114–15. Hooker observes that the pattern of Christian obedience set out in Phil 3 and elsewhere is "conformity to the way of the Cross: Paul is content to be found in Christ—to know the power of his resurrection and the fellowship of his sufferings; to be conformed to his death, in confident hope of resurrection" (*Adam*, 93).

talking about the convergence of *morphē, eikōn,* and *doxa* here, but Paul's argument is that Christ has provided the pattern of suffering and vindication that believers will have to replicate in their own lives if they are to be fellow heirs with him (cf. 8:17). The Jesus who appears to Paul on the road to Damascus embodies not perfect manhood but the persecuted community: "Saul, Saul, why are you persecuting me?" (Acts 9:4–5).

Conclusion

It seems unlikely, in light of the preceding discussion, that Paul would have intended *morphē theou* as a reference to the being or some essential attribute of God. There is no evidence even in the more esoteric literature that *morphē* was ever used in such an abstract sense. The thought is consistently of the *outward* appearance of an object or being, not of some *inner* quality. Moreover, the association of the term with pagan religious practice and discourse (on which more later) probably marked it as singularly inappropriate for speaking about the one God of Jewish belief. So perhaps we are indeed to think of the "form of God" in more human terms. We shall see.

5

Being in Human Form

IF WE CANNOT REDEFINE *morphē* in terms compatible with the traditional idea that the one God is strictly invisible and unimaginable and therefore *form-less*, an alternative approach would be to grant that *morphē theou* denotes an essentially humanlike form and ask how that might work in the context of the encomium. In the first place, we have a set of interpretations that takes the being of Jesus in the "form of God" to be roughly equivalent to the being of the biblical Adam in the "image of God." This is usually understood directly to preclude the idea that Christ pre-existed his earthly life as a second Adam. In its standard form the interpretation is associated especially with Dunn, but we will also look at Murphy-O'Connor's attempt to ground an anthropological reading in the account of the "righteous man" in Wisdom of Solomon and Oscar Cullman's argument about a pre-existent *human* Son of Man. More radically, it has been argued on the basis of various religious analogies that the pre-existent form of Christ mirrored the humanlike appearance of God himself. Interpretation proceeds, in other words, not from God to *morphē* to Christ, as traditionally, but in the opposite direction—from Christ as obviously human in appearance to *morphē* to God. We will look at the contributions of Bockmuehl and Gieschen.

Dunn: Christ in the Form of God as Second Adam

The basic thesis is that the assertion that Jesus was "in the form of God" corresponds to the assertion that Adam was "in the image of God," and that whereas Adam sought to be like God, Jesus remained obedient and did not seek either to gain or to retain (depending on how we interpret the second half of the verse) equality with God. Dunn has been the standout proponent of the view in recent years. He argues in his *Christology in the Making* that *morphē theou* "probably refers to Adam having been made in the image . . . of

God and with a share of the glory . . . of God."[1] Like Martin, he suggests that *morphē* and *eikōn* are near synonyms and that in Jewish thought the *morphē* of God is his glory.[2] *Morphē* is preferred to *eikōn* because the "image of God" that Adam possessed is not abandoned or exchanged and because it better serves the contrast with "form of a slave." But whereas Martin assumes a pre-existent glory for Christ, Dunn here thinks in terms of the glory which Adam had before the fall, which he lost, becoming a slave either to corruption (cf. Rom 8:18–21) or to the "elemental spirits" (cf. Gal 4:3). So the encomium conforms to a two-stage Christology evidenced elsewhere: "free acceptance of man's lot followed out to death, and exaltation to the status of Lord over all, echoing the primitive association of Ps. 110.1 with Ps. 8.6."

In a later essay Dunn defends the Adamic interpretation but argues that it leaves the question of pre-existence open.[3] The self-emptying and taking the form of a slave could refer to an act of self-abasement during Jesus' life, but he now thinks it more likely that a pre-incarnate decision is in view: Jesus is "to be envisaged as making an Adamic choice at some time (!) in eternity," which reduces the Adam Christology to a metaphor. The alternative would be to suppose, more literally, that Adam himself made some sort of "mythic" transition—from Adam as humankind to Adam as father of children, for example; or from Adam in the garden to Adam in the world, subject to corruption. So Jesus "freely embraced the lot of humanity, as slave to sin and death . . . . he freely accepted the death that was the consequence of Adam's disobedience."

That there is a parallel, on the face of it, between the refusal of Christ "in the form of God" to seize or hold on to equality with God and the attempt of Adam "in the image of God" to be like God (Gen 3:5) is hard to deny. No doubt much of the criticism has been driven by a desire to rescue the traditional view that the pre-existence of Christ as (Son of) God is intended, but I am not persuaded that the Adam-Christology thesis adequately accounts for Paul's language here.[4]

1. Dunn, *Christology*, 115; cf. Cullman, *Christology*, 175; Brown, *Christology*, 134; Chester, *Messiah*, 392; Hooker, *Adam*, 96–97. For the nineteenth-century origins of the view see Glasson, "Two Notes," 137–38.

2. For the evidence, he cites Martin (Dunn, *Christology*, 311n69); cf. Dunn, "Pre-existence," 77. On the basis of a similar chain of reasoning, Talbert concludes that the phrase *en morphēi theou* is "part of the Adam/Christ typology and is intended to speak of Christ as the second Adam who has reversed the decision of the first Adam" ("Problem," 151); also Murphy-O'Connor, "Anthropology," 41–42; Howard, "Human Christ," 376–77; Brown, "*Kyrios* Jesus Revisited," 26–27; Hooker, *Adam*, 98.

3. Dunn, "Preexistence," 78–79; see also Fee, *Christology*, 501n2.

4. For the arguments against the Adam-Christology interpretation see Strimple, "Philippians 2:5–11," 257–59; Hurst, "Pre-existent Christ"; Wanamaker, "Philippians

First, it has become clear that "form of God" is not a substitute for "image of God." While "form of a slave" is intelligible, to speak of the "outward appearance" of the one God is problematic on any reading. We have to keep in mind that the *morphē* is not Christ's but God's. How was the earthly Jesus—or, for that matter, a pre-existent Jesus—in the outward appearance of God? Conversely, if *morphē* means "image" in verse 6, how are we to understand "form of a slave" in verse 7?[5] The idea of a *derived* character or manner of being or, perhaps better, function entailed in the "image of God" figure simply does not work here.

Secondly, Morna Hooker addresses what she regards as the chief objection to the Adamic interpretation, which is that "at this point in the story the true Adam is said to *become* man; how can this be?" The answer is found in the central "paradox and irony" of the passage: "the one who is truly what man is meant to be—in the form and likeness of God—becomes what other men *are*, because they are in Adam."[6] This would account for the "shadowy" language of *schēma* and *homoiōma*: "Men have ceased to be what they were meant to be."[7] The comment may well be generally pertinent, but it still does not solve the problem of *morphē theou*, which cannot signify an essential humanity which might in principle be overlaid with the "form of a slave." The ambiguity of *schēma* and *homoiōma* is easily overstated: the point need only be that the now exalted and transcendent Lord was formerly encountered as another instance of the human species. But in any case, in common usage *morphē* so closely and consistently refers to the particular *appearance* that an object, person, or god takes that the transformation from *morphē theou* to "form of a slave" must have been *apparent* to observers in some way. A person cannot be in two different *forms* at the same time.

Thirdly, what Adam and Eve were offered was not equality with God as such, or to be treated as equal to God, but a likeness to God in knowing good and evil, which in fact humanity attained *without becoming God-equal*.[8] Some support for the argument may be gained from the parallelism

---

2:6–11," 180–83; O'Brien, *Philippians*, 263–68; Bockmuehl, "Form of God," 9–11; Hurst, "Preexistence," 85–90; Hurtado, *How on Earth*, 98–101; Lee, *Preexistent Son*, 306–7; Hansen, *Philippians*, 239; Keown, *Philippians 1:1–2:18*, 358–59. Hurtado says that "the alleged use of *en morphē theou* as an allusion to Adam . . . would be a singular phenomenon, and a particularly inept one as well" (*Lord Jesus Christ*, 122).

5. Cf. O'Brien, *Philippians*, 264; Hawthorne and Martin, *Philippians*, 111–12.

6. Hooker, *Adam*, 98 (her emphasis). For the objection see Hurst, "Preexistence," 85–86.

7. Hooker, *Adam*, 98–99.

8. Cf. Vincent, *Philippians*, 86: "it is nowhere asserted or hinted in Scripture that Adam desired equality with God in the comprehensive sense of that expression"; O'Brien, *Philippians*, 265; Kuschel, *Before All Time*, 252–53; Bockmuehl, "Form of

constructed in Rom 5:12–21 between the disobedience of the "one man" Adam, which led to death, and the obedience of the "one man Jesus Christ," which led to life; but this does not explain his "being in the form of God." As we have seen, it is the *resurrected* Jesus who is the "last Adam," whose image resurrected believers will share (1 Cor 15:45–49).

That said, we may wonder—running ahead of ourselves a little—whether the story of Adam is recalled *indirectly* in Phil 2:6 by way of the account of the fall of the ruler of Tyre in Ezek 28:1–19 LXX. He was "in the delight of the paradise of God," a "signet of likeness," "born blameless in your days from the day you were created," blessed with great wisdom and knowledge (Ezek 28:4, 12–15*). But "acts of iniquity" were found in him, he prospered commercially and became corrupt, he arrogated for himself the status of a god, and he was driven by the cherub from the holy mountain (28:2–10, 15–16).[9] This narrative of pagan kingship is much closer to the thematic interests of the encomium, but it has been conceived as an approximate re-enactment of the tragedy of Adam's disobedience. Christ is not here presented as a second Adam, but he will attain kingship by not emulating—for example—the career of the ruler of Tyre, who *was*, in effect, a second Adam.

Murphy-O'Connor and the Anthropology of Wisdom of Solomon

Taking his cue from Dieter Georgi, Murphy-O'Connor sets out to show how in particular the "theological anthropology" of Wisdom of Solomon "constitutes a homogeneous background which permits a coherent interpretation of the hymn."[10] The "anthropological perspective" of the book is that "God created man in incorruption and made him the image (*eikona*) of his own eternality" (Wis 2:23*).[11] Murphy-O'Connor cites the argument

God," 9.

9. Cf. Allen, *Ezekiel 20–48*, 94: the passage speaks of "the garden of Eden and expulsion from it, of moral perfection before a fall and of one cherub who is the agent of expulsion."

10. Murphy-O'Connor, "Anthropology," 36–37; see also the summary of Murphy-O'Connor's argument in Howard, "Human Christ," 369–71; Kuschel, *Before All Time*, 251–53. Oakes discusses the proposal of Seeley, "Background," that the encomium draws on Isa 53, stories of the suffering righteous from the Maccabean period, and the language of Greek-Roman ruler worship (*Philippians*, 133–36).

11. It is difficult to avoid the gendered form of expression if we are to preserve the individuality entailed in *ton anthrōpon . . . auton*. NETS has "God created human beings for incorruption and made them the image of his own nature."

of Reese that *ep' aphtharsiai* refers to the state *in which* humanity was created ("*in* incorruption"), not the state *for which* humanity was destined ("*for* incorruption").[12] The background to the language of the passage is Epicurean. On the one hand, Epicureans believed that, while gods were corporeal like humans, they possessed "incorruption," which meant that their bodies existed endlessly and did not disintegrate. On the other, "Plutarch attributes to Epicurus a statement that God's nature is incorruptibility, and that this is his eternity."[13] In the Jewish text, however, the thought derives from Gen 1–3, as is suggested both by the phrase "image of his own eternality" and the claim that "through the envy of the devil death entered the world" (Wis 2:24).[14] So under the present conditions "immortality is God's gift offered in recompense for success . . . in the struggle against a corrupt environment."[15] The anthropological narrative then acquires a more concrete form. The death of the righteous person is the result of the plotting of the wicked (2:17–20), and the reward is more than just immortality: "Clothed in royal raiment . . . , the righteous stands with the confidence born of full authority in the midst of those who afflicted him . . . 'to govern nations and rule over peoples.'"[16]

Murphy-O'Connor supports Hoover's translation of the *harpagmos* clause: "It is a question . . . of something considered to be in Christ's possession. It was a gain which he already had, a right of which he was free to dispose." But he argues that the anthropology of Wisdom of Solomon provides "an appropriate background on the assumption that the author of the hymn was thinking of Christ as man."[17] So if, for the author, "man as he came forth from the hand of God had the right to incorruptibility, a right that he lost through sin," we may suppose that the sinless Christ had the "right to incorruptibility"—had the "right to be treated as if he were god"—but did not "turn this situation to his own advantage."

---

12. Murphy-O'Connor, "Anthropology," 32–33.

13. Murphy-O'Connor, "Anthropology," 34: "Therefore they do not well who make God's eternal existence to be the result of watchfulness and the thrusting aside of destructive agencies" (Plutarch, *Def. orac.* 20).

14. Murphy-O'Connor thinks that Isa 54:16 LXX ("I have created you not for destruction") has influenced the language of Wis 2:23: "Thus, a form of Adam speculation attested in *Isaiah* is carried over into *Wisdom* where the first man is alluded to . . . " ("Anthropology," 35). The statement, however, has reference to Israel, and the text has been misunderstood.

15. Murphy-O'Connor, "Anthropology," 32.

16. Murphy-O'Connor, "Anthropology," 36.

17. Murphy-O'Connor, "Anthropology," 39–40.

The link with the anthropology of Wisdom of Solomon is established on the basis of Phil 2:6b–7: the sinless Jesus enjoyed an original incorruptibility, which was a "divine prerogative"; he chose not to exploit the right to be treated as a god; on the contrary, he suffered like the righteous man in the Wisdom tradition, only willingly, emptying himself in an act of *self-renunciation*.[18] This then provides the framework for understanding verse 6a. Murphy-O'Connor takes up the argument of Eltester and Martin that *eikōn* and *morphē* are "used as interchangeable terms in the LXX," suggesting that *morphē* has been substituted here in order to underline "the distinction between Christ and other men." The Israelite, according to Jewish tradition, remained in the "image of God" even when he failed to live up to the standards of his vocation. "The absolute fidelity of Christ," therefore, "justified the choice of an alternative term, and permitted the contrast between μορφὴ θεοῦ [*morphē theou*] and μομρφὴ δούλου [*morphē doulou*]."

Two basic objections are by now immediately clear: *eikōn* and *morphē* are not interchangeable terms, and *morphē* has reference to an outward appearance that is difficult to reconcile with the emphasis on an inherent sinlessness and incorruptibility. But Murphy-O'Connor has also misrepresented the anthropology of Wisdom of Solomon.[19] Humanity is created "in incorruption" and is made as an *eikōn* of God's "eternality," but "by the envy of the devil death came into the world, and those who have a part in him experience it" (Wis 2:23–24*). Although Adam transgressed (10:1), the problem is not that all have sinned but that the "righteous man" or "divine son," who keeps the Law and is blameless (2:12, 16–18, 22), nevertheless may be killed by the wicked who plot against him.[20] The solution to this quandary is the belief that the righteous are being tested through their suffering, that they have a hope full of "immortality," that "in the time of their visitation they will shine out, and as sparks through the stubble, they will run about" (3:7; cf. Dan 12:3; Matt 13:43), and finally that they will "judge nations and rule over peoples" (3:8). There is nothing in this narrative to warrant the attribution of sinlessness and incorruptibility to Jesus. Quite the opposite. It is possible to be a righteous man even though the *incorruptibility* of the divine image has been removed from humanity and death is universal. This may well foreshadow in certain respects the

18. Murphy-O'Connor, "Anthropology," 40–41.

19. See also the critique in Howard, "Human Christ," 371–72.

20. Murphy-O'Connor notes that there is no mention of "human responsibility" in Wis 2:23–24 but thinks that it is indicated by the reference to Adam's transgression in 10:1 (cf. 1:16) ("Anthropology," 35). There is no thought, however, of the transmission of sinfulness to all. There are righteous people and unrighteous people; the problem is that they are all subject to death.

story of Jesus, culminating in judgment of and rule over the nations, but it does not explain the language of Phil 2:6–7.

Cullman's Pre-existent Son of Man Argument

In his *Christology of the New Testament* Cullmann proposes a reconstruction of the background to Paul's thought which leads to the conclusion that *morphē* "firmly establishes the connection between Jesus and the creation story of Adam from the very beginning."[21] The Aramaic expression *bar 'enash* denotes one who "belongs to the human classification." The Greek expression *huios tou anthrōpou* ("son of man") is, therefore, too literal; *bar 'enash* should be translated *anthrōpos* or "man."[22] The Son of Man figure in apocalyptic Judaism, therefore, is simply the "man," but he is nevertheless a pre-existent heavenly figure. This is most clearly the case in Ethiopic Enoch, but it is true also of the Son of Man figure in Daniel and 4 Ezra. Cullman takes it that there must be some connection here with "non-Jewish speculations about an 'Original Man,'" though the germ of the concept is also present in the Old Testament idea of the creation of man in the image of God.[23] The problem is that the Jews did not clarify the relation between the first man Adam and the eschatological man or Son of Man. But the "otherwise completely inexplicable fact that the eschatological redeemer is called 'man' shows that the two concepts really do belong together."[24]

The Original Man in Judaism, therefore, comes in two forms.[25] He is the eschatological Heavenly Man of Daniel, Enoch, and 4 Ezra, who is now hidden but who will come at the end of time to judge and establish the "nation of the saints"; and he is the ideal Heavenly Man "identified with the first man at the beginning of time" (emphasis removed), who appears in Philo, the Pseudo-Clementine *Preaching of Peter*, and rabbinical Adam speculation. The link between them is established in the fact that the eschatological Son of Man is a pre-existent figure. "When one thinks of him as existing before the end time, the question of his origin is implicitly raised."

It is Cullman's view that Paul is chiefly interested in the second version of the Original Man—the incarnate Heavenly man as the "second Adam," but he also knows of a Heavenly Man who *will come* on the clouds

---

21. Cullman, *Christology*, 176.

22. Cullman, *Christology*, 138.

23. Cullman, *Christology*, 142.

24. Cullman, *Christology*, 144.

25. Cullman, *Christology*, 150–51.

(1 Thess 4:17).[26] The "ideal divine Man, the Heavenly Man, the perfect prototype of men," cannot be identified with the first Adam; he does not belong in the creation story. Like the Son of Man in the apocalyptic texts he is pre-existent, but Paul does not speculate on the circumstances of this pre-existence; he just takes it for granted.[27] Cullman is also persuaded, by J. Héring, that *morphē* is equivalent to *eikōn*; the reference, therefore, is not to Christ's "divine nature" but to the "image of God which he possessed from the beginning."[28] Jesus is the "Heavenly Man who is the only one to fulfil the divine destiny of being the image of God" (cf. 2 Cor 4:4; Col 1:15). The "form of God" is the form of the Heavenly Man, who existed as such from the beginning, who is also the Son of Man of apocalyptic thought and, implicitly, the Original Man of non-Jewish speculation.[29] The final transformation or metamorphosis of believers is into the "image of the man from heaven" (1 Cor 15:49; cf. Rom 8:29; 2 Cor 3:18; Col 3:10).

I see a number of difficulties with this as an argument for pre-existence, many of which we have touched on already in other contexts.[30] In the first place, the interpretive narrative setting is missing. Paul does not say of Christ that "before the creation of the sun and the moon, before the creation of the stars, he was given a name in the presence of the Lord of the Spirits," or that he was "concealed in the presence of (the Lord of the Spirits) prior to the creation of the world, and for eternity" (1 En. 48:3, 6). Why *should* this be taken for granted? The suggestion that the "one like a son of man" in Daniel is a pre-existent figure is doubtful: he is no more pre-existent than the beastly empires are pre-existent. In 1 Cor 15:42–49 Christ is "last Adam" and "man from heaven" in a specific eschatological sense: having been raised from the dead, he now has a "spiritual body" that makes him the beginning of a new mode of existence, in which the dead in Christ will share at the *parousia*. The argument at no point demands the pre-existence of the one who was crucified. If Paul thought of the future "coming" of the Son from heaven as an outworking of Dan 7:13–14, it is not because he identified Christ as the "man," whose pre-existence had been mooted, but because he believed that Christ had received vindication and eventual rule over the nations in like

26. Cullman, *Christology*, 166–67. If anything, it is the reverse: Paul is chiefly interested in the Man who will come on the clouds, who by his resurrection is the beginning of a new somatic existence as a second Adam.

27. Cullman, *Christology*, 168–69. Cullman says that to the question "Where was the pre-existent Christ?" the New Testament gives the answer: he was the Logos, "with God."

28. Cullman, *Christology*, 176.

29. Cullman, *Christology*, 177.

30. See also the critique of Ridderbos, *Paul*, 75–78.

manner. So if *morphē* were equivalent to *eikōn*, Paul would be talking about the crucified, risen, and regnant Christ as the pattern for the suffering and hope of the apostles and the churches. But that is not the case.

Bockmuehl: The Outward Appearance of the Pre-existent Christ

Having dismissed the relevance of both "glory" and "image" for interpretation of *morphē theou*, Bockmuehl proposes taking "form" as a quite straightforward reference to "the visible identifying features of a person or object."[31] His argument is that 1) the expression "form of a slave" in verse 7 points us in the direction of a rather literal understanding of *morphē* as "visible form"; 2) despite the "fierce resistance" of the Old Testament to the idea that God may be visually represented, there are persistent prophetic, apocalyptic, and mystical traditions in which God is spoken about in richly anthropomorphic language; 3) there is occasional reference to the *morphē* of God in Jewish writings; and 4) there is speculation about the form or immense body of God in later rabbinic literature.[32] On the basis of these propositions, Bockmuehl suggests that we must locate Paul "in a similar mystical tradition in which it was possible to speak of the Lord's majesty and greatness by alluding to the inconceivable size and beauty of his bodily appearance." There is reason to think that Paul was something of a visionary and a mystic (cf. 1 Cor 9:1; 2 Cor 12:1–4). The association of the "mystical theme of God's *form*" with the name above all names in the Christ encomium has parallels in Jewish mystical texts. Phil 3:21 makes apparent Paul's "concern with the Lord's heavenly body as relevant not merely to Christ's pre-incarnate state, but also as that which holds the key to the future existence of Christians." It is a mistake, therefore, in Bockmuehl's view, to suppose that the "form of God" is the appearance of the human person of Jesus: it rather "pertains to the beauty of his eternal heavenly appearance, which is expressed in the eternally present but historically realised act of taking on 'the form of a slave.'"[33]

What are we to make of this? The first proposition is certainly correct: interpretation of *morphē theou* should reckon with the concrete visual aspect of *morphē doulou*, as a reference to the "appearance" of Isaiah's

---

31. Bockmuehl, "Form of God," 11; see also Bockmuehl, *Philippians*, 126–29.

32. Bockmuehl, "Form of God," 11–19.

33. Bockmuehl, "Form of God," 21; cf. Bockmuehl, *Philippians*, 126–29: the form of God "probably means simply the visual characteristics of his heavenly being, which Christ shared but took on the characteristics of a servant"; and Gorman, "Form of God," 160: "Christ's divinity, and thus divinity itself, is being narratively defined as kenotic and cruciform in character."

suffering servant perhaps (Isa 52:14; 53:2) or simply to the wretchedness of the slave's condition.

The appeal to biblical anthropomorphisms, secondly, is of limited value. Literary context is important. These are not visions of God in heaven; they capture the *ephemeral* appearance of God on earth—in the garden, under the oaks of Mamre, beside a ladder,[34] on the mountain, in the temple, by the Chebar canal. Even Daniel's "Ancient of Days," who is clothed and whose hair is like pure wool, appears when wheeled thrones are "put in place" *on earth* specifically for the purpose of judging empires (Dan 7:9–10).[35] God is envisaged in human guise *when he appears in the earthly realm*, presumably as an accommodation to human perception. There is no precedent for speaking about the *heavenly* humanlike appearance of God. Moreover, visualization is persistently oblique and ambiguous in keeping with the "fierce resistance" to the depiction of God. God is only *heard* walking in the garden (Gen 3:8). The relationship between YHWH and the three men who appear to Abraham remains enigmatic (Gen 18). God appears to Jacob at the foot of the ladder but is not described, only heard, and only in a dream. When Moses and the elders of Israel ascended Sinai, it is said that they "saw the God of Israel" and safely ate and drank in his presence (Exod 24:9–11). Their vision is restricted by the fact that they are prostrate on the ground: they see what looked like a pavement of translucent sapphire stone beneath his feet but not the figure or "form" of God. The Septuagint is even more circumspect: "they saw the place, there where the God of Israel stood . . . they appeared in the place of God . . . ." The visual presence of the Lord in the temple is strictly ineffable; merely the extreme hem of his robe filling the temple is mentioned, along with the vividly depicted seraphim (Isa 6:1–3). Only the wheeled throne visions of Ezekiel and Daniel venture to fill in the details of the appearance of the humanlike divine figure.

Thirdly, we saw in the previous chapter that neither of the texts that Bockmuehl cites (Philo, *Moses* 1 66; Josephus, *Ag. Ap.* 2:190) can properly be construed as attributing a *morphē* to God. What Moses sees in the burning bush is not the "form of God" but—as a matter of theological necessity—the form of an angel; and Josephus *denies* that God has either "form" or great

---

34. It is debated whether *nitsav ʿalayw* means "stood above him" or "stood above it" (Wenham, *Genesis 16–50*, 222), but the sense may be "against" or "in front of." In another epiphany Abraham saw three men "standing in front of him" (*nitsavim ʿalayw*) (Gen 18:2). Cf. LXX: Jacob dreamed and saw "a ladder set firmly (*estērigmenē*) on the earth . . . . And the Lord leaned against it (*epestērikto ep' autēs*) . . . ." The ensuing conversation and Jacob's response ("YHWH is in this place") suggest that God is present with Jacob at the base of the ladder.

35. See Perriman, *Son of Man*, 54.

size. As with the biblical anthropomorphisms, the point at issue is whether God may be visualized, either directly in epiphanies or indirectly by artistic representation, *in an earthly setting*. There is no evidence that "talk of God's 'form' could belong to the context of Jewish mystical thought about the ascent to behold the heavenly appearance of God."[36] The argument from the use of the Hebrew *tvnyt* in the Songs of the Sabbath Sacrifice is doubtful and inconclusive. There is reference to various "forms" in the worship that is taking place in the heavenly temple: the glorious forms of the "princes of the spiritual kingdom" (4Q403 f1ii:2–3), the form of the chariot throne (4Q405 f20ii22:8–9), the forms of "wondrous spirits" (11Q17 8:3); but not clearly to the "form of God" as Bockmuehl suggests. The phrase *r'sy tvnyt 'lwhym* (4Q403 f1ii:16) more likely refers to the glorious form of angelic figures or to other forms in the heavenly temple.[37] Beyond this, very little is gained by noting that *tvnyt* corresponds to *morphē* and is used in the Old Testament for the "pattern" of the temple furnishings or the "form" of an angel's hand (Ezek 8:3).

Fourthly, apocalyptic and mystical speculation regarding the gigantic body of God will be considered in the next section. Bockmuehl connects this only implicitly with Paul, apart from the speculative suggestion that he was familiar with Jewish mystical reflection on the body of the beloved in the Song of Songs, and even this has only "tangential" relevance for the reading of Philippians.[38]

Finally, as with the argument about form and glory, the attempt to link the Jewish traditions with Paul founders repeatedly on the fact that his visionary experience is directed towards the risen Christ (1 Cor 9:1; 2 Cor 12:1; Gal 1:12, 16; cf. Acts 9:3–9; 22:6–10; 26:13–18). If the Essenes and others had "an intense interest in the glorious and transcendent names of the heavenly beings," Paul is interested only in the name that Christ received *after his resurrection and exaltation* (Phil 2:9–11).[39] There is no basis for the inference that mention of the "body of his glory" in Phil 3:21 has relevance for "Christ's pre-incarnate state." The expectation here, as in 1 Corinthians 15:20, 48–49, is that resurrected believers will share in the same *resurrected* bodily life. The reference to the "measure of the stature of the fullness of Christ" in Eph 4:13, 15–16 offers no support for the idea

36. Bockmuehl, "Form of God," 15.

37. Wise, Abegg, and Cook translate "the chiefs of the divine building" (*Scrolls*, 372).

38. Bockmuehl, "Form of God," 22–23. With regard to the mystical texts, Reumann says that the "lexical and contextual jumps" required are not persuasive (*Philippians*, 343).

39. Bockmuehl, "Form of God," 19–23, page 20 for the quotation.

that Paul or the Pauline tradition would have conceived of Christ as being in the form of the immense body of God: the author expects believers to attain to this standard.[40] So we may agree that these visions must be set "in close proximity to the traditions about visions of God," but the recognition that the risen and highly exalted Christ, seated at the right hand of God, is closely associated with God does not, perforce, entail a pre-incarnate life. Resurrection does not in itself presuppose pre-existence; nor does Paul say anything to suggest that he felt the need to relate the body of the resurrected Jesus to, or to reconcile it with, some manner of pre-incarnate bodily life on a grand scale from eternity.

Gieschen and the *Macranthropos* Myth

Gieschen's thesis is that angelomorphic traditions played a substantial role in the development of Paul's Christology.[41] Much of the evidence for this is considered sporadically elsewhere in this book. The argument about the expression "form of God" is that it presupposes, on the one hand, certain Jewish and early Jewish-Christian beliefs regarding the gigantic body of God, and on the other, the existence of a heavenly *anthrōpos* or proto-Adam. For this Gieschen relies chiefly on separate investigations of the relevant materials by Jarl Fossum and Gedaliahu Stroumsa. He assumes that Bockmuehl was not aware of this research.[42]

1. There is some evidence, from perhaps as early as the first century AD, for a quite literal Jewish belief in the bodily form of God. The "most clearly anthropomorphic, or rather, macrocosmic conceptions of the deity in late antique Judaism" are to be found, Stroumsa maintains, in *Shi'ur Qomah* ("Measurement of the Stature"), a Jewish mystical text which catalogues the size of the limbs of the divine body.[43] Dating of the work is difficult, but Stroumsa thinks that the "original Jewish speculation on the macrocosmic divine body is pre-Christian."[44] Fossum notes the view of Scholem that there is a reference to the *Shi'ur Qomah* doctrine in the short version of the highly syncretistic and undateable 2 Enoch: "You, you see the extent of my body, the same as your own; but I, I have seen the extent of the LORD, without measure and without analogy, who has no end" (2 En. A 39:6).[45] The Pseudo-

---

40. Bockmuehl, "Form of God," 17.

41. Gieschen, *Angelomorphic Christology*, 315.

42. Gieschen, *Angelomorphic Christology*, 338n76.

43. Stroumsa, "Form(s) of God," 276.

44. Stroumsa, "Form(s) of God," 277; Fossum, "Christology," 261.

45. Fossum, "Christology," 261, claiming that the work "in all probability is

Clementine writings are thought to give expression to an "Ebionite" doctrine of the divine body.[46] God has a "most beautiful form (*morphēn*)" and a brilliantly shining "body," though his limbs are "solely for the sake of beauty and not for use" (*Ps.-Clem. Hom.* 17.7).[47] The form of God is perceptible to the pure in heart, "that they may rejoice because they suffered." Justin makes reference to certain Jewish teachers who held that "the Father of all, the unbegotten God, has hands and feet, and fingers, and a soul, like a composite being; and they for this reason teach that it was the Father Himself who appeared to Abraham and to Jacob" (*Dial.* 114).[48]

2. A Jewish sect known as the Maghārīyans (an Arabic word meaning "cave-dwellers") reportedly opposed the literalism of the Sadducees, arguing that biblical anthropomorphisms applied to "the angel who created the world."[49] The Jewish-Christian *Book of Elchasai*, was supposedly revealed by an angel 96 miles in height called "Son of God," accompanied by a female of similar proportions called "Holy Spirit" (Hippolytus, *Haer.* 9.8).[50]

3. In gnostic cosmogonies a primordial heavenly man appears, who in various ways is closely identified with God.[51] The "Self-constructed Father" is full of "ineffable light"; in the beginning he decided "to have his likeness become a great power," and immediately "the principle . . . of that Light appeared as Immortal Androgynous Man" (*Eugnostos* 76.16–24). The earthly Adam is a copy of the heavenly "Adam of Light" (*Orig. World* 112.31—113.2; cf. 107.25–27; 108.8–9).

The most important of the gnostic texts considered is *Poimandres*, not least because it is thought to provide evidence for the interchangeability of

---

pre-Christian"; and Gieschen, *Angelomorphic Christology*, 342. Enoch has seen the Lord from a distance in the seventh heaven, seated on his throne, with angels serving before his face (2 En. A 20:3—21:1). When he attempts to describe the appearance of the Lord from close up, he can only ask, "Who (is) to give an account of the dimensions of the being of the face of the Lord, strong and very terrible?" (2 En. A 22:1–2).

46. Fossum, "Christology," 264–65.

47. Cf. *Ps.-Clem. Hom.* 17.10: "beauty cannot exist apart from shape; nor can one be attracted to the love of God, nor even deem that he can see Him, if God has no form" (Schaff).

48. See Stroumsa, "Form(s) of God," 271. Origen censures those "carnal men" who infer from a passage such as Isa 66:1 that "God has so large a body that . . . he sits in heaven and stretches out his feet to the earth" (*Hom. Gen.* 1.13); and because the scriptures record that God speaks to people, not only the Jews but also some Christians have "supposed that God should be understood as a man, that is, adorned with human members and human appearance" (3.1).

49. Stroumsa, "Form(s) of God," 278; also Wolfson, "Pre-existent Angel," 90.

50. Hippolytus records that Elchasai preached a new remission of sins in the third year of Trajan's reign (*Haer.* 9.8).

51. Fossum, "Christology," 266–69.

eikōn and *morphē*.[52] Poimandres, the Man-Shepherd, is an "enormous being completely unbounded in size" (*Corp. herm.* 1.1).[53] He is god, father, and *nous* or mind. From mind comes the "lightgiving word" or "son of god." Mind and word, "god the father" and the son of god, "are not divided from one another for their union is life" (1.6). The visionary sees in mind the "archetypal form (*archetypon eidos*), the preprinciple that exists before a beginning without end" (1.8). He asks how the elements of nature came into existence, and is told that mind "by speaking gave birth to a second mind, a craftsman," who fashioned the "seven governors" which encompass the material world (1.9). Subsequently, the heavier elements of nature sink downwards, but the word ascends to be reunited with the "craftsman-mind," so nature is left devoid of reason and only "living things without reason" are created.

Mind, however, then gives birth to a human person, an *anthrōpos*, "like himself (*autōi ison*) whom he loved as his own child" (*Corp. herm.* 1.12). The *anthrōpos* has the father's "image" (*eikona*); and god, being in love with "his own form (*morphēs*)," gave to the human "all his craftworks."[54] Stroumsa says that the myth posits an "essential duality" between two divine entities: "Nous, the supreme God, who remains invisible and formless, and his hypostatic Form, who is his Son, the Primordial Man."[55]

The *anthrōpos* enters the sphere of the "craftsman" or *dēmiourgos* and gains all the wisdom of the seven governors. Now having acquired "all authority over the cosmos of mortals and unreasoning animals," he desires to see what is happening in the natural world. Stooping to look down through the "cosmic framework," he reveals to the lower natural order "the fair form (*morphēn*) of god" (*Corp. herm.* 1.14). It is love at first sight. Nature becomes besotted with the form of god in the *anthrōpos*; and the *anthrōpos* falls in love with the "form like himself as it was in nature," and desires to inhabit the "unreasoning form" (*alogon morphēn*). So nature and the *anthrōpos* embrace, "for they were lovers," which explains why, "unlike any other living thing on earth, mankind is twofold—in the body mortal but immortal in the essential man" (1.15).

4. According to Fossum, the Pseudo-Clementine writings indicate that the early Jewish-Christian "Ebionites" were likely to have identified the "brilliant bodily Form of God" with the Son.[56] The argument is speculative in parts. The Son of God, who is "the beginning of all things," became man

52. Gieschen, *Angelomorphic Christology*, 337–38; Fossum, "Christology," 268–69; see also Jervell, *Imago Dei*, 228–29.

53. For the translation Copenhaver, *Hermetica*.

54. See Hamerton-Kelly, *Pre-Existence*, 160–68; and Stroumsa, "Form(s) of God," 273–74, who notes that *eikōn* appears to be equivalent to *morphē*.

55. Stroumsa, "Form(s) of God," 274; see also Fossum, "Christology," 265.

56. Fossum, "Christology," 267; cf. Gieschen, *Angelomorphic Christology*, 338.

and was called Christ, in that he was the anointed king among the Jews (*Ps.-Clem. Rec.* 1.45). Fossum maintains, however, that in an earlier passage (1.28) "Adam-Christ" is spoken of as the pre-existent "form" or "appearance" of the true incarnate prophet. This is less clear. The text reads: "But after all these things He made man, on whose account He had prepared all things, whose internal species is older, and for whose sake all things that are were made" (Schaff). The phrase "internal species" renders the Latin *interna species*, but the Syriac translation of the *Recognitions* has *dĕmûthâ*, which Fossum thinks corresponds to *morphē* in Phil 2:6, for which the Peshitta uses *dĕmûthâ*.[57] But the thought may rather be of the pre-existence of souls. In *Homilies* 16.16 Peter says that the souls of humans have come from God and are of the same substance as God.

5. Fossum also finds in these traditions evidence for the identification of the heavenly man with the glory of God revealed in human form in Ezek 1:26. Elchasai's followers, to start with, would have identified the Son of God with Christ and would have "regarded Christ as the Kabod, the heavenly Makranthropos."[58] It appears from the Valentinian *Tripartite Tractate* 66.10–14 that Christians in the second century could speak of the Son as "man of the Father . . . the form of the formless, the body of the bodiless." Since *morphē* and *doxa* are used interchangeably (supposedly) in Greek translations of Old Testament theophanies, it appears that the Son who is the *morphē* of the formless God is also the glory of God. Justin said, on the one hand, that God has "ineffable Glory and Form (*morphēn*)" (*1 Apol.* 9.1–3), and on the other, that the original "rational Power" begotten by God before all creatures is variously known as the "Glory of the Lord," "Son," "Wisdom," "Angel," "God," "Lord," and "Word" (*Dial.* 61.1).[59] Justin also identified Christ with the "Glory of man-like form" in Ezek 1:26 (*Dial.* 126.1). Further evidence for the association of Christ with "the Glory" in early Jewish Christianity may be found in the "Ebionite" teaching that God has a radiant body and "the most beautiful Form (*morphēn*) on account of man, so that the pure in heart may be able to see Him" (*Ps.-Clem. Hom.* 17.7.2–4).[60]

6. Stroumsa argues that a "random suggestion" made by Gershom Scholem that the "body of glory" in the *Shi'ur Qomah* is related to the expression "body of his glory" in Phil 3:21 is too speculative.[61] But he thinks that

57. Fossum, "Christology," 267–68.

58. Fossum, "Christology," 263. According to Epiphanius, Elchasai identified the gigantic angel as Christ, though Epiphanius is unsure whether *Jesus* Christ was intended; he says that Elchasai later joined the Ebionites and Nazarenes (Epiphanius, *Pan.* 19 3.4; 4.1; 5.4; see Klijn and Reinink, *Jewish-Christian Sects*, 157, 159, 161).

59. Fossum, "Christology," 263–64.

60. Fossum, "Christology," 265.

61. Stroumsa, "Form(s) of God," 281–82. Gieschen to the contrary, makes it a key part of his argument (*Angelomorphic Christology*, 338).

there may be traces of the Jewish mythologoumenon in the christological encomia of Phil 2:6–11 and Col 1:15–20. So Christ's being "in the form of God" may presuppose the original idea that "his cosmic body filled the whole world and was identical to the *pleroma*."[62] The incarnation, therefore, required Christ to *empty himself* of this cosmic fullness.[63] The description of Christ in the Colossians encomium as "image of the invisible God"—"first creature" or "First Adam"—and as the "head of the body" clearly suggests, in Stroumsa's view, "the macrocosmic conception of Christ as the image, or form, of the invisible God."[64]

Stroumsa concludes cautiously that there existed in the first century "a cluster of mythologoumena about the archangelic hypostasis of God, also identified with the First Adam (and therefore the true image of God), whose body possessed cosmic dimensions. This figure, moreover, who bore God's name, had created the world at his command."[65] Gieschen then argues on the strength of the philological and tradition-historical insights generated by these studies that the pre-incarnate Christ is presented in Philippians as the "visible manifestation" or "form" of God, the glory in "the likeness of a man" depicted in Ezek 1:26 and related texts.[66]

Can the argument be sustained? Two of the texts considered attribute a *morphē* to God. In the Pseudo-Clementine romance God has a most beautiful humanlike form, and humanity has been fashioned in the image of that form: "For He moulded man in His own shape (*morphēi*) as in the grandest seal, in order that he may be the ruler and lord of all, and that all may be subject to him" (*Ps.-Clem. Hom.* 17.7).[67] In the more elaborate cosmogony of *Poimandres* the beautiful form of God is represented in the primordial *anthrōpos* which precedes the emergence of an earthly, bipartite humanity.

62. Stroumsa, "Form(s) of God," 283.

63. A similar conceptuality is found in Odes Sol. 7:3–6 if *rabūtā* in verse 3 is translated "greatness," "size," rather than "dreadfulness" or "grandeur" (Stroumsa, "Form(s) of God," 283–84). In that case, the Lord is said to have diminished his size to become like Solomon in *form* and nature.

64. Stroumsa, "Form(s) of God," 284. Gieschen thinks that Stroumsa is mistaken in ascribing to Paul the notion of a cosmic, rather than merely a gigantic, body of the pre-existent Christ (*Angelomorphic Christology*, 339).

65. Stroumsa, "Form(s) of God," 279.

66. Gieschen, *Angelomorphic Christology*, 338. Gieschen further suggests that Paul's "body of Christ" imagery, particularly as it is associated with the "glory of God" as in Eph 1:17–23, and his characteristic "in Christ" language are to be explained with reference to his understanding that Christ was the "manifestation of God with a mystical body of gigantic proportions" (*Angelomorphic Christology*, 340).

67. Cf. Steenburg, "Case Against," 84: *morphē* is used "precisely because its connotations are more clearly supportive of the concept that there exists a bodily manifestation of God."

This is the only point of contact with Paul's statement in Philippians 2:6. Speculation regarding the divine body or angelic proxies carries little weight unless it is established that Paul's *morphē theou* draws on this cluster of mythologoumena. The historical value of the evidence is obviously precarious.[68] Perhaps ideas and ways of speaking were around in the early first century that prompted Paul or some other author to identify the crucified Christ with a pre-existent figure in the visible *morphē* of a humanlike God. That he became subsequently, by way of contrast (*all'*), in "likeness of humans (*anthrōpōn*)" and was "found in outward appearance as a human person (*anthrōpos*)" makes it less likely that the "form" of a heavenly *anthrōpos* is in view in verse 6. But the argument from the Jewish texts about *morphē*, which we have seen is not interchangeable with *eikōn* or *doxa*, is valid only because God is conceived in sharply *anthropomorphic* terms. Given Paul's patent and pervasive dependence on Old Testament traditions it seems unlikely that he thought of God in this way—and in any case, it would be difficult to differentiate Jesus from any other person molded "in the form of" an anthropomorphic God. The evidence from the earlier Jewish sects is of dubious relevance. It is unclear whether either Elchasai or his followers identified the gigantic angel with Christ, despite Fossum's endeavors to claim as much.[69] Elchasai, according to Hippolytus, promoted a blend of Jewish-Christian beliefs (he required his followers to be circumcised) and Pythagoreanism, and taught that Christ had been born many times on earth, "having his soul transferred from body to body" (*Haer.* 9.9).

Conclusion

I have placed repeated emphasis on the fact that *morphē* and *eikōn* are not synonymous terms. This and the fact that, when Paul speaks of Christ as "image of God," the sense is eschatological weigh heavily against interpretations that take *en morphēi theou* to be a reference to either the earthly or the pre-incarnate *human form* of Jesus. In the end, it seems to me, neither Bockmuehl nor Gieschen has shown that the phrase "form of God" was available to Paul as a way of asserting the spectacular anthropomorphic pre-existence of Jesus. But there is one other option open to interpreters at this stage, which is that the "form of God" in which Christ pre-existed was not human as such but angelic—so anthropomorphic indirectly, without relying on the equation of "form" and "image."

68. See Lee, *Preexistent Son*, 20.

69. Fossum, "Christology," 262–63.

6

Being in the Angelic Form of God

AGAINST A BACKGROUND OF interest in divergent forms of Jewish monotheism and the impact that traditions about angels had on the development of early Christology, some scholars have proposed an "angelomorphic" interpretation of *morphē theou*.[1] Jesus pre-existed as a heavenly figure whose "form" or outward appearance was angel-like—as one of the "sons of God" (Sanders), as a "spiritual messiah" (Horbury), as the apocalyptic Son of Man (Holloway), or as the Son of God who appears as though in a pagan epiphany (Vollenweider). We begin, however, with the argument, occasionally touted, that in one place at least Paul directly identifies Christ as an angel.

As an Angel of God, as Christ Jesus

There is little direct evidence that may be cited in support of an "angelomorphic Christology" in Paul's writings. One passage that has attracted attention is Gal 4:14*, where he says, "as an angel of God you received me, as Christ Jesus." Gieschen has argued that this reflects Paul's conviction that "he had been united with a very specific angel: God's Angel, Christ Jesus."[2] He thinks, in the first place, that Paul regarded himself as an *angelos*—an angel from earth rather than an "angel from heaven" (Gal 1:8)—whom the Galatians did not "spit out" as demon-possessed but embraced as a "Christ-possessed" messenger, "as God's Angel."[3] The identification is to be understood against the background of Paul's claim to have received his gospel by a direct revelation or mystical vision of Christ Jesus, particularly in view of the fact that "visionary ascent experiences can involve the transformation of the seer into

1. Zeller, "Christology," 313.

2. Gieschen, *Angelomorphic Christology*, 316–22; cf. Ehrman, *How Jesus*, 252–53, who cites Garrett, *No Ordinary Angel*, 11.

3. Gieschen attributes the argument to Schweitzer and Schlier (*Angelomorphic Christology*, 320 and n20).

the likeness of the Divine Image" (cf. 2 En. 22:8–10). Secondly, Gieschen maintains that the *hōs* ("as") clauses assert real, not hypothetical, comparisons, and that the relationship between them is epexegetical: "as Christ Jesus" explains "as God's Angel."[4] So he rearranges the sentence and translates: "You received me as God's Angel, namely Christ Jesus."

The identification of Christ as God's angel does not depend on the claim that Paul believed himself to be united with the angelic Christ. Still, Gieschen's argument at this point seems muddled. Paul speaks not of himself alone in Gal 1:8 but of himself "and all the brothers who are with me" (Gal 1:2), so he means: "even if we as an apostolic team or an angel from heaven should preach . . . ." The comparison between false apostles disguised as apostles of Christ and Satan disguised as an "angel of light" in 2 Cor 11:13–15 does not blur the distinction between the two realms. The false apostles are "servants" of Satan but they are not demons. It is not the *person* of Paul but the "trial" that he presented on account of his bodily affliction ("in my flesh") that was not despised or "spat out" by the Galatians (Gal 4:14). It is not certain that he is talking about his own mystical journey to the third heaven in 2 Cor 12:2–4, but in any case, the emphasis is on the ambiguity of the *bodily* experience ("whether in the body or out of the body I do not know"), not on anything that might be construed as an angelic transformation.

The argument that the *hōs* clauses entail a *real* identification of Paul with God's Angel, who is Christ, is also weak.[5] The difference between welcoming Onesimus "*as if* this slave were Paul" and welcoming him "*as* Paul" (Phlm 17) is purely rhetorical. Onesimus is *not* Paul. The instruction in Did. 11:3–4 to welcome every visiting apostle *hōs kyrios* is pragmatic; it does not carry the idea that "Christ lives and speaks" in the true apostle. A teacher is also to be welcomed *hōs kyrion* "if his teaching contributes to righteousness and knowledge of the Lord" (Did. 11:2), but there is no suggestion that every teacher is somehow a real embodiment of the Lord. The point is simply that itinerant teachers, apostles, and prophets should be treated as though the Lord himself were in their midst, *provided that the visitor behaves correctly* and does not "teach a different teaching," overstay his or her welcome, or ask for money (11:2, 5–6).[6]

The main question for us here, however, is whether "as Christ Jesus" *interprets* "as an angel of God." A similar construction is found in two other passages in Paul's writings: "but as fleshly, as infants in Christ" (1 Cor 3:1*);

4. Gieschen, *Angelomorphic Christology*, 323.

5. Gieschen, *Angelomorphic Christology*, 323.

6. Cf. Waddell, *Messiah*, 142n46.

"but as from sincerity, but as from God" (2 Cor 2:17*). Gieschen thinks that the "organic connection" between the two clauses in both cases points to the identification of Christ with, in effect, the "Angel of YHWH" in Gal 4:14.[7] But "organic connection" is too vague. The Corinthians are both "fleshly" and "infants in Christ," but the terms are not synonymous. The apostles act "from sincerity" and are "from God," but the second *hōs* clause is clearly not epexegetical. The most likely reading of Gal 4:14 is still that the Galatians received Paul *both* as an angel of God *and* as Christ Jesus, without thereby implying any identification of the two.

In the Form of One of the Sons of God, According to Sanders

J. A. Sanders begins with Poimandres. The "cosmograph" of the descent and ascent of the gnostic Anthropos, he argues, provides only a partial analogy to the itinerary of the one "in the form of God."[8] It lacks the depth of Christ's descent and the height of his exaltation, and although it gives us the image of one "in the form of God," it does not answer "the essential question of the status of ὃς ἐν μορφῇ θεοῦ [*hos en morphēi theou*] before the drama of emptying and humbling." A more complete analogy to Paul's image, he argues, is to be found in the stories of rebellious angels and other "sons of heaven" in Hellenistic Judaism and at Qumran who conspicuously *did not humble themselves.*[9] A common and serious indictment against these dissenting sons of heaven in Enoch, for example, is that they lead people astray in the specific sense that they act "as if they were the Lord" (1 En. 68:4); but their "vanity and self-seeking ambition" are especially evident in the Latin Life of Adam and Eve 12–17. When the devil refuses to worship Adam and is threatened with the wrath of God, he responds: "If God becomes angry with me, I shall set my seat above the stars of heaven and will be like the Highest" (L.A.E. 15:3). This appears to be an allusion to the boast of the king of Babylon in Isa 14:10, and Sanders conjectures that this sort of Jewish *mythos* accounts for the language of *eritheia* ("selfish ambition"), *kenodoxia* ("conceit"), and *harpagmos* ("thievery") in Phil 2:3–6. The descending "dissenting deities," therefore, provide an "excellent foil" for the image of the one who descended, but without such hubris, with no wish to rival God, motivated rather by humility (*tapeinophrosynē*).

Sanders argues further that we find in a pesher on the Enochic tradition of the rebellious angels in 4Q Ages of Creation the same ironic inversion

7. Gieschen, *Angelomorphic Christology*, 324–25.
8. Sanders, "Dissenting," 283.
9. Sanders, "Dissenting," 284–86.

that we have in the Philippians encomium. On the one hand, the angels descended from heaven because they "rejected the authority of God and rebelled seeking their own selfish ends" (4Q180 f1:7–10; 4Q181 f2:1–2).[10] On the other, God caused his glory to draw near "from among the children of the world to counsel with him in the heavenly council" (4Q181 f1:3). For the lowly community at Qumran this was really a contrast between themselves and the apostate Hasmoneans in Jerusalem. In Philippians the contrast remains "patently on the mythic level" between the self-serving "dissenting deities" and the self-denying "consenting deity"; but in both Palestine and Philippi "the historical counterparts of the mythic drama would have been the humble, obedient Jesus, on the one hand, and all those who failed to acknowledge him, on the other."[11]

The thesis, therefore, is that an early Palestinian disciple of Paul generated a unique "mythic amalgam" out of the two traditions: Jesus is the heavenly Anthropos in the form of God, whose descent from heaven was not like that of the rebellious angels, who sought to usurp the place of God, but was undertaken in humility for him then to be elevated to a position of supreme authority in the divine council.

Even allowing for the extensive Hellenization of Palestinian Judaism, such a synthesis seems inherently improbable.[12] We have seen good reason to discount Poimandres as a source for *en morphēi theou*, and the attribution of selfish ambition to the rebellious angels is by no means a prominent element in the tradition. As Sanders recognizes, the crime of the angels was primarily the corruption of humanity by their illicit sexual union with women and the transmission of heavenly mysteries—the various forms of knowledge that brought death into the world (e.g., 1 En. 16:3; 64:1–2; 67:10; 69:4–15). This is accurately reflected in the Qumran pesher on Azazel and the angels. The passages cited from 2 Enoch speak only of a self-willed revolt against God and a descent from heaven to ravish the daughters of men and defile the earth with their deeds (2 En. 7:3; 18:3–4). In the case of the devil's refusal to worship Adam as the image of God in Life of Adam and Eve, the descent from heaven to earth is expulsion, not revolt. The threat made by the devil is presumably that he will retaliate by inspiring such blasphemous examples of kingship as the king of Babylon; but now it is the king rather than the outcast devil who in fact provides the

10. Sanders, "Dissenting," 287–88.

11. Sanders, "Dissenting," 288–89.

12. The argument that the fall of Satan provides the antitype for the descent of the pre-existent Christ is given some credence by Keown, citing Stauffer and Knox (*Philippians 1:1–2:18*, 359–60). He doubts any direct influence but allows that the idea may be "in the conceptual background of the hymn."

counterpoint to Christ. It seems more reasonable to think that these divergent traditions constituted different ways of addressing the same problem
of human arrogance than that the Hellenistic-Jewish material accounts for
the conceptuality of Phil 2:6.

Horbury's Angel-Christology and the Argument
for a Pre-Existent Messiah

William Horbury's argument about the origins of the cult of Christ is
straightforward enough.[13] That we may speak, in the first place, of such a
cult is established by the presence in the New Testament of acclamation
and hymnody directed towards Christ. The cult had its origins in Jewish
messianic traditions, developed against the background of the Herodian
and Roman ruler cult. These traditions principally took the form of the
"praise of Jewish rulers," meaning that the cult of Christ is to be understood
fundamentally as the "worship" of Christ as the messianic ruler of the nations: "Homage to the messiah was important in a Jewish messianism which
formed a counterpart to gentile ruler-cult. Recognition of Christ as messianic king . . . led directly to the scenes of acclamation and obeisance, the
hymns and the titles preserved in the New Testament."[14]

Horbury also thinks, however, that the ruler cult of Christ was substantially underpinned by Jewish expectations of "angelic deliverers," by the
belief that "favoured mortals might be transformed into angels," and by the
"appearance in apocalypses and mystical texts of one exalted angel almost
indistinguishable from God himself."[15] Roughly speaking, the picture of a
supreme deity surrounded by a host of angels was continuous with earlier
ideas of a pantheon or divine council, to the extent that the angelic beings
"retained much of their demigod-like power in the thought of the later Second-Temple period."[16] Horbury notes the absence of unambiguous evidence
for an angel-Christology in the New Testament but argues nevertheless
that angelology influenced the development of early Christology through
the medium of messianism, so that Christ as messiah was "envisaged as an
angel-like spiritual being."[17] Specifically, he thinks that such a conceptual-

13. Horbury, *Jewish Messianism*, 109–52. See also the summary in Chester, "Christology," 26–27; and the analysis of Lee, *Preexistent Son*, 99–115.

14. Horbury, *Jewish Messianism*, 150; cf. Ehrman's "exaltation Christology" (*How
Jesus*, 230–35).

15. Horbury, *Jewish Messianism*, 119.

16. Horbury, *Jewish Messianism*, 120.

17. Horbury, *Jewish Messianism*, 126.

ity would provide an appropriate background for the "metamorphosis from divine to servile form" that we find in Phil 2:6–8.[18]

The proposition, in the first place, that Jews entertained notions of an "angel-like messiah" is debatable. Horbury stresses the close association and coordination between angelic and human figures.[19] He argues, for example, that while Daniel's "one like a son of man" has been identified with Michael or Gabriel by modern commentators, in the late second temple period he was widely interpreted to be a messianic king (1 En., 2 Esd, Sib. Or. 5:414–33). The "angel" sent before Israel at the exodus is closely coordinated with human leadership but also served as a model for John the Baptist. The Qumran community hoped both for angelic aid and for messianic deliverers. More significant is the view that the messiah could be thought of as an "angel-like spirit," as having a spirit that pre-existed birth, presupposing the "conception of God as lord of godlike angels and spirits."[20] The evidence is in the first place general: the idea that humans have semi-independent spirits or that angels are disembodied souls which can enter humans. But Horbury also adduces instances of the specific belief that the messianic king could be regarded "as the manifestation and embodiment of a spirit sent by God."[21]

1. In Isa 9:5 LXX the royal child who will sit on the throne of David is named "angel of great counsel." Horbury links this with the prediction that a spirit of God will rest upon the rod which will sprout from the root of Jesse (Isa 11:1–3 LXX), and infers that "angel of great counsel" is a recognition that the messiah will possess a "spirit of wisdom."[22] This seems to fall some way short of an affirmation of pre-existence. Joshua the son of Nun was "full of the spirit of wisdom" (Deut 34:9; cf. Dan 5:11, 14).

2. Texts in the prophets suggest that the messianic king has been associated by the LXX translators "with divinely-sent spirit." But the announcement of "his Christ" (*ton christon autou*) to people in Amos 4:13 LXX is wrongly associated with creation: the announcement comes amid the *present* activity of God who produces thunder and wind, dawn and mist, and "treads on the heights of the earth." Lam 4:20 may associate the anointed king with the breathing of life into humanity at creation, but the metaphor, in that case, works firmly against any thought of a unique pre-existence for the messiah: the verse is a statement about the significance of the king for the people—under whose shadow "we shall live among the nations"—not

18. Horbury, *Jewish Messianism*, 125.

19. Horbury, *Jewish Messianism*, 83–86.

20. Horbury, *Jewish Messianism*, 86, 88, 89.

21. Horbury, *Jewish Messianism*, 90.

22. Horbury, *Jewish Messianism*, 90–91.

about the pre-existence of the king's spirit. There is no ground for the claim that the messianic king could be "understood as a spiritual messiah, in touch with or embodying a spirit sent from God."[23]

3. That the association of a king from Judah with a star in Balaam's prophecy carries angelic connotations is also doubtful (Num 24:17). The stars are not so clearly regarded as angels in the literature. They are created objects (cf. Pss 8:4; 135:9; 146:4; Isa 45:12 LXX); they are exhorted to praise God but *along with* the angels, the "water above the heavens," and all created things (Ps 148).[24] The Israelites are commanded not to do obeisance to sun, moon, and stars, which have been allotted—as the whole "ornamentation" (*kosmon*) of the sky—to all the nations (Deut 4:19 LXX). People are mistaken in thinking that the luminaries of heaven are "gods that rule the world" (Wis 13:2). The stars are simply part of the natural order (Wis 7:19); they are there to give light (Isa 13:10; Joel 3:15). Horbury is able to show that the star prophecy was widely used, notably in conjunction with Isa 11:1–2, but not that the messiah was expected to be the incarnation of an angelic being.[25] The rising star in Balaam's prophecy is simply a metaphor for the appearance of a new king.[26]

4. If *anatolē* in Jer 23:5; Zech 3:8; 6:12 means "rising" or "dayspring" rather than "shoot" or "branch," the angelic connotations remain nevertheless tenuous. The attempt to connect the "man whose name is *anatolē*" in Philo with the angelic Logos fails.[27] On the one hand, Moses is presented as an example of a good "dawning (*anatolēs*) in the soul" and is therefore aptly named "Rising" or "East" (*anatolē*) by one of his companions; but this is in contrast to Balak, who dwelt "in the east" (*anatolais*) but cursed the Israelites. So "this dawning, having the same name as the former one, has nevertheless an opposite nature to it, and is continually at war with it" (*Confusion* 60, 62–64). On the other hand, Philo exhorts those who wish to be called "sons of God" to be conformed to his "first-born word, the eldest of his angels," so that they "may deserve to be called the children of his eternal image, of his

23. Horbury, *Jewish Messianism*, 92.

24. According to Heiser the "sons of God" are referred to as "stars" in Job 38:7 (*Unseen Realm*, 80), but the point seems to be that the angels celebrated *along with* the stars of morning when the foundations of the earth were laid. This is certainly how the LXX understands it. Goldingay, *Daniel*, 308: "The stars can be taken to represent celestial beings: cf. 8:10; also Judg 5:20; Job 38:7; IEnoch 104; *T. Moses* 10.9; IIApocBar 51. It is difficult to tell how literal and how metaphorical these passages are."

25. The nearest we get is Eusebius's statement that "Barcocheba (which signifies a star) . . . pretended that he was a star that had come down to them out of heaven to bring them light in the midst of their misfortunes" (Eusebius, *Hist. eccl.* 4.6.2, Schaff).

26. Cf. Budd, *Numbers*, 270.

27. Horbury, *Jewish Messianism*, 94.

most sacred word" (146). The argument is only that people were made in the image of God and should behave accordingly—that is, rationally. Again, there appears to be no ground for the conclusion that *anatolē* is another Septuagint title that is "associated with an understanding of the messianic figure as a luminary and a heavenly being."

5. Horbury asks whether second-century Christian testimony concerning the pre-existence of Christ based on interpretation of Pss 72 and 110 points to "an opinion current in the Second-Temple period, that the messiah existed in glory before the world."[28] The assertion that "before the sun came to be his name was determined" (*Targum Ps.* 72:17)—in contrast to the Hebrew "May . . . his fame continue as long as the sun"—is not the same as saying that the messiah existed or was born before the creation of the sun.[29] The Greek translation of Ps 110:3* is more suggestive: "With you the rule in a day of your power among the splendors of the holy ones; from the womb before morning star I begot you."[30] But if, as Horbury thinks, Psalm 2:7 has impinged upon the translation, "before morning star" may only be a poetic substitute for "today," perhaps adding the thought that the rising of the daystar is a figure for the ascendancy of a ruler of the nations (Isa 14:12 LXX): the Jewish king who will rule in the midst of his enemies and receive the nations as his heritage will have a status comparable to that of the king of Babylon. In any case, the connection with a supposedly pre-existent Son of Man or messiah in Similitudes of Enoch and 4 Ezra is not apparent. The naming of the Son of Man "before the creation of the stars" (1 En. 48:2–3) and the begetting of the king before the morning star are two quite different tropes.[31] Hesperus, in this symbolic world, is not a star that is created but a star that *rises*, literally or figuratively, as new light dawns on the peoples.

6. There is now little reason to link the "beauty" of the messianic king in Pss. Sol. 17:42 with the "beauty of the holy one" in Theodotion's version

---

28. Horbury, *Jewish Messianism*, 94–95. Lee disagrees with Horbury that Ps 109:3 LXX constitutes evidence for belief in a pre-existent messiah before Christianity but argues that this does not rule out the possibility that the text was "interpreted as entailing the pre-existence of the messiah at a later stage by early Christians" (*Preexistent Son*, 115).

29. See also Yarbro Collins and Collins, *King and Messiah*, 58; Bates, *Trinity*, 55.

30. Horbury, *Jewish Messianism*, 95–96; also Yarbro Collins, "How on Earth," 61; Yarbro Collins and Collins, *King and Messiah*, 57–58.

31. Horbury thinks that "before the daystar came to be" is a plausible translation (*Jewish Messianism*, 96), but this is at odds with Ps 2, with the Hebrew text of Ps 110:3, and with the narrative context, which has to do with the recent or impending establishment of the king's rule among the nations.

of Ps 110:3 and conclude that we have here a reference to the king's origin "before the daystar."[32]

7. The suggestion that "when God engenders (*ywlyd*) the messiah" in 1QSa 2:11–12 implies that God "brings the pre-existent spirit of the messiah to birth" seems gratuitous.[33] The allusion to Ps 2:7 ("Today I have begotten (*yelidti*) you") again indicates not physical birth but appointment or endorsement. The passage stipulates protocol and seating arrangements for the banquet to celebrate the revelation of the identity of the messiah, who will enter and bless the congregation of the Yahad (2:11–22). There is no thought of pre-existence.

8. The rabbinic material is late (third to fourth century) and characteristically midrashic in its exegetical logic.[34] A fourth-century interpretation of Daniel 2:22 reads: "'The light dwells with Him'—this is the Messiah, as it says . . . : 'Arise, shine, for your light has come'" (*Gen. Rab.* 1:6). But this could just as well mean that the messiah, when he comes, will reveal the deep and secret things of God *as Daniel did*. That the interpretation entails the idea that the messiah dwells with God in heaven "as a being of light" is not demonstrated. Similarly, the doctrine of the restoration of the "radiant light of Adam . . . in the days of the messiah" does not mean that the messiah existed as light from creation. If the spirit or soul of the Davidic messiah pre-exists, then so too do all the "souls" that must inhabit physical bodies before he appears (*Yebam.* 63b; *Gen. Rab.* 24:4).[35] Finally, that the Spirit, which hovered over the water at creation and was breathed into the first man, was expected to rest upon the messiah offers no further evidence in support of the claim that throughout the Greek and Roman periods the messiah was conceived of as "a star-like being of light, an angelic spirit hidden with God from of old in celestial beauty until the day when he should come forth as the conquering king of Israel."[36]

9. The last set of texts to be considered are "late Herodian apocalyptic and Sibylline."[37] The Most High has kept the messiah until the end of days; he will "arise from the posterity of David"; he will denounce the iniquity and impiety of the kings of Rome and then will judge and destroy them (4 Ezra 12:31–33); after four hundred years of rejoicing the messiah will die, along

32. Horbury, *Jewish Messianism*, 97–98. In Pss. Sol. 17:42 "this" (*Autē*) beauty, "which God knows," refers back to the strong and just actions of the messianic king, not to his intrinsic personal beauty.

33. Horbury, *Jewish Messianism*, 98.

34. Horbury, *Jewish Messianism*, 99–102.

35. Horbury, *Jewish Messianism*, 100.

36. Horbury, *Jewish Messianism*, 102.

37. Horbury, *Jewish Messianism*, 102–4.

with all humanity, and perhaps will be taken back to heaven (7:28–29; cf. 2 Bar. 30:1). In another vision the "Son" has been kept "for many ages" in the heart of the sea, meaning that "no one on earth can see my Son or those who are with him, except in the time of his day" (13:26, 32, 52). A more or less literal pre-existence of the Davidic messiah may be intended here, but pre-existence may pertain only to the symbolic vision. Is it the messiah himself who has been kept for many ages, or the "figure of a man," who is stirred up by the wind, emerges from the heart of the sea, and flies with the clouds of heaven—a clear reworking of Daniel's "one like a son of man" (13:1–3)?[38] If the latter, then the point may only be that the *thought* of the messiah, much like his name, as part of a symbolic narrative of *ideas*, has been kept in mind by God from eternity. The man coming from the sea is *interpreted* as the "Son" who will be revealed; and the "sea" stands explicitly for the ignorance that will precede the revelation of the Son's identity on earth (13:21, 32, 37, 52). In any case, Paul says nothing like this about Jesus.

The vision of the Elect One "in those days" has a future orientation: he is seen "underneath the wings of the Lord of the Spirits" along with the "righteous and elect ones" (1 En. 39:6–7). On a day of judgment he will "sit on the seat of glory," vindicate the spirits of the righteous, and dwell among them (45:3–4). Enoch sees "another individual, whose face was like that of a human being" in the presence of God and asks the angel: "Who is this, and from whence is he who is going as the prototype of the Before-Time?"[39] The figure is identified as the Son of Man, whom the Lord of Spirits has chosen, who will overthrow the unjust kings who oppose the God of Israel (46:1–5). He was given a name before the creation of the sun, moon and stars; he was "concealed in the presence of (the Lord of the Spirits) prior to the creation of the world, and for eternity."[40] He will become a staff for the righteous and a light of the gentiles; all who "dwell upon the earth shall fall and worship before him; they shall glorify, bless, and sing the name of the Lord of Spirits" (48:2–6). The premise for the language of pre-existence in this case is the wisdom narrative.[41] Wisdom originally had failed to find a dwelling place among people and had returned to heaven to settle

38. See Stone, *Fourth Ezra*, 384.

39. Manuscripts vary here. Nickelsburg and VanderKam, *1 Enoch 2*, 153, have "who he was and whence he was (and) why he went with the Head of Days."

40. Isaac suggests literally, "he concealed (him) in his (own) presence" (Charlesworth, *OT Pseudepigrapha 1*, 35n48f).

41. Nickelsburg and VanderKam, *1 Enoch 2*, 118: "while the Parables' protagonist is not identified with Wisdom as he is with the Servant, the Anointed of YHWH, and the one like a son of man, this figure takes on characteristics of Wisdom, also a heavenly figure."

"permanently among the angels" (42:1–2). In the vision of chapter 48, the thirsty drink from "numerous fountains of wisdom," and the Elect One reveals the "wisdom of the Lord of the Spirits to the righteous and the holy ones" (48:1, 7; cf. 49:1–4; 51:3). The pre-existence of the messiah, therefore, is rather narrowly determined: when he appears, he will be the embodiment of, or conduit for, divine wisdom, which was present with God before creation but became a stranger to humanity.

The blessed man who "came from the expanses of heaven with a scepter in his hands which God gave him" to destroy the cities of the nations and rebuild Jerusalem and the temple seems, on the face of it, to be a pre-existent messiah, but we may suspect the hand of a Christian redactor here (Sib. Or. 5:414–33). There is an earlier reference to "one exceptional man from the sky (who stretched out his hands on the fruitful wood)" (5:256–57). That the man comes from heaven already with a scepter in his hand may suggest the *parousia* of Jesus, who was seated at the right hand of God to rule in the midst of his enemies and given the nations as his inheritance (cf. Pss 2:7–8; 110:1–2), and who will come from heaven with the authority to judge and rule invested in him as Son of Man (cf. Dan 7:13–14). The "blessed man" is not *makarios* but the rare *makaritēs*, which has the connotation of "*dead*, esp. of one *lately dead*."[42] The reference to "a certain king sent from God" against the returning Nero, which Horbury also cites, does not clearly have a messianic ruler in view (Sib. Or. 108; cf. the sending by God of Cyrus and an Egyptian king in Sib. Or. 3:286, 652). The "great star" that will burn up the sea and destroy Rome is less likely to be a messianic deliverer than an angelic power (cf. Rev 8:10; 9:1).

Finally, Horbury maintains that theophanic language is sometimes applied to the messiah in such a way as to endow him with divine and angelic traits.[43] For example, we read in 1 Enoch that mountains will become "like a honeycomb . . . before fire" in the presence of the Elect One (1 En. 52:6; cf. Ps 97:5; Mic 1:3–4). But the transference of traits is more readily explained on the basis of transferred authority. In this instance, Enoch is told that the things he has seen "happen by the authority of his Messiah so that he may give orders and be praised upon the earth"; and the destruction of the earth occurs "when the Elect One shall appear before the face of the Lord of Spirits" (1 En. 52:4, 9). The messiah remains an independent agent. Horbury suggests that the pattern constitutes an antecedent for the application of Old Testament YHWH texts to Christ, but again we have to ask about

42. LSJ s.v. μακαρίτης, 1074. Lactantius seems to have understood the passage in this way (*Inst.* 7.24).

43. Horbury, *Jewish Messianism*, 103–4.

the rationale: is it because the messiah is being in some way *identified* with YHWH or because he has been *authorized* to act on occasion in the place of YHWH that similar effects are attributed to him?

Horbury concludes that the "pre-existent angel-like figure" of the Philippians encomium recalls "the Lord begotten before the daystar . . . the messianic title 'angel of great counsel' . . . the Philonic link between the heavenly Adam and the dayspring-man, and the pre-existent 'spirit of the messiah' in rabbinic exegesis"; he may be linked with the thought in Psalms of Solomon that "the beauty of the coming Davidic king of Israel is known (beforehand) to God," and has a particular affinity with the exalted messiah described, in language drawn from Dan 7, in Similitudes of Enoch, 2 Esdras, and Sibylline Oracles 5.[44] The claim, however, has seemed less than secure, and the link with the actual words *en morphēi theou hyparchōn* is barely considered. Josephus's comment on the noble *morphē* of Aristobulus (*Ant.* 15:51), which "attracted acclamation," is noted, implying, it seems, that Christ was likewise acclaimed for the "royal beauty and majesty" of his form.[45] As an explanation of the meaning of *morphē* this is very much to the point, but Paul speaks of the form *of God* or *of a god*, not of Christ, and public acclamation obviously belongs to his post-resurrection reign as Lord. There is a brief mention of "similarities between angelomorphism in ancient conceptions of Christ, and anthropomorphism in ancient Jewish mysticism," supported by reference to Bockmuehl's argument about the "majestic body of God." But that appears to shift the interpretation of the expression on to a different footing altogether.[46] Do we have a pre-existent figure in Phil 2:6 because Judaism entertained the idea of a pre-existent angel-like messiah, or because God was thought to have a glorious human-like body? Otherwise, it is merely asserted that a "spirit-messianism" would account very well for "the metamorphosis from divine to servile form, and subsequent superexaltation, celebrated in Phil. 2.5–11."[47]

Holloway's Angelic Son of Man Interpretation

We move from angel-like messiah as model for the pre-existent Christ to angel-like Son of Man, and a fuller attempt to show how the thought explains "being in the form of God." In general terms, Paul Holloway finds a "striking analogy" for Paul's heavenly Christ in the "Enochic Messiah/Son

44. Horbury, *Jewish Messianism*, 113.
45. Horbury, *Jewish Messianism*, 111, 137.
46. Horbury, *Jewish Messianism*, 123–24, 198n65.
47. Horbury, *Jewish Messianism*, 125.

of Man" figure of Jewish apocalyptic. He takes it that in Daniel's vision the "one like a son of man" is the angel Michael, the agent of eschatological deliverance, at the head of a multitude of "holy ones" (Dan 7:13, 18; 12:1); pious Jews are the "people of the holy ones," "those whose cause was supported by the angels" (7:27).[48] In Similitudes of Enoch this "angelic hero" became "that Son of Man" and was associated with older predictions, becoming the heavenly Messiah who would ascend to the throne of God to judge the world. The figure was then invoked by early Christians in their endeavors to explain the apocalyptic Jesus.[49] Enochic Jews were further able to conceive of their Messiah/Son of Man as their "heavenly counterpart": he was the "Righteous One," they were the "righteous ones," and so on. This was paradigmatic for Paul's understanding of the relation between Christ and believers: they die with him in baptism, suffer with him at the hands of the wicked, and will be raised with him.

The apocalyptic literature also affords us parallels, in Holloway's view, for the two-way transformation or *metamorphosis* of Christ. Angels are inherently glorious, even to the point of bearing the divine "Name" (Exod 23:20–21), but in their dealings with humans they "typically veiled their splendor and took humbler forms similar to the way the immortal gods of Greek and Roman metamorphic myths transformed themselves in order to interact with mortals" (e.g., T. Job 6:4; 17:2; T. Reu. 5:6; 1 En. 86:3; T. Sol. 20:13; cf. Heb 13:2).[50] Holloway suggests that Paul thought of Christ's "incarnation" as "a kind of metamorphosis." He was a mighty angel existing originally in the "form of God"; he "enjoyed a luminous appearance of the sort a powerful angel might possess."[51] But he *metamorphosed*, so to speak, into the "form of a slave," taking on human "likeness" and "appearance." After his death he was restored to his "original angelic form, but now as the even more glorious ruling angel who bears the divine Name and shares the divine throne."[52]

---

48. Holloway, *Philippians*, 45–46. Cf. Hannah, *Michael*, 35: the one like a son of man "can only be either a symbolic figure who represents the angelic host or their leader." He thinks the latter more likely but maintains that the identification of Jesus as "Son of Man" in the Gospels presupposes a messianic rather than angelic interpretation of Dan 7:13 (156–57).

49. Piñero argues, to the contrary, that Similitudes "contains an Enochic response to the Son of Man christology developed in different strata of the New Testament" ("Enoch as Mediator," 6–7).

50. Holloway, *Philippians*, 48.

51. Holloway, *Philippians*, 118.

52. Holloway, *Philippians*, 49–50.

For the specific link with Paul's statement about the "form of God" Holloway references the arguments of Behm, Fossum, Stroumsa, Horbury, and Bockmuehl regarding the glorious humanlike, angel-like *appearance* of the pre-existent Christ. He points out that God is sometimes thought of as having a "gigantic humanlike body," seated on a throne (e.g., Isa 6:1–3), which is also the luminous "image of the likeness of the Glory of Yahweh" (Ezek 1:26–28). In 1 Enoch 14:20 the figure on the throne is the "Great Glory," whose "raiment was like the appearance of the sun." On the grounds that "glory" and "form" are closely associated in the LXX and that angels were imagined to have radiant humanlike forms, he concludes that for Christ to have been "in the form of God" meant that he "enjoyed a luminous appearance of the sort a powerful angel might possess."[53] He finds the alignment of "form," "glory," and "angel" reproduced in Philo's account of the burning bush. Moses saw at its heart "a certain very beautiful form (*morphē*), unlike any of the things that are seen, a most godlike image (*agalma*), flashing forth with a light more brilliant than fire, which one might have surmised to be an image (*eikona*) of the Being" (*Moses* 1 66*).[54]

Holloway's reading of the phrase *en morphēi theou* draws on lines of interpretation that have been considered already. The view that *morphē* equates to "glory" has been rejected. There is no precedent for the idea that God has a *morphē* as such. The "form" that Moses saw in the bush, Philo says, whatever anyone may imagine it to have been, cannot have been the form of God and must be called an angel, because "it merely related the events which were about to happen." God is suggestively "humanlike" in the visions of Isaiah and Ezekiel, but these are epiphanies, not descriptions of a heavenly appearance that the pre-existent Christ might have shared. In the Book of Watchers God is seen on his throne in a heavenly temple, but the description draws directly on the prophetic epiphanies.[55] It is difficult to attribute an *angelic* form to the divine figure when it is stated that "no angel could pass into this house and see his face on account of the honor and glory" (1 En. 14:21*). Nor could any flesh look upon him, so Enoch keeps his gaze averted, glimpsing no more than the dazzling cloak, which was "as the appearance (*eidos*) of the sun."

The suggestion, however, that Paul's conception of Christ as an exalted divine figure owes something to Jewish notions of a heavenly or angelic Son of Man who undergoes metamorphosis needs some further consideration.

---

53. Holloway, *Philippians*, 118 and n24, n30.

54. Cf. Bockmuehl, "Form of God."

55. See Nickelsburg, *1 Enoch 1*, 254–55.

It is not clear, in the first place, that Daniel's "one like a son of man" is an angelic figure or that he was introduced into New Testament traditions on that basis. Michael is the "great prince" who has charge of Israel during the course of the conflict with Greece and who fights on behalf of Israel (Dan 10:13, 20–21; 12:1); according to the War Scroll, God will "exalt the authority of Michael among the gods and the dominion of Israel among all flesh" (1QM 17:7–8). But he is sent with authority *at the time of* the conflict to support "the company of His redeemed" (17:6). The "one like a son of man," by contrast, is not described as a combatant; he receives dominion, glory and a kingdom only *after* the fourth beast has been destroyed and the other empires tamed.[56] Michael suffers no loss of authority and glory that these things need to be restored to him. The "holy ones of the Most High" are readily identified with the pious Jews persecuted by Antiochus Epiphanes. The "people" of the holy ones of the Most High (Dan 7:27) is then the *nation* which has been saved by the faithfulness of the persecuted righteous. The story, therefore, more plausibly in my view, is that with the support of Michael righteous Jews, represented by the symbolic human figure, overcome the blasphemous oppressor and are rewarded with dominion, glory, and a kingdom.

Daniel sees in his vision by night, and "behold, the four winds of heaven were stirring up the great sea. And four great beasts came up out of the sea . . . " (Dan 7:2–3). The first three beasts are in the *likeness* of a familiar animal: "like a lion," "like a bear," "like a leopard." The fourth beast exceeds any such analogy in its terrifying aspect, but the little horn has eyes "like the eyes of a man" (7:8). Once judgment has taken place, he again sees in the night visions, and "behold, with the clouds of heaven there came one like a son of man, and he came to the Ancient of Days and was presented before him" (7:13). The parallelism between the two parts of the vision strongly suggests that the figure in human form is a symbolic counterpart to the four beasts. The dominion that is given to the one like a son of man is the dominion that is taken from the beasts, not from their angelic champions, much as the kingdom was earlier transferred from the Babylonians to the Medes (5:30).

Multiple thrones are *put in place,* not for rule but for judgment. The scene does not take place in heaven, where it would be unnecessary to have thrones specially set up; judgment of the nations must take place *on earth,* which is why the thrones have wheels, and the Ancient of Days must *come* in order to take his seat (Dan 7:9, 22). A court—consisting of members of

---

56. Note the argument of Rillera that the faithful Jews represented by the "one like a son of man" offer *passive* resistance to Antiochus; Michael fights on their behalf, but the *maskilim* do not fight ("Resistance," 766–67).

the divine council—comes to sit in judgment in a tribunal that has been constructed specifically for that purpose (Dan 7:26). It is not said that the "one like a son of man" will sit on one of the thrones in order to exercise the dominion that is taken from the beasts and given to him. According to the angel's interpretation, it is the "saints of the Most" or the "people of the saints of the Most" who receive the kingdom and are served and revered by all peoples, and nothing points to this being a rule *from heaven*.

Secondly, there is a line of interpretation that sees in Dan 7:13 a reference to two divine figures. Daniel Boyarin, for example, has argued that the older god invests the younger god with an eternal kingship over all peoples, and that this vision "will become in the fullness of time the story of the Father and the Son."[57] The younger god has his own throne; and that he comes with the clouds of heaven renders his appearance a theophany. The Ancient of Days is the Canaanite ʾEl, the transcendent "sky god"; the one like a son of man is Baʿal, known to the Israelites as YHWH, the "god of war." These two are fused in biblical religion, but only imperfectly, and in the two thrones theophany of Dan 7:13 we find an "unreconstructed relic of Israel's religious past."[58] Boyarin recognises that the "angelic decoding of the vision" later in the chapter makes the one like a son of man a symbolic representation of righteous Israel, but this is because the author of the book "wanted to suppress the ancient testimony of a more-than-singular God, using allegory to do so."[59]

Even if we allow that a residual two gods tradition lies behind Dan 7:13, we must surely assume that the second-century *suppression* of that tradition in the actual text of Daniel would have prevailed through to the time of Jesus, and that the angelic decoding would have been taken as determinative for interpretation of the "one like a son of man." It is unlikely, therefore, that the Jesus of the Synoptic Gospels consciously identified himself with a pre-existent god in the form of one like a son of man, or that the author of the Philippians encomium was drawing on such a belief. We could refer back here to the earlier argument in relation to 1 Cor 8:6 regarding the *dissociation* of the two divine functions of creation and government: what controls Paul's thought is the *assignment* of the right to judge and rule over the pagan nations to the one who suffered and was vindicated.

Thirdly, the "Son of Man" whom Enoch sees, who is closely identified with the righteous, is revealed as one who has righteousness, who will

57. Boyarin, *Jewish Gospels*, 44; cf. Barker, *Angel*, 153–54; Boyarin, "Two Powers," 343–46.

58. Boyarin, *Jewish Gospels*, 48.

59. Boyarin, *Jewish Gospels*, 47.

depose kings and crush sinners, and who will "sit on the seat of glory" and vindicate the righteous (1 En. 45:3; 46:1–8). He is "that Son of Man" of Daniel's vision, but whereas Daniel has the Ancient of Days execute judgment, in Similitudes of Enoch it is the Son of Man who acts to destroy the oppressors and reward the righteous. It appears that some manner of pre-existence is attributed to this Son of Man. He was not only named but also concealed "in the presence of the Lord of Spirits" before the creation of the world (48:2–6).[60] Arguably this reproduces the dynamics of a wisdom narrative. Enoch has learned that Wisdom failed to find a place to dwell "with the children of men" and so returned to her place in heaven and "settled permanently among the angels"; iniquity went out and was warmly welcomed (42:1–3). The Son of Man has the appearance of one who is "among the holy angels"; he has revealed (Isaac), or has been revealed by (Nickelsburg and Vanderkam), the wisdom of the Lord of Spirits because he has "preserved the portion of the righteous" (46:1; 48:7). The righteous drink from the "fountains of wisdom" (48:1). The "spirit of wisdom" dwells in the Son of Man, "the spirit which gives thoughtfulness, the spirit of knowledge and strength, and the spirit of those who have fallen asleep in righteousness" (49:3; cf. Isa 11:2). On this basis he will "judge the secret things" (49:4). The eschatological intervention of the Son of Man at the behest of the Lord of Spirits to destroy unrighteousness and his dwelling among the righteous (45:4–5) are, therefore, a reversal of the wisdom poem.[61] Wisdom failed when she went out in her own person but succeeded in the person of the Son of Man.

There is some justification, fourthly, for associating the exalted Christ of Phil 2:9–11 either with the Enochic Son of Man or with an angelic figure, if only because the resurrected Christ has become a glorious heavenly figure, invested with the authority of God, who will judge and rule, etc. But it is by no means obvious that this glorious heavenly *post-existence* must be projected back as a glorious heavenly *pre-existence* on the basis of the opening assertion that Jesus was *en morphēi theou* or that he refused equality with God. Being *en morphēi theou* cannot be construed as a way of speaking about primordial wisdom. The Enochic Son of Man is one who is chosen (1

60. Cf. Nickelsburg and VanderKam, *1 Enoch 2*, 172–73: "the text's reference to his hidden existence in God's presence as well as to his continued existence into eternity support the notion that it is the Son of Man himself and not just his name that preexists his eschatological functions." See also Yarbro Collins and Collins, *King and Messiah*, 89–90; Waddell, *Messiah*, 62–63. Moreover, Enoch's Son of Man seems more likely to be the actual "person" than the symbolic man from the sea in the carefully interpreted dream of 4 Ezra 13.

61. Waddell discusses the relationship between wisdom, the Son of Man, and Enoch (*Messiah*, 63–68).

En. 46:3), not one who chooses. In appearance he is both humanlike and angel-like, but not God-like (46:1). Both the "Head of Days" and the Son of Man sit on thrones of glory, but God sits on his throne in advance of judgment, in response to the prayers and suffering of the righteous (47:3–4; 60:2; 62:2); the Son of Man takes his seat, or is placed "on the throne of glory," in order to carry out the judgment (45:3; 55:4; 61:8; 62:5; 69:29). Any such association, therefore, is placed in the future, not in the past.

Vollenweider's Angelomorphic Christology

Samuel Vollenweider first argues that the use of *morphē* in the Philippians encomium is best explained by reference to the widespread figure of "hidden epiphanies" in Greek and Roman texts, many examples of which we will consider in the next chapter.[62] The Philippians encomium, therefore, begins in a pagan milieu, "in which the incarnation of the pre-existent Son of God is expressed by means of epiphanic themes from the world of the gods of Greece."[63] The encomium ends, however, with a thoroughly Jewish affirmation of the lordship of Christ. The pivot between these two perspectives is to be found in Jewish mystical reflection on angels, who "not only occupy the highest positions in the divine throne room, but also appear on earth, and this in human form."[64]

Philo is put forward as chief evidence that in Greek-speaking Judaism angelophanies were naturally expressed in the "conceptual horizon of Hellenistic divine epiphanies."[65] The substance of angels is spiritual, Philo says; but it sometimes happens that "on emergencies occurring they have imitated the appearance of men, and transformed themselves so as to assume the human shape" (*QG* 1 92). Abraham supposed that the three men who appeared to him by the oaks at Mamre were, if not prophets, "angels who had changed their spiritual and soul-like essence (*ousias*), and assumed the appearance of men (*anthrōpomorphon idean*)" (*Abraham* 113; cf. Gen 18:1–8). They condescended to make their presence known to his senses by a simulation of eating and drinking: "these beings who were incorporeal presented the appearance of a body in human form (*idean*

---

62. Vollenweider, "Metamorphose," 288–93. Cf. Müller, "Christushymnus," 25, quoting Dibelius: "The underlying idea behind Phil 2:6f. should nevertheless be that of the metamorphosis of deities: The word *morphē* 'has an almost self-evidently mythical meaning in relation to gods and god: it denotes the divine form that the god occasionally exchanges for a human . . . .'"

63. Vollenweider, "Metamorphose," 286.

64. Vollenweider, "Metamorphose," 296.

65. Vollenweider, "Metamorphose," 296.

anthrōpōn memorphōsthai) by reason of their favour to the virtuous man"
(*Abraham* 118). Given that Philo also defends the essential anthropomorphism of God by appealing to Homer, who says that "the Deity in the
likeness of a beautiful human form is believed to appear many times" (*QG*
4 2),[66] we now have the elements necessary for understanding the clause
"being in the form of God": God manifests himself in angels, "who in turn
reveal themselves in human form."[67]

The thesis is supported by evidence from the New Testament for an
early Christian appreciation of hidden epiphanies, not only with regard
to angels (Heb 13:2; cf. Gal 4:14; Acts 12:15), but also in relation to Jesus
(1 Cor 2:8). The resurrection appearances, in particular, lend themselves
to this interpretation. Epiphanic narratives are prominent in Acts (Acts
14:8–18; 28:6). There are supposedly indications of an "angelic Christology"
in earliest Christianity. Vollenweider concludes that Jewish ideas about
angels provided "an essential matrix for the emergence of a pre-existence
Christology, and in turn quickly attracted elements of wisdom theology."
For Jesus to have been "in the form of God" is not a direct statement about
pre-existence. Rather, the "earthly life of Jesus is depicted as the hidden
epiphany of an angelomorphic heavenly nature." Vollenweider suggests that
this came about as an extrapolation from an angelological conception of the
exalted Christ, as described in Phil 2:9–11.[68]

At a general level, I will suggest that the identification of gentile Christianity as the cultural milieu for the opening of the encomium is correct,
but it is doubtful that the detailed interpretation leaves us with a coherent
narrative. First, in the hidden epiphanies, the perceived figure is not a man
in the form of a heavenly being—a god or an angel—but a heavenly being
in the form of a human person or some other creature. So it is difficult to
read *morphē theou* as the disclosure of an actual pre-existence. Secondly,
if "being *en morphēi theou*" is a statement about the human Jesus in Galilee and Judea, when does he make the decision entailed in the *harpagmos*
clause, when does he "empty himself"? Vollenweider says that the "preexistent Christ lays down his glorious form in the divine throne room and
assumes the form of the slave."[69] That seems to locate the decision *before* he

66. Cf. Philo, *Dreams* 1 232: "to those souls which are still in the body he must
appear in the resemblance of the angels, though without changing his nature (for he is
unchangeable), but merely implanting in those who behold him an idea of his having
another form, so that they fancy that it is his image, not an imitation of him, but the
very archetypal appearance itself."

67. Vollenweider, "Metamorphose," 297.

68. Vollenweider, "Metamorphose," 300–301.

69. Vollenweider, "Metamorphose," 302.

was the hidden epiphany of a heavenly being. In the encomium, however, it is *while being* in the form of God that Jesus decides not to count *to einai isa theōi* as *harpagmon*. If the pre-existent Christ then undergoes a "radical kenosis," surely the whole idea of an "epiphany," hidden or otherwise, has been lost. Thirdly, as Dieter Zeller observes, Judaism barely allows us to speak about a heavenly figure becoming a historical person; for this there are "far more precedents in the pagan milieu."[70]

Finally, the angelomorphic element in the explanation appears to be redundant. It is not required to account for the expression *morphē theou*, which is supplied by the epiphany paradigm. Nor is the exaltation (*hyperypsōsen*) of Christ stated in terms that suggest the return of an angel to heaven. Indeed, there is little reason to think that an ascent to heaven is in view at all in Phil 2:9–11. The resurrection is not mentioned, there is no "ascension," there is no reference to Jesus being seated at the right hand of God.[71] It seems very likely that the compositional impetus for the second part of the encomium came from Ps 96:7–9* LXX: those who do obeisance to carved images will be put to shame; but the Lord is "most high over all the earth," therefore he was "greatly exalted (*hyperypsōthēs*) above all the gods." Angels, in fact, are commanded to do obeisance to this Lord. There is no *ascent* motif here. The point would be only that the one who was crucified has been granted a status—not a location—an elevated reputation, above all gods, and that sooner or later the idolatrous nations will be put to shame and will confess Jesus as Lord, to the glory of the God who has done all this. Responsibility for the public effacement of the old gods in history has been assigned to Jesus. But if the encomium does not actually speak of Christ's *going up* in the second paragraph, is there any reason to think that it speaks of an angel-like *coming down* in the first? All we may need, therefore, is a pagan explanation of *morphē theou* and perhaps an evocation of its narrative setting, supposing that in the context of the Pauline mission it sometimes made sense to register the very *unJewish* perception that Jesus was "in the form of a god."

---

70. Zeller rejects Vollenweider's proposal of an "angelomorphic Christology" at this point because it does not account for the historical and human application: "In Christian use, the surrendering of divinity has the hard consequence of death" ("Christology," 322).

71. Against, for example, Hawthorne and Martin, who say that the encomium is "a piece of cosmic drama, involving a 'descent' of a heavenly being and his elevation and enthronement" (*Philippians*, 103).

Conclusion

Sanders's remapping of the cosmograph works little better than the gnostic model it was designed to replace. If the "self-willed reascension of the Anthropos of Poimandres" is unlike the elevation of the resurrected Christ to heaven, the self-denial of Christ—the rejection of godlikeness and self-emptying—is unlike the expulsion of the sons of God from heaven.[72] Neither Horbury's pre-existent messiah nor Holloway's pre-existent Son of Man seems a reliable enough construct to account for Paul's language, and we are still without a satisfactory explanation of the particular expression "in the form of God." Vollenweider's appeal to pagan epiphanies gets us on to firmer ground in this regard, but we must then ask whether we need to retain the idea of an angelomorphic pre-existence. Indeed, we have been left wondering whether a "cosmograph" of descent and ascent is required at all—in either direction—in order to explain the language of the encomium.

72. Sanders, "Dissenting," 282.

7

Being in the Form of a God

THE ARGUMENT PUT FORWARD by Vollenweider that in Phil 2:6 Paul speaks of the incarnation of the angelomorphic Christ *as though it were* a pagan epiphany is an acknowledgment of the problematic character of the translation "in the form of God." It seems likely that Jews were loath to talk about the *morphē* of the one God not only because he was thought to be beyond visual depiction but also because the term was strongly associated with the practice of idolatry and the visual appearance of pagan gods and of divine people. This language and the contexts in which it proliferates need to be examined.

The Forms of the Gods

The visible manifestation of gods in the sublunary sphere in their own form or in other forms is commonplace in Greek mythological, religious, and philosophical texts.[1] The gods are mostly understood as corporeal beings, blessed with immortality, larger, more beautiful, and more powerful than their mortal analogues. According to the philosophers, divine corporeality consisted in a unity of body and soul far superior to that found in humans: "the gods and heroes . . . differ from mankind, having first a great superiority in regard to the body and then in regard to the soul" (Aristotle, *Pol.* 7.13 1332b18–20).[2] A typical Stoic account denies the coarse physicality of the bodies of the gods; rather "they are endowed with supreme beauty of form (*forma*), they are situated in the purest region of the sky, and they so control their motions and courses as to seem to be conspiring together to preserve and to protect the universe" (Cicero,

---

1. See Behm, "μορφή," 746; Hengel, *Cross*, 37; Moss, "Transfiguration," 76–84; Talbert, *Christology*, 17–19.

2. See Litwa, *Transformed*, 121; and Levene, D. S. "Defining the Divine," 64–66. Cf. Plato, *Phaedr.* 246c–d; Aristotle, *Top.* 5.1 128b39–129a2; *Cael.* 2.3 286a10–11.

Nat. d. 2.60). Xenophon has Socrates advise Euthydemus to get on with worshiping the gods for what they do rather than waiting, most likely in vain, to see "the forms (*morphas*) of the gods" (*Mem.* 4.3.13). When the gods do enter the physical world, they become to a degree constrained in time and space. "Such divine bodies were not omnipresent," David Litwa says, "but had to move from place to place by bounding from mountain to mountain or by flying on the winds or in a chariot."[3]

Polymorphic Polytheism

Transformations are the order of the day, either from the brilliant heavenly form to an earthly guise or from one earthly body to another. At the opening of *Bacchanals* Dionysius, son of Zeus, strides on to the stage and declares, "I have exchanged my divine form (*morphēn . . . ek theou*) for a mortal one and have come to the waters of Dirce and Ismenus" (Euripides, *Bacch.* 4–5). He later explains why. He has been deprived of libations by Cadmus and plans to demonstrate to him that he is a god: "That is why I have changed to mortal appearance and have turned my form (*morphēn*) into the nature of a man" (53–54*). The chorus concludes the drama: "Many are the forms (*morphai*) of the daemons, many things the gods bring about in unexpected ways" (1388–89*). Dionysius of Halicarnassus says of Demosthenes's oratorical style that it has a character not unlike that of the sea god Proteus as portrayed by the poets, who "effortlessly assumed every kind of form (*morphēn*), whether a god or daemon" (Dem. 8*). The Stoics differentiated between substance and the diverse forms that a god might take: "The Stoics thus define the essence (*ousian*) of a God. It is a spirit intellectual and fiery, which acknowledges no shape (*morphēn*), but is continually changed into what it pleases, and assimilates itself to all things" (Plutarch, *[Plac. philos.]* 1.6). So even in this more rationalistic understanding no difficulty is found with the idea that an *essentially formless* god may appear to human perception in some *morphē* or other.

Helen has heard it said that Zeus flew to her mother "taking the form (*morphōmat' . . . labōn*) of a swan" (Euripides, *Hel.* 19). The poet Moschus describes how Zeus, having transformed himself into a bull in order to abduct Europa, "took his own form (*morphēn*) again" in order to bed her (*Eur.* 162–64*). But such liaisons could go tragically wrong. Angered that Zeus/Jove has impregnated Semele Juno adopts the guise of the elderly nurse and maliciously advises the girl: "let him give proof of love if he is indeed true; as great and as glorious as he is welcomed by heavenly Juno,

3. Litwa, *Transformed*, 120, citing Homer, *Il.* 5.363–66; 8.41–52; 14.298–99.

so great and so glorious—ask him!—let him embrace you, having first put on his splendors" (Ovid, *Metam.* 3.284–86*). So Jove enters the palace in appearance as Juno would see him when he comes looking for love; poor mortal Semele cannot bear the "heavenly tumult" and is incinerated by the "conjugal gift" (3.292–95, 308–9*).

Diodorus Siculus reports that the Egyptians believe that Zeus and the gods of the elements "travel all the inhabited world, appearing to people in the forms (*morphais*) of sacred animals, and at times turning into the shapes of people or of other things."[4] He then quotes Homer: "The gods, looking like strangers from another people, taking all manner of likenesses, visit cities . . . " (*Bib. hist.* 1.12.9–10*). Plato has Socrates object to this opinion on the grounds that a god who has many forms (*morphas*) must be less than perfect: a change from ideal beauty and virtue can only be a deterioration (*Resp.* 2 381b–d). So we should expect a god "to remain always simply in his own form (*en tēi hautou morphēi*)." In Pseudo-Lucian's *Philopatris*, Triepho finds the whole sordid business of Zeus's metamorphoses disgraceful: "Didn't he become swan and satyr out of wantonness, yes and bull too? . . . The episode of the eagle and Mount Ida and his being pregnant all over his body I'm ashamed even to mention!" (*[Philopatr.]* 4).

Vollenweider draws particular attention to the popularity of the story of the servitude of Apollo and Poseidon among mortals, when they are sent to help rebuild the walls of Troy.[5] Poseidon reminds Apollo: "Do you not remember all the ills that we two alone of all the gods suffered at Ilios, that time when we came at the command of Zeus and served the lordly Laomedon for a year at a fixed wage, and he was our taskmaster and laid on us his commands?" (Homer, *Il.* 21.441–45). Apollo "put on mortal form" (*mortalem induitur formam*) to help Laomedon rebuild the walls of Troy, "having first agreed upon a sum of gold for the walls" (Ovid, *Metam.* 11.199–204). Lucian says that the two gods "were so poor that they had to make bricks and work upon the wall" (Lucian, *On Sacrifices* 4).[6]

The visible manifestation of the gods may be expressed, of course, in other terms, not always with reference to the *morphē*, reflecting the potency and pervasiveness of the topos in such narratives. In the *Homeric*

---

4. A prayer to Lord Hermes affirms the names by which he is known in the four corners of heaven: "in the east you have the *morphēn* of an ibis, in the west you have the *morphēn* of a dog-headed monkey, in the north you have the *morphēn* of a snake, but in the south you have the *morphēn* of a wolf" (*PGM* 8.1–3; Betz, *Greek Magical Papyri*, 145).

5. Vollenweider, "Metamorphose," 290.

6. Also Apollodorus, *Library* 2.9; Euripides, *Alc.* 1–2; Diodorus Siculus, *Library* 4.71.3–4.

Hymn to Apollo the god intercepts a ship "in the likeness of a dolphin," addresses the crew "in the likeness of a sturdy yeoman," and the leader of the Cretans says to him, "Sir, . . . you don't seem at all like a mortal in body and stature, but like the immortal gods" (*Hom. Hymns* 3.398–401, 448–51, 463–67). When pirates attempt to abduct Dionysius, who appears as a "stripling in the first flush of manhood," they are unable to bind him. The helmsman realizes the error: "Madmen! what god is this whom you have taken and bind, strong that he is? Not even the well-built ship can carry him. Surely this is either Zeus or Apollo who has the silver bow, or Poseidon, for he looks not like mortal men but like the gods who dwell on Olympus" (7.1–24). So this person who has the likeness of a well-built fellow in the prime of youth is perceived also to be—so to speak—in the form of a god. Aphrodite, daughter of Zeus, stands before Anchises "like an unmarried girl in stature and appearance, so that he should not be afraid when his eyes fell on her" (5.81–83). Demeter flees Olympus and journeys across the earth, "effacing her beauty, and no man or deep-girt woman looking upon her knew who she was" (2.91–97). Athene approaches the bewildered Odysseus on his return to Ithaca "in a body like that of a young man, a herdsman from the orchard" (Homer, *Od.* 13.221–23*).

If the gods are going to appear on earth, then their outward appearance or form, whether mundane or ethereal, nondescript or superhuman, whether it cloaks or discloses divinity, inevitably becomes a matter of great curiosity to the ancient mind.

Statues of the Gods

The fascination spills over into discussions of statuary. The Jewish critique of idols finds its counterpart in occasional Greek unease about the power of the manufactured form. So, on the one hand, Isaiah speaks of the artisan who chooses a piece of wood and makes it "like the form (*morphēn*) of a man, like human beauty, to set it up in a house" (Isa 44:13 LXX). Josephus blames the Greek legislators of old for popular ignorance concerning the true God and for allowing the poets to "introduce whatever gods they pleased, subject to every passion." The painters and sculptors were given the power to "imagine a certain form (*morphēn*)" for a god, to be shaped from clay or depicted in paint (*Ag. Ap.* 2:250–52*).[7] On the other hand, the

---

7. Cf. Strabo, *Geogr.* 16.2.35: Moses said that "the Greeks were also wrong in modelling gods in human form (*anthrōpomorphous*); for, according to him, God is this one thing alone that encompasses us all and encompasses land and sea—the thing which we call heaven, or universe, or the nature of all that exists."

pagan mind is struck with both wonder and disquiet by the material representation of divinity. It is said of a statue of Apollo, for example, that the "lovely form (*morphē*) of the god shone through, bringing adornment to the bronze," but attention is on the details of the physical appearance: the abundant hair curling over both shoulders, the intense gaze of the inspired god (*Greek Anthology* 2.283–87*).

Of especial interest is Dio Chrysostom's (AD 40–120) imagined dialogue with the renowned Athenian sculptor Phidias (c. 480–430 BC), whose statue of Zeus at Olympia was one of the seven wonders of the ancient world.[8] Dio acknowledges the excellence of the work, but asks a troubling question: "Did you fashion a fitting shape and a form (*morphēn*) worthy of the nature of a god, having not only used a pleasing material but also having brought to light the form (*morphēn*) of a man of exceptional beauty and proportions . . . ?" (*Dei cogn.* 52*). Phidias produced the definitive *schēma* and *morphē* of Zeus, thus putting an end to the uncertainties and disagreements regarding the god's appearance: "you by the power of your art first conquered and united Hellas and then all others by means of this wondrous presentment, showing forth so marvellous and dazzling a conception, that none of those who have beheld it could any longer easily form a different one." But why had this not been done by previous generations? Was it not because they "feared that they would never be able adequately to portray by human art the Supreme and most Perfect Being"? Was not the statue a piece of dangerous presumption?

In the Nemrud Dağı East Terrace Inscription, Antiochus I of Commagene (c. 69–36 BC) proclaims himself as "the God, Just, Manifest, a Friend of the Romans and a Friend of the Greeks," and gives the reasons for erecting a statue of himself on his tomb alongside those of the gods, including Heracles.[9] He explains that, having acceded to the throne, he had decided to make his kingdom a home for all the gods of Persia and Greece and therefore had widely displayed the "images of their form" (*morphēs . . . ikonas*) by different artistic means and honored them with sacrifices and festivals. The tomb would contain the preserved "body of my form" (*sōma morphēs emēs*) and was sited "in closest proximity to the heavenly throne"

---

8. See also the discussion of the differences between Egyptian and Greek iconography in Philostratus, *Vit. Apoll.* 6.19. Apollonius ridicules the Egyptian practice of representing the gods not in "godlike form" (*theoeidōs*) but as "dumb, worthless animals" (6.19.1). Apollonius extols the imagination of Phidias and Praxiteles and dismisses the argument that the Egyptians "are not presumptuous about the forms taken by the gods. They make these forms symbolic and suggestive, since in that way they seem more venerable" (6.19.2–5).

9. Commagene BEc; SEG LIII, 1769; for the Greek text and translation see Crowther, "Inscriptions," 199–200; and Rose, "New Relief," for relief images.

on Mount Nemrud. So it was fitting that a statue having the "features of my own form" (*charaktēra morphēs emēs*) should be placed alongside those of the gods.[10] BDAG suggests that Antiochus's body is the framework for his *morphē* or "essential identity as a descendant of divinities," which takes us back to our earlier discussion of the relation between form and substance. But the correlation between "images of their form" and "body of my form"—preserved by good fortune into old age—points rather to *outward appearance*, not to the abstract idea of "essential identity." It seems to have been a matter of some concern to Antiochus that the four colossal statues set alongside his own recognizable image should bear a real visual likeness to the gods represented. With the phrase *charaktēra morphēs emēs* we may compare: "We impress upon the tender nature of a child a remarkable likeness (*charaktēra*) both of soul and of form (*morphēs*)" (4 Macc 15:4). So *morphē* in these inscriptions indicates less the godlike identity or essence of Antiochus than the humanlike appearance of the gods.

Incidentally, Plutarch punctures the vanity of kings and rulers who "act like unskilful sculptors." In their affectation and posturing they are no different from "colossal statues which have a heroic and godlike form on the outside (*tēn exōthen hēroikēn kai theoprepē morphēn*), but inside are full of clay, stone, and lead" (*Princ. iner.* 780a–b). He is speaking metaphorically, but the point is underlined that a "godlike form" is an *external* reality: it has to do with how the figure *appears* to the world.

Conclusion

From this survey, it is clear that the phrase *morphē theou*, problematic as it was in a Jewish context, would have evoked readily in the pagan or post-pagan mind a prodigious body of reflection on the outward appearance and visible behavior of the gods. Bockmuehl insists that "given the clearly Jewish Christian tenor of our passage, a direct dependence on this material must be deemed highly unlikely."[11] But that begs the question. The point is that *morphē theou* is *not* a Jewish-Christian expression. Typically, the proper form of the transcendent being is either revealed in the perfections of the human form or masked by its ordinariness. But if a god may become perceptible in the form of a human person, it also may be that a person has the "form of a god." There is something about the manner and appearance of

10. Strait discusses the relationship between divine and royal statuary ("Wisdom," 611–13). Josephus says that the Colossus of Augustus at Caesarea was "not less than that of Jupiter Olympius, which it was made to resemble" (*J.W.* 1:414).

11. Bockmuehl, "Form of God," 7; cf. Bockmuehl, *Philippians*, 127.

the person that suggests a divine provenance or character or power, either literally or figuratively. In a discussion of poetic comparisons of people with the gods, notably in Homer, Lucian says that "with regard to form (*morphēs*) it is acceptable if someone is said to be like a god." Indeed, the gods "did not take revenge against the best of philosophers for saying that the human person is an image (*eikona*) of a god" (*Pro imag.* 27–28*). He takes the comparison of people to gods, therefore, to be commonplace, particularly with respect to outward appearance or "form." Homer says of Agamemnon that "in eyes and head he was like to Zeus, in waist to Ares, and in chest to Poseidon, dismembering the man for the sake of comparing him with all those gods" (25). The poets *portray* people as being *in the form of a god*, which is half the point of the old "divine man" hypothesis.

The "Divine Man" Hypothesis

The thought that Jesus might have been perceived or represented as a divine figure specifically in pagan terms is not a new one. For much of the twentieth century the view held sway in New Testament scholarship that Mark's portrayal of Jesus was shaped, either positively or negatively, by the Hellenistic concept of the "divine man" (*theios anēr*). As Jack Kingsbury tells the story, in a first phase, represented by Wrede and Bultmann, it was thought that Mark presented Jesus in the form of a "divine man," as the earthly counterpart to the Hellenistic myth about Christ that was found, for example, in Phil 2:6–11. In the second phase, associated with Keck, Achtemeier, Weeden, and Perrin, the contention was broadly that Mark had reinterpreted or *corrected* the tradition of Jesus as a Hellenistic *thaumaturge* by inserting the cycle of miracle stories into a narrative that moved resolutely towards the cross. The miracle-working "Son of God" became the suffering Son of Man.[12] Theodore Weeden made the point bluntly: "If the only portion of Mark's Gospel one possessed was 1:1—8:9, one would have to assume that Mark understood Jesus to be a *theios aner* and that his messiahship was to be interpreted only within this perspective."[13]

12. Kingsbury, "Divine Man," 244–47. Kingsbury includes within the second phase a minority view (Georgi and Schulz) that Mark adopted the Hellenistic divine-man Christology but that as a result we end up with a Christology that is inferior to Paul's. Achtemeier uses "divine man" rather loosely (a "broad category") for a person in whom "the characteristics of the gods were evident, such as, foreknowledge, persuasive speech, the ability to heal and to perform miracles; and in addition they were frequently set apart by an extraordinary birth and death" ("Divine Man," 187).

13. Weeden, *Traditions in Conflict*, 56. Achtemeier concludes that there is much in the Gospel stories that would "identify Jesus as a more or less conventional Hellenistic wonder-worker," though it must be recognized that the miracles remain subservient to

Kingsbury argued 40 years ago, however, that the "divine man" hypothesis, in whatever form, was untenable, mainly because there was no longer agreement that a sufficiently stable and coherent "divine man" concept was available in the Hellenistic world in the first century to account for Mark's Christology.[14] Scholars were now more likely to look to Jewish sources for the background to Mark's designation of Jesus as "Son of God," despite the difficulty of documenting the use of the expression as a messianic title in pre-Christian Judaism.

More recently, some efforts have been made to reinstate the Hellenistic hypothesis in modified form, largely as part of a broader enquiry into the importance of the imperial cult for understanding early Christian confessions, on two grounds: first, that the dividing wall between Judaism and Hellenism was less solid than commonly assumed and in places quite derelict—an insight usually accredited to Hengel; secondly, that the *reappropriation and reimagination* of the Jewish Jesus by Greek-Roman onlookers, believers among them, from the earliest period, might plausibly have left its mark on the New Testament witness.[15] The point has been recognized even by those who reject the genetic hypothesis. So Aage Pilgaard concludes his assessment of the *theios anēr* argument: "In their meeting with the pagan world and their traditions Mark and the community to which he belonged could adopt traits from traditions about pagan charismatic types, but a *theios aner* based on a specific pagan anthropology they did not adopt."[16] Zeller grants that *theios* is not used for Jesus in the New Testament, but he thinks that in Mark "there are devices by which Jesus' divine sonship is recognized that have astonishing parallels in the biographies of such men"—Pythagoras's disclosure of his divine identity to Abaris or the appearance of omens

eschatology and the proclamation of the gospel ("Divine Man," 185).

14. Kingsbury, "Divine Man," 247–50. Liefeld says that "Only occasionally has any substantial work appeared to challenge the assumption that there is a coherent divine man type which lurks behind the Gospels' portrayal of Jesus" ("Divine Man," 197). Also Marcus, *Mark 1–8*, 76–77; Hengel, *Cross*, 29–30; Blackburn, *Theios Anēr*; Pilgaard, "Hellenistic *Theios Aner*," 111; Evans, *Mark 8:27–16:20*, lxxii; Edwards, *Mark*, 105–9. For the history of research see Smith, "Prolegomena," 188–95; Litwa, *Iesus Deus*, 23–27; Pérez i Díaz, *Mark*, 192–200.

15. See especially Litwa, *Iesus Deus*, 6–21; also Yarbro Collins, "Readers," 85–86; and the discussion in Bird, *Eternal Son*, 73–75, though the proper historical analysis is then confused with a much more open-ended reader response approach. Achtemeier, in fact, asked the question very precisely: "Did the early Christian tradition . . . also use the hermeneutical device of divine man in interpreting the figure of Jesus? That is, did early Christology attempt to understand and present the earthly Jesus by making use of motifs belonging to the Hellenistic concept of *theios anēr*?" ("Divine Man," 188). For Hengel's thesis see Hengel, *Judaism and Hellenism*.

16. Pilgaard, "Hellenistic *Theios Aner*," 122.

at the death of a hero, for example. He concludes: "Thus, even if the christo-logical kerygma Mark wants to communicate has Jewish roots, the way he does it shows consideration for his non-Jewish readers as represented in the pagan centurion."[17] Brennan Hill similarly insists that the Gospel writers did not get their source material from Greek miracle traditions, but he allows that the stories about Jesus may have been shaped according to "Greek liter-ary models."[18] In a useful survey of the debate Mar Pérez i Díaz affirms the skeptical consensus among scholars regarding the influence of a Hellenistic *theios anēr* motif on Mark's presentation of Jesus, but she acknowledges the possibility that "when Jesus was presented to the pagans, he was given some traits proper to the divine men in order to demonstrate that he was the high-est fulfilment of all their theological aspirations."[19]

The same shift of perspective may apply to Paul. Against interpreta-tions of the Christ encomium grounded in "angelological speculations," Zeller suggests that if we ask how the text "might have been received in a community made up mainly of former pagans," we find that there are closer models to hand—men deified because of their merits, foremost among them Hercules, whose "career is exemplary for the Stoic-Cynic sage, in a similar way to that in which Christ's self-humiliation is recommended as an example for Christians." Judaism may account for the origin of the topos of the exaltation of the righteous man following self-abasement or humili-ation, but at most "the suffering pious is counted among the 'sons of God' (Wis 5.5)."[20] Familiarity with the "divine man" concept may, therefore, have facilitated pagan acceptance of the Jewish idea. Zeller finds support for this in Justin's comparison of the Logos—"who is the first-birth of God, was produced without sexual union . . . , was crucified and died, and rose again, and ascended into heaven"—with what pagans believe about the "sons of Zeus," including Hercules, who "committed himself to the flames to escape his toils" and ascended to heaven (Justin, *1 Apol.* 21). The only distinction that Justin makes is that, in his view, "those only are deified who have lived near to God in holiness and virtue."

The approach, finally, has also been developed by Litwa: "My argument asserts *not* that early Christians *borrowed* their divine christology from Hel-lenistic theology, but that certain conceptions of deity were part of the 'preun-derstanding' of Hellenistic culture—a culture in which Jews and Christians

17. Zeller, "Christology," 328.

18. Hill, *Jesus, the Christ*, 68.

19. Pérez i Díaz, *Mark*, 198.

20. Zeller, "Christology," 317–18.

already participated."[21] He notes, in this case, how the stories about Heracles were allegorized in Socratic and Cynic traditions to lend them moral weight down to the first century AD, when the grammarian Heraclitus wrote that Heracles "should be thought of not as someone so trained in bodily power that he was the strongest man of his time, but as a sensible man and an initiate of heavenly wisdom who brought to light philosophy which had been plunged into the depths of fog . . . " (*All.* 33:1).[22] In fact, Wilfred Knox long ago stressed the importance of Heracles for Christology—"the type of the missionary philosopher who goes up and down the world, saving men from vice and ignorance," the tragedy of whose death is "reversed by his exaltation to the rank of the Olympian gods."[23] If the language of such christological passages as Phil 2:6–11 shows "a close affinity with the descriptions and panegyrics of these figures in the pagan world," it need not be attributed to willful invention or imitation, Knox argued. It may only be that the stories were told "on the principle of St. Paul's speech at Athens 'what therefore ye ignorantly worship, Him we declare unto you.'"[24] The importance of Heracles for understanding the ex-pagan understanding of Jesus that lies behind the Philippians encomium is brought out by Hengel: "Of all the 'sons of Zeus' in Greek religion, Heracles might be most likely to provide analogies to christological ideas, but he never became a god of the mysteries: he only had a strong influence as a model for the ruler cult . . . ."[25]

21. Litwa, *Iesus Deus*, 20; cf. Zeller, "Christology," 314–15.

22. The philosopher Epicurus is praised by Lucretius: if the swashbuckling Heracles is to be regarded as a god, all the more so Epicurus, "from whom even now spreading abroad through great nations come sweet consolations of life to soothe our minds." Is it not fitting that a man who subjugated such great psychological enemies should be "held worthy to be counted in the number of the gods" (Lucretius, *De rerum* 5.19–21, 49–51)?

23. Knox, "Divine Hero," 232.

24. Knox, "Divine Hero," 233. Also: "While . . . it seems inconceivable that Paul was borrowing, either deliberately or unconsciously, from the ideas of pagan religion, it is nonetheless true that he had in fact described Jesus in terms which represented Him in very much the same light as some of the most popular cult-figures of the hellenistic world, an active deity who was partly human and partly divine" (231).

25. Hengel, *Cross*, 23. Also Huijgen and Versluis, "Unity," 223–24: Hellenistic thought did not entertain a sharp distinction between Creator and creature, and "Jesus Christ was more likely to belong somewhere in between God and humans, neither truly God nor truly man, but a demigod like Hercules." For the relevance of Heracles and possible evidence for his cult in Philippi see Reumann, *Philippians*, 363–64.

A Few Godlike Men

If we ask after analogies for Christ in the form of a god apart from the larger-than-life superman Heracles, the two figures who most readily come to mind are the sixth-century BC philosopher Pythagoras and the first century AD Neopythagorean Apollonius. Iamblichus (c. AD 242–327) considered it certain that the soul of Pythagoras, having enjoyed some exceptional status perhaps as a personal attendant on the god, was "sent to mankind from the empire of Apollo" (*Vit. Pyth.* 2 §5).[26] But many "celebrated him as one of the Olympian Gods, who, in order to benefit and correct the mortal life, appeared to the men of those times in a human form (*en anthrōpinēi morphei*), in order that he might extend to them the salutary light of felicity and philosophy" (6 §19). Pythagoras, we are told, did little to discourage the opinion that he was in fact Apollo, having "assumed human form (*anthrōpomorphos*) lest men disturbed by the novelty of his transcendency should avoid the discipline he advised" (19 §68). He was by nature and education "of beautiful form" (*eumorphotatos*), "fit to be a god," and of "godlike appearance," and "deserved his present prerogatives." Quite reasonably, many regarded him as "the son of a God" (*to theou paida*) (2 §6–7). Philostratus describes the arrival of Apollonius of Tyana, a first-century Pythagorean philosopher and miracle-worker, in Alexandria: "As he proceeded from the ship to the city, they looked on him as a god (*theōi isa*)" (*Vit. Apoll.* 5.24.1).[27] When Damis discovered that Apollonius preferred to stay imprisoned even though he had miraculously slipped from his chains, he understood for the first time that his nature was "godlike (*theia*) and more than human" (7.38.2; cf. 8.13.2).

The point of these analogies is limited. The texts are late but they provide a more or less plausible template for the Greek perception of the unfamiliar, pre-exalted Jewish Jesus. Specifically they illustrate the common use of *morphē* to speak of both the human and godlike appearance of an exceptional person. Barry Blackburn wonders whether Philostratus's *Life of Apollonius* was influenced by the Gospels.[28] If this could be established, it would weaken arguments for the *formative* force of a supposed *theios anēr*

26. For the translation: T. Taylor, *Iamblichus' Life of Pythagoras* (London: J. M. Watkins, 1818). For a detailed overview of Philostratus's account of the life of Apollonius, see Blackburn, *Theios Anēr*, 73–85. On the parallels between the critical investigations of the lives of Jesus and Apollonius, see Ehrman, *How Jesus*, 11–18.

27. Cf. Philostratus, *Vit. Apoll.* 1.19.2: "The Assyrian worshiped him when he said this, regarding him as a supernatural being (*daimona*), and he became his companion, growing in wisdom and remembering everything he learned."

28. Blackburn, *Theios Anēr*, 74–75.

tradition, but it would also demonstrate just how easy it was to *translate* the life of Jesus into somewhat alien Hellenistic cultural forms.

We should also not overlook the fact that Hellenistic Judaism developed its own *theios anēr* propaganda.[29] In his syncretistic embellishment of the biblical stories the Jewish historian Artapanus (third to second century BC) says that Moses was considered by the Egyptian priests to be "worthy of respect equal to the gods (*isotheou*)" and was called Hermes because he had taught them "interpretation of letters" (Artapan. 3:6). Josephus tells the story of the adoption of Moses by Thermuthis, the daughter of Pharaoh. She presents the boy to her father, proposing to make him her father's successor and heir to the kingdom, "if it should please God she should have no legitimate child of her own." She explains that she has brought up a "child divine in form" (*paida morphēi . . . theion*) (*Ant.* 2:232*; cf. 3:180). Thermuthis speaks as a pagan, but she differentiates between the boy who is in divine form and the God who will determine whether or not she has a child. This presumably echoes God's response to Moses when he complains that he is too weak-voiced to speak to Pharaoh: "Look, I have given you as a god to Pharaoh, and Aaron, your brother, shall be your prophet" (Exod 7:1 LXX; cf. 4:16). But her statement also illustrates the sort of fluid narrative intersection of the two religious traditions that we are beginning to find in the Philippians encomium.

Philo says of Moses that he had "utterly discarded all desire of gain and of those riches which are held in the highest repute among men," therefore God "honoured him, and . . . gave him the whole world as a possession suitable for his heir" (*Moses* 1 155). But he enjoyed an even closer partnership with God, "being thought worthy of the same form of address; for he was named god and king of the whole nation" (158*). Having entered into the presence of God on Mount Sinai, where he beheld what is normally hidden from mortals, he has "put himself at the center of things as a well-wrought composition, a beautiful and godlike (*theoeides*) work, and has established a model for those willing to imitate it."[30] The thematic significance of the passage for our reading of Phil 2:6–11 is immediately apparent. Moses abjures wealth and status (cf. Phil 3:8), gains an inheritance in the whole world, is given the name of "god," is *perceived* as "beautiful and godlike," and serves as a model for imitation (cf. Phil 2:5; 3:17).[31]

29. Achtemeier says that "Hellenistic-Jewish propaganda . . . described as, and on occasion identified as, divine men" such figures as Abraham, Elijah, Solomon, and most importantly Moses ("Divine Man," 187–88).

30. On the passage see Yarbro Collins and Collins, *King and Messiah*, 115.

31. Litwa observes that "Beauty was one of the trademarks of divinity," citing Diotima's question: "do you not say that all gods are happy and beautiful?" (Plato, *Symp.*

According to Litwa, Philo distinguishes between two types of deity: "primal deity," which is the true God or the "Existent" (*ho ōn*), and "mediate deity," which is "deity in the realm of becoming, and thus shareable."[32] He regards Moses as a god according to the second category. The Logos or *nous* ("mind"), which Philo also calls the "second God," functions as "Prime Mediate divinity," so that deification is "the process of becoming wholly and purely *nous*." The deification of Moses, therefore, is the outworking of his "philosophical vocation." This obviously does not account for Paul's *en morphēi theou hyparchōn*. Moses begins with an innate divinity inasmuch as every human is born with a fragment of the Logos or *nous*; but he *becomes* a god, on the one hand, through a training in "the full Platonic curriculum" (Litwa) and on the other, by way of his ascent to enter the presence of God on Mount Sinai to behold the pure Logos, which becomes symbolic of the whole process, culminating in his final assimilation to the cosmic Mind at death.[33] But if the phrase *morphēi . . . theion* ("in form divine") had any currency amongst Hellenistic Jews of the diaspora as a way of speaking about Moses, or if he was remembered as a beautiful and godlike person, we may still suppose that the motif was available for the reconceptualization of the one who would redeem Israel from its captivity to the Law. Why should Jesus, the prophet like Moses, not get similar treatment?[34]

Jesus as "Divine Man" in Mark

How the insight works in exegetical practice can be illustrated from the work of two scholars—Adela Yarbro Collins in overview and Robert Guelich in some detail. Yarbro Collins has examined a number of incidents in Mark's Gospel with a view to understanding not so much how the portrayal of Jesus was initially produced but how it might have been *received* by "those members of Mark's audience who were more familiar with Greek and Roman religious traditions than with Jewish traditions."[35] She compares Jesus's baptism with the endowment of Aesop with the gift of story-telling, and with the epiphany experienced by the poet Archilocus. People in Mark's

202c) ("Deification," 18).

32. Litwa, "Deification," 7–9.

33. See Litwa, "Deification," 9–26.

34. Blackburn is at pains to deny that Moses is portrayed in Artapanus, Josephus, and Philo as being essentially divine and thus to preclude the possibility that he constituted a template for a *theios anēr* construction of Jesus (*Theios Anēr*, 59–72). But his study demonstrates clearly enough the fully credible, and unsurprising, tendency to reimagine the Jewish figure in Hellenistic terms.

35. Yarbro Collins, "Readers," 86.

audience familiar with such traditions were likely to interpret Jesus's baptism "as an analogous legend and to view Jesus as an heroic figure analogous to the great poets and sages of Greek tradition."[36] Likewise, she compares his healing ministry with traditions about Empedocles, who declared himself an "immortal god, mortal no more," and the healer Asclepius, the son of Apollo and a mortal woman; the transfiguration with the transformation of the disguised Demeter from old woman to goddess; the prophetic discourse of Mark 13 with prognostications from the oracular shrines; and the acclamation of Jesus as "Son of God"—notwithstanding some ambiguities of grammar—with the deification of the emperors.[37] She argues that these episodes comprise a narrative culminating in the recognition of Jesus as "Son of God" that would inevitably have evoked in the pagan mind "traditions of divine men": "workers of miracles, philosophers and other wise men, inspired diviners, and benefactors, especially Heracles, who labored for the benefit of humankind and died a noble death."[38]

The narrative section in Mark 7:24—8:26, on the other hand, may have been shaped by a more sustained and intentional gentile perspective on Jesus the miracle worker. Having programmatically redrawn the boundary between clean and unclean (Mark 7:14–23), Jesus pointedly sets out for the "region of Tyre and Sidon," where he is confronted by a Greek woman, a Syrophoenician by race, whose daughter he begrudgingly heals. The woman understands that she is not one of the children and can expect no more than the crumbs that fall from Israel's table. In "the region of the Decapolis" (7:31) a deaf man with a speech impediment is brought to him for healing—presumably a Jew since there is no controversy, and Isa 35:6 is clearly in the background.[39] Guelich notes that spittle was thought to

36. Yarbro Collins, "Readers," 88.

37. Yarbro Collins, "Readers," 89–97. Moss makes a similar case for the transfiguration ("Transfiguration"). Mark's account betrays both Jewish and Hellenistic influence. The Jewish elements are constitutive, but there are indications that Mark has accommodated the story to a Greek audience: he "presents his ideas on two wavelengths, one for those more familiar with Jewish traditions and another for those more familiar with Greek religious thought" (76). In particular, the transfiguration may be understood as an epiphany-like event, analogous to the Greek metamorphoses, that discloses not the pre-existent divine essence or *ousia* of Jesus but his relation to the Father (84–85). See also Holloway, *Philippians*, 49n390. It seems to me more likely that the transfiguration anticipates the future glory of the vindicated Son of Man (see Perriman, *Son of Man*, 68–69).

38. Yarbro Collins, "Readers," 100. For further examples of miracle workers in the Greek world see Achtemeier, "Divine Man," 179–82.

39. The rare word *mogilalos* ("mute," "with a speech impediment") is found only here and in Isa 35:6 in the Greek Bible; and Isa 35:6 is alluded to at the end of the healing story (Mark 7:37). According to Guelich, however, the emphasis on the privacy of

have a "therapeutic function" in both the Greek-Roman and the Jewish world.[40] The looking up to heaven and the sighing are also actions that may have resonated with both pagans and Jews.[41] It appears that Mark has adapted the miracle story to its pagan setting by enhancing its Hellenistic thaumaturgical features—unless, of course, the adaptation should be attributed to Jesus himself.[42] If the people who zealously proclaim what has happened and express their admiration in the words of Isa 35:5–6 are gentiles, then we have a faint anticipation of the gentiles' worship of YHWH because Jesus became a servant to Israel (Rom 15:8–9), or of the confession of Jesus as Lord by the nations because he rejected the prevailing paradigm of supreme kingship (Phil 2:6–11).

The feeding of the four thousand is generally regarded as a Hellenized version of the feeding of the five thousand (Mark 6:30–44; 8:1–10). Conceivably, there were gentiles among those fed.[43] Shortly after, Jesus rebukes the disciples for their inability to grasp the significance of the baskets of leftover bread following the two feeding miracles. They have aligned themselves with obtuse Israel: "Do you not yet perceive or understand? Are your hearts hardened? Having eyes do you not see, and having ears do you not hear?" (8:17–18). They have seen the works that he has performed, but they have failed to draw the right conclusions. The reference to the "leaven of Herod" directs the reader back to Herod Antipas's superstitious belief that Jesus was able to perform miracles because he was John the Baptist raised from the dead (6:14–16).

Before the question of Jesus's identity comes up for serious discussion, however, we have the healing of a blindman in Bethsaida (Mark 8:22–26). Bethsaida is on the north-eastern shore of the Sea of Galilee, beyond the border of Galilee in territory governed by Herod Philip. Caesarea Philippi lies to the north. Philip enlarged the original village and renamed it Julias after the daughter of Augustus (Josephus, *Ant.* 18:28); he may have built an imperial temple there. In Matthew and Luke Bethsaida is condemned along with Chorazin as a Jewish town that would fare worse on the day

the healing points to the man being a gentile (*Mark 1–8:26*, 394).

40. Guelich, *Mark 1–8:26*, 394–95.

41. Guelich says of Jesus's sighing: "like the previous gestures, this gesture with apparent thaumaturgic parallels in pagan miracle stories takes its own special twist here" (*Mark 1–8:26*, 395).

42. Lane comments with reference to Mark 6:56: "The works of Jesus appear to be an epiphany of divine power and the people treat him as a miracle worker or divine man whose power is released through touch" (*Mark*, 240–41).

43. Guelich, *Mark 1–8:26*, 403; cf. Lane, *Mark*, 271–75; Donahue and Harrington, *Mark*, 246.

of judgment than Tyre and Sidon, because "mighty works" had been done in it but the people had not repented (Matt 11:21–22; Luke 10:13–14). As with the deaf man earlier, Jesus takes the blind man to a more private location—according to Guelich, "a thaumaturgic trait suggesting a desire to conceal the means of the healing."[44] He concludes: "The materials involving a Syrophoenician woman, two miracle stories laced with an inordinate amount of hellenistic thaumaturgical traits . . . , and a second, 'hellenized,' Feeding located in the Decapolis aptly constitute all but two events . . . of this 'itinerary' since the discussion of the purity laws in 7:1–23 set aside that critical social boundary between Jew and Gentile."[45]

When the question of Jesus's identity is directly broached, however, in the neighborhood of Caesarea Philippi, the narrative of the Son of Man who must suffer many things is immediately introduced (Mark 8:27–31). We are still in gentile territory, and the political-religious significance of the location (Herod the Great built a white marble temple here dedicated to Augustus) may not have been entirely lost on Mark's readers.[46] But the point to note is that the answer given to the question raised by these mighty works is subverted by the decision to go the way of rejection and death. As he strayed into gentile territory, Jesus may well have acquired something of the "form of a god" in the eyes of pagan onlookers, but he is clear in his own mind that the stunning demonstration of divine power is subsidiary to a painful eschatological vocation. No doubt the harsh response to Peter is motivated by the memory of the testing by Satan in the wilderness, and the offer of rule over the nations resonates with the anti-imperial motif. The story of the Son of Man culminates in his coming "in the glory of his Father with the holy angels," but it entails a very realistic imitation by his followers, who must deny themselves and take up their own crosses (8:34—9:1).

These are stories told about a powerful miracle-worker on the border between the Jewish and gentile worlds, on the ragged fringe of Jesus's mission to the lost sheep of the house of Israel. Their immediate significance for the gentiles is incidental—no more than crumbs that fall from the table. But the stories are not being told *immediately*; they are being told decades later in a very different world, and the manner of telling may reflect the fact that the pre-exalted Christ appeared to outsiders less as a charismatic Jewish prophet, born under the Law, than as a Greek thaumaturge; and it is possible that some

44. Guelich, *Mark 1–8:26*, 432.

45. Guelich, *Mark 1–8:26*, 431.

46. Marcus, *Mark 8–16*, 603: "The city was thus associated with imperial rule, messianic hopes, and violent death—all of which make it a fitting backdrop for our story." See Josephus, *J.W.* 1:404–6; *Ant.* 15:363–64. Also Yarbro Collins, "Worship," 255–56.

of the gentiles saw what the leaders of Israel mostly did not see—that these miracles were a sign of a radically new future, and not for Israel only. We may also wonder here whether there is not some point to the thesis that—in the words of Joel Marcus—the "purpose of Mark's Gospel is to prevent the Pauline kerygma from floating off into space by grounding it in the story of Jesus of Nazareth."[47] Some adjustment, however, is needed, which would have the effect of reducing the tension between Mark and Paul: from the perspective of the gentile mission, Mark fills out the story of the one "in the form of a god," who pre-existed the otherwise *ungrounded* exalted Lord.

Godlike People and People-Like Gods

The story of the reception of Paul and Barnabas in Lystra also needs to be taken into consideration—and may even tell us something eventually about the composition of the encomium. According to Luke, the apostles heal a man crippled from birth and are at once acclaimed as gods by the people of the city: "when the crowds saw what Paul had done, they lifted up their voices, saying in Lycaonian, 'The gods have come down to us in the likeness of men!'" (Acts 14:11). At the end of the book, when Paul survives a snake bite, it is again assumed by astonished onlookers that he must be a god (28:6)—indeed, Paul Achtemeier suggests that throughout this sea journey and shipwreck narrative Paul "functions as a model divine man."[48] Luke Timothy Johnson makes the important point that this sort of misapprehension is a commonplace of the Hellenistic novel.[49] The currency of the idea is also demonstrated by Philo's allusion to an "old word" from Homer's *Odyssey* which tells how "the Divinity, assuming the resemblance of men of different countries, goes round the different cities of men, searching out the deeds of iniquity and lawlessness" (*Dreams* 1 233).[50] Ehrman wonders, a little fancifully, whether the people of Lystra may have remembered the story of the elderly and impoverished couple Baucis and

47. Marcus, *Mark 1–8*, 75.

48. Achtemeier, "Divine Man," 195.

49. Johnson, *Acts*, 248, noting Chariton, *Chaer.* 1.1.16; 1.14.1; 3.2.15–17; Xenophon of Ephesus, *Anthia and Habrocomes* 1.12.1; Heliodorus, *Aeth.* 1.2.1.

50. The suitors reproach Antinous for striking the disguised Odysseus: "Doomed man that you are, what if perchance he be some god come down from heaven? And the gods do, in the guise of strangers from afar, put on all manner of shapes, and visit the cities, beholding the violence and the righteousness of men" (Homer, *Od.* 17.484–87). I noted above Diodorus Siculus's familiarity with the passage (*Library* 1.12.9–10).

Philemon, who offered hospitality to Jupiter and Mercury when they came "in mortal guise" (Ovid, *Metam.* 8.626–34).[51]

Jesus is perhaps depicted in Mark in a way that would have conjured up in pagan minds the image of a "divine man"—a demigod, a human person with godlike qualities and abilities. The people of Lystra and Malta jump to the conclusion that the wonder-working apostles are gods manifested in human form. Here we have the systematic distinction that Talbert makes in his analysis of the cultural models underlying the two basic "christological patterns"—one entailing pre-existence, the other not.[52] He quotes Diodorus Siculus: "As regards the gods, then, men of ancient times have handed down to later generations two different conceptions: Certain of the gods, they say, are eternal and imperishable . . . . But the other gods, we are told, were terrestrial beings who attained to immortal honour and fame because of their benefactions to mankind, such as Heracles, Dionysus, Aristaeus, and the others who were like them" (*Bib. hist.* 6.1.2).[53] Cicero likewise differentiates between two classes of gods: "those who have always been regarded as dwellers in heaven, and also those whose merits have admitted them to heaven; Hercules, Liber, Aesculapius, Castor, Pollux, Quirinus" (*Leg.* 2.19).[54]

Either pattern lends itself to the perception that Jesus had been "in the form of a god." The terse rhetoric of the encomium probably does not require us to press for an exact resolution, but arguably it was, most immediately, the sort of confrontation and misunderstanding that Luke describes that prompted either the apostles or post-pagan believers to reformulate the existence of Jesus in such terms.[55] Again, if to the pagan mind Paul and Barnabas could appear as gods, then surely the exalted Lord whom they proclaimed may initially have been adjudged to have been, in his previous earthly existence, godlike, "in the form of a god."

---

51. Ehrman, *How Jesus*, 21; also Fitzmyer, *Acts*, 530.

52. Talbert, *Christology*, 7–10.

53. Talbert, *Christology*, 7. What Diodorus means by the "eternal and imperishable" gods are not the Olympian pantheon but natural phenomena such as sun, moon, stars, and winds.

54. Plutarch says that his native tradition promoted Apollo "from among those deities who were changed from mortals into immortals, like Heracles and Dionysus" to the ranks of those gods who are "unbegotten and eternal" (Plutarch, *Pel.* 16.5).

55. The slave girl at Philippi with the "python spirit" says: "These men are servants of the Most High God, who proclaim to you the way of salvation" (Acts 16:17). Does she mean Zeus? If so, this is another pagan perspective on the activity of the apostles. Cf. Fitzmyer, *Acts*, 586: "What the phrase 'the Most High God' would have meant on the lips of a pagan slave girl is hard to say: probably Zeus, the highest god of the Greek pantheon . . . ."

In an article that pushes back firmly against attempts to explain Paul's Christology in exclusively Jewish terms, Zeller asks how the encomium of Phil 2:6–11 might have been received by former pagans, given that the eschatological or "heilsgeschichtliche" background to such expressions as "Son of Man" or "Christ" would not have been immediately accessible to ordinary Greek hearers of the apostolic preaching.[56] The account of the transition from divine to human status as an angelomorphic epiphany is doubtful because there is little basis in Jewish thought for its application to a historical figure.[57] The idea of Christ's pre-existence may have owed something to Jewish Wisdom traditions, but the "idea of incarnation in a concrete man apparently is not anticipated in the wisdom tradition."[58] There are, however, abundant precedents in the pagan milieu. Zeller proposes, therefore, that the movement from divine to human status is "expressed by the terminology of *metamorphosis* which is customary in the secret epiphanies of gods on earth," and in the further idea that certain humans, especially rulers and wise men, are manifestations of gods on earth.[59]

It is merely assumed, however, that Phil 2:6–8 speaks of the appearance of a "celestial being" on earth. Zeller notes that the gods would "appear in human form, sometimes in the shape of poor beggars," but nothing like this is asserted in the text. Rather, Jesus was *en morphēi theou* but took the form of a slave; he was in the "likeness of human persons" and he was "found in appearance (*schēmati*) as a human person." There is no reference to a manifestation or epiphany here; and it is not clear that *taking* the form of a slave amounts to a metamorphosis in the sense required by the model. Indeed, the point is made that the motif is not fully suitable: "first because it implies only an external change, and second because the hidden stay of gods on earth did not end with death, but with self-disclosure."[60] The first concern shows that Zeller is still hankering after a definition of "form of God" that retains an ontological aspect when the language precisely speaks of a change in *outward appearance*, from god to slave, which I think makes sense only if

56. Zeller, "Christology," 314.

57. Zeller notes that "Jacob embodies the angel Israel, representative of the people of God" in Pr. Jos. ("Christology," 322n57).

58. Zeller, "Christology," 323–24.

59. Zeller, "Christology," 321–22; and Fletcher-Louis, "Being," 582–83. The attraction of the epiphanic model for Christians from a Hellenistic background is confirmed, in Zeller's view, by its appearance in texts from the early second century (323). Yarbro Collins recognises that some details of the poem are drawn from Jewish tradition but argues that the "more complete and illuminating analogies are to be found in Greek and Roman traditions" ("Readers," 97); cf. Yarbro Collins, "Worship," 244–46.

60. Zeller, "Christology," 322.

the earthly person of Jesus is at all times the actor in this drama. The second concern is addressed if we allow that the statement is rhetorical: the Jewish prophet-messiah Jesus was not a god but he would have appeared as such to pagan observers, much as Paul and Barnabas were mistaken for gods by the people of Lystra. What happens next subverts the pagan perception, just as—one supposes—the stoning and near killing of Paul would finally have convinced the Lystrans that these really were just two ordinary mortals. The contrast, in Luke's telling of the story, is striking, though some time must have elapsed for Jews to arrive from Antioch and Iconium: one moment the people are barely restrained from offering sacrifices to them, the next Paul is left for dead outside the city (Acts 14:18–19).

Paul and Barnabas had done their best to correct the misapprehension: "We also are men, of like nature with you, and we bring you good news, that you should turn from these vain things to a living God, who made the heaven and the earth and the sea and all that is in them" (Acts 14:15). For a long time this God has "allowed all the nations to walk in their own ways" but has left enough evidence in the working of the natural order for people to find him if they so wish. This is the first stage of an argument that in Acts 17:22–31 and Rom 1:18–32 will lead to the warning that the patience of God is wearing thin and judgment is in the offing. But the point to note here is that there is no mention of Jesus: the basic message or gospel to the nations could be proclaimed, in principle, without invoking the name of Jesus. The effect of this is to reduce the "theological" distance between Jesus and the apostles. In the pagan context, in pagan eyes, the apostles appear as godlike miracle-workers who make themselves slaves (cf. Phil 1:1) for the sake of a mission that will culminate in the judgment of the religiously and morally corrupt nations.

There are differences, of course, but they have to do with *priority* rather than with ontology. What marks the miracle-worker Jesus out is that he *first* took the way of humiliation and suffering, was raised from death, and was given authority to judge and rule at the right hand of the living God. The apostles must endure the same things among the nations, in the expectation that they will share in Christ's vindication at the *parousia*—each in his or her own order (1 Cor 15:23). Thus Jesus is the "*firstborn* among many brothers" (Rom 8:29). But in the context of their mission they find that the concrete experience of being tempted to exploit a godlike status, of a countervailing self-abasement, and of suffering provides a compelling window back on the mission of Jesus to Israel. Admittedly, this reconstruction is heavily dependent on Acts, but Luke's account is not implausible, and we know at least that Paul struggled with spiritual pride because of the revelations he received (2

Cor 12:1–10). It is also possible, in any case, that someone other than Paul
was responsible for the composition of Phil 2:6–8.

Being in the Form of a God

The literary and linguistic evidence considered in the last few chapters leads
us to two conclusions, one negative, one positive. First, it seems very unlikely that Paul would have attributed a *morphē* to the one God of his fathers
in which Jesus might at some point have existed. Secondly, the phrase *en
morphēi theou hyparchōn*, heard in a pagan or post-pagan Christian context,
would surely have elicited the thought of a man who appeared to the world
in the form of a god, looking and behaving like a god. "On the evidence,"
Paula Fredriksen says, "a divine human, whether in the first century or
thereafter, for pagans and even for Jews and, later, for Christians, was not
that hard a thought to think."[61] The reference, therefore, is not to a speculative pre-incarnate existence—it is, after all, "Christ Jesus" who is in view, not
some pre-Jewish, pre-human being—but to a flesh and blood, *pre-exalted*
existence as a godlike man, evoking with marvelous concision diverse modes
of popular pagan mythologizing.[62] Caligula was a sham Apollo, Philo says, a
pathetic imitation of the "true Apollo," utterly devoid of the moral character
to warrant displaying himself in the "form of a god" (*Embassy* 109–10). The
charismatic Jesus—an "excellent prophet," which is what Philo calls Apollo—
had been what Caligula could only pretend to be.

It is very difficult to discern any pattern in Paul's use of the verb
hyparchō ("exist, be present, be") that would suggest that the present
participle in Phil 2:6 of itself connotes the pre-existence of Christ. Kuschel highlights the *archē* component and finds in the word a reference
to Christ's "origin" in God's "world," but such a nuance is unattested
elsewhere in Paul, if anywhere in Hellenistic Greek.[63] Perhaps *hyparchōn*
is a little more emphatic than *ōn*, with context accounting for any

61. Fredriksen, *Apostle*, 144.

62. This is to be distinguished from the view, associated with Hilary, Erasmus, and
Luther (Lightfoot, *Philippians*, 131), that the *already incarnate* Christ is "in the form
of God."

63. Kuschel, *Before All Time*, 259; Martin proposes "being originally" (*Confession*,
16). LSJ s.v. ὑπάρχω gives "to be already in existence" and "exist really" as possible
meanings (italics removed). Lightfoot says that "The word denotes 'prior existence,'
but not necessarily 'eternal existence.' The latter idea however follows in the present
instance from the conception of the divinity of Christ which the context supposes"
(*Philippians*, 110). Reumann takes the participle to be "virtually an equivalent" of *ōn*:
"neither philosophical concepts of ontology nor notions about '*being from the beginning*' are to be read in" (*Philippians*, 367).

particular temporal connotation that may attach to it (cf. Ps 54:20 LXX), but that is probably the most we can say. Keown thinks that the present participle "suggests an ongoing essential status," which is not interrupted by the self-emptying and self-abasement—so Jesus remains "in the form of God," and therefore "divine," even after he has become human.[64] The grammatical argument is unconvincing. Paul says, for example, that he had been advancing in Judaism, "being (*hyparchōn*) extremely zealous for the traditions of my fathers" (Gal 1:14*), until God "was pleased" (aorist) to reveal his Son, *at which point he ceased* to be zealous for the traditions of his fathers. But even if we suppose that Christ's being *en morphēi theou* persists after he takes the form of a slave, this does not require the premise of pre-existence. We need only think that the characteristics that gave him a godlike appearance *from the beginning of* his ministry were not completely effaced (he still performed impressive works, he still spoke with remarkable wisdom) when he chose to make himself of no account and took the way of suffering. We have a rather close parallel—perhaps even something of a literary antecedent, a torn scrap of storyline blowing around in the cultural wind—in Apollo's declamation: "O, House of Admetus, in which I submitted to doing menial labor, despite being a god (*theos . . . ōn*). . . . Zeus the father forced me to be a slave in the house of a mortal"—as punishment for having killed the Cyclopes (Euripides, *Alc.* 1–7*). Pre-existence is not the point of "despite being a god."

The debate over whether the participle has concessive or causal force[65] may also be beside the point if we suppose that the rhetorical contrast is not with the *harpagmon* clause but with "emptied himself": he was in the *form* of a god but he emptied himself, taking the *form* of a slave. Support for this shift of emphasis may be found in the analogous 2 Cor 8:9, where "being rich" (*plousios ōn*) is the condition under which he "became poor" (*eptōcheusen*). The causal sense (*because* he was rich, he became poor) is obviously out of place here, but the concessive interpretation is barely more coherent since *only* a rich man can impoverish himself.[66] The simple constative or descriptive sense of the present participle, therefore, may be adequate.[67]

64. Keown, *Philippians 1:1–2:18*, 385.

65. In favor of the causal interpretation: Wright, *Climax*, 83n110; Bockmuehl, "Form of God," 21–22; Bockmuehl, *Philippians*, 133–34; Fowl, *Philippians*, 94; Gorman, "Form of God," 160–63. But as Holloway points out, this "makes sense only if we force μορφή [morphē] to mean Christ's essence instead of his appearance" (*Philippians*, 118–19).

66. Against, e.g., Holloway, *Philippians*, 119.

67. Cf. Dunn, *Christology*, 310–11n67. Focant suggests that if Paul had meant to assert the pre-existence of Christ in this clause, "a relative pronoun with an imperfect verb would have suited better" (cf. John 17:5) ("La portée," 282).

The possibility that *en morphēi theou* should be translated "in the form of *a god*" has rarely been considered by interpreters. Fredriksen is one exception: "Jesus is not 'in the form of the [high] God,' but in the form of '[a] god'"; he "does not demur from equality with God the Father, but from 'god-status' or . . . equality with '[a] god.'"[68] The god who exalts Jesus in verse 9 is *the* high god (*ho theos*), but the contrast apparent in the Greek is obscured by the convention of capitalizing the high "God" in English. In fact, discussing the statement, "I am the God, the one seen by you in the place of a god," Philo distinguishes between the correct singular and the incorrect plural use of *theos*: "Therefore, the holy word in the present instance indicates the true reference by means of the article, saying, 'I am the God' (*egō eimi ho theos*), but asserts the improper usage without an article: 'the one seen by you in the place . . . ' not 'of the God' but only 'of a god'" (*Dreams* 1 229*). Philo understands the anarthrous form (without the definite article) to refer to God's "most ancient word," which is a "second god" (*QG* 2 62; cf. *Providence* 1), and we cannot extrapolate beyond this "present instance"; but it demonstrates at least that the conceptual distinctions were manageable.

The argument merely from the absence of the article in Phil 2:6 seems precarious—it is, in any case, not the absence of the article but the meaning of *morphē* that chiefly recommends this line of interpretation.[69] But we do need to highlight the inherent ambiguity of the language, the misleading nature of the systematic theological distinction between "god" and "God," and the grammatical plausibility of the translation "in the form of a god."[70] The expression would be comparable to such phrases as "voice of a god" (*phōnēn theou*) (Deut 4:33; cf. Acts 12:22) or "heart of a god" (*kardian theou*) (Ezek 28:2, 6), which speak of a divine attribute possessed—or supposedly possessed—by a person. It is said of the "man of lawlessness" that he "opposes and exalts himself over every so-called god or object of

68. Fredriksen, *Apostle*, 138, who seems to have relied on Focant, "La portée."

69. Keown maintains that *theos* in the phrase *en morphēi theou* refers not to the emperor or any pagan god but to the "Jewish God Yahweh," because the one God is in view in the phrase *isa theōi* and in verses 9–11 (*Philippians 1:1–2:18*, 387). But if "in the form of a god" evokes the religious environment of paganism, arguably *to einai isa theōi* should be read in the same way: the one who appeared to the world in godlike form did not want to be honored as a god—including, perhaps, the god of Israel. When we get to *ho theos* (with the article, and as subject rather than as object) in verse 9 we have shifted into a conceptual sphere determined by the *anti*-pagan polemic of Isa 45:18–25.

70. See Litwa, "Deification," 5–6; Kleinknecht, "θεός," 67: "There is similar variation between θεός and ὁ θεός [*ho theos*] with no obvious distinction of sense. We also have variations, often close together, between 'the gods,' 'the god,' 'god,' and 'the godhead,' as though they were all monistic terms referring to a single power"; and Heiser, "Elohim," 263: "The absence of the article may point to indefiniteness when the subject complement is the lemma θεός [*theos*] (especially when it is plural), but it can also point to a specific, definite entity. Building an interpretation on this argument is a poor strategy."

worship, so that he takes his seat in the temple of God, presenting himself as a god" (2 Thess 2:4*). We do not need to think that this satanically inspired opponent would claim specifically to be *the* God of Israel. Behind him are the prince of Tyre, who said, "I am a god, I have inhabited the dwelling of a god in the heart of the sea" (Ezek 28:2* LXX), and Antiochus Epiphanes, who "will be enraged and will be exalted against every god and against the God of gods he will speak remarkable things" (Dan 11:36* LXX). The contrast with the testimony about Jesus is intriguing. The "man of lawlessness" exalts (*hyperairomenos*) himself over whatever is called "god," including, presumably, the god whose temple is in Jerusalem, and proclaims (*apodeiknynta*) himself "that he is a god." Jesus is "in the form of a god," and Luke has Peter speak of him as "a man presented (*apodedeigmenon*) to you from God in mighty works and wonders and signs which God did through him"—almost as a *theios anēr*, who is "crucified and killed by the hands of lawless men" (Acts 2:22–23*). Jesus does not exalt himself but is highly exalted (*hyperypsōsen*) by God. If 2 Thessalonians is late, it may still recollect traditions in which Jesus is conceived in pagan terms as an antitype to the blasphemous pagan ruler.

Conclusion

The upshot is that *en morphēi theou hyparchōn* most likely expresses a popular pagan appraisal of the Jewish person of Jesus according to a broad typology ranging from the epiphanies of Greek mythology to such super-human figures as Heracles, Pythagoras, or Apollonius. If it is essentially a matter of Hellenistic rhetoric, there is little need for precision: different Greeks would have heard the stories about Jesus in different ways. Justin was happy to discuss Jesus among the gods and demigods of antiquity, as being like Mercury, Asclepius, Bacchus, Hercules, Perseus, Ariadne, or the deified Caesars (Justin, *1 Apol.* 21–22). Litwa argues that "many other Christian writers—including those of the New Testament—consciously or unconsciously re-inscribed divine traits of Mediterranean gods and deified figures into their discourse concerning Jesus."[71] But the pre-exalted Jesus not only started out "in the form of a god"; he made a decision, he took a course of action; and it is to this critical dramatic moment that we turn now.

---

71. Litwa, *Iesus Deus*, 3. Veyne suggests that the "divine man" conception remained operative for ex-pagans into the fourth century: "This was an age that was very receptive to 'divine men' (*theioi andres*) and to miracle workers and prophets who lived among ordinary people and were revered by some as masters" (*Our World*, 23).

8

The *Harpagmos* Incident

JESUS WAS IN THE form of a god *but* he took a quite incongruous course of action. The first step we cannot translate yet: *ouch harpagmon hēgēsato to einai isa theōi*; but from there we can proceed more or less literally. He "emptied himself," took the "form of a slave," was in the likeness of people, was found in human appearance, humbled himself, and was obedient to the point of death on a Roman cross (Phil 2:6–8). The meaning of the clause with *harpagmos* has been extensively discussed, to put it mildly. I will not venture to review the debate here. My view is that having attuned ourselves to a pagan frame of mind, we can get to a very satisfactory understanding of the clause by pursuing the path of what has become a dominant opinion in recent years. But we must be careful not to get knocked off course at the last minute when an unconventional resolution suddenly comes into view.

Hoover's Solution

The "philological solution" to the conundrum of *harpagmos* proposed by Hoover in a 1971 article has been widely accepted by commentators.[1] A critical essay by J. C. O'Neill did little to dent the consensus, but doubts

1. Hoover, "*Harpagmos*." Among those persuaded are Murphy-O'Connor, "Anthropology," 38–39; Strimple, "Philippians 2:5–11," 263–65; Wright, "ἁρπαγμός"; Fowl, *Story of Christ*, 55–56; O'Brien, *Philippians*, 214–16; Wright, *Climax*, 77–90; Witherington, *Narrative*, 122–23n46; Fee, *Philippians*, 206–7; Bockmuehl, *Philippians*, 130; Byrne, "Pre-Existence," 316–17; Hawthorne, "Form of God," 102; Fowl, *Philippians*, 94; Hurtado, *How on Earth*, 95–96; Lee, *Preexistent Son*, 306; Silva, *Philippians*, 104; Fee, *Christology*, 381–83; Gorman, "Form of God," 155–56; Reumann, *Philippians*, 345–47, 367; Hansen, *Philippians*, 145–46; Hellerman, *Honor*, 133–34; Hellerman, "Μορφη Θεου," 787–88n22; Thurston and Ryan, *Philippians*, 81–82; Weymouth, "Christ-Story," 251–55; Focant, "La portée," 284–85; Keown, *Philippians 1:1–2:18*, 399. See also the listing in Martin, "ἁρπαγμός Revisited," 176n3. Martin briefly affirms the "adverbial sense of ἁρπαγμὸν ἡγεῖσθαι [*harpagmon hēgeisthai*]" suggested by Hoover (*Hymn of Christ*, lxviin51).

raised by Vollenweider on philological grounds have been taken more seriously.[2] More recently Martin has attempted to address the objections
and consolidate Hoover's argument.[3]

The verb *harpazō* has the straightforward meaning "seize, snatch, carry
off." In Phil 2:6 we have the noun *harpagmos*, which formally would have the
active sense of "robbery" or "a violent seizure of property."[4] It is found only
here in the Greek Bible and is rare in non-biblical literature. More common
is the passive noun *harpagma*, signifying *that which is seized*—"booty, prey."[5]
Hoover argued, however, that what we have in Phil 2:6 is not the simple lexical meaning of the noun but a metaphorical and idiomatic expression which
is more than, or other than, the sum of its parts. The idiom typically consists
of a verb such as *hēgeisthai* or *poieisthai*, meaning "think of, regard, consider," and a double accusative construction consisting of the direct object
of the verb and the complement *harpagma*. In this particular case the idiom
is negated, giving: he did not consider *harpagmon* (complement or predicate accusative) the being-like-a-god (object accusative).[6] Interpretation is
complicated by the fact that Paul uses *harpagmos* rather than *harpagma*, but
Hoover maintained, for reasons which we will come to, that at least in this

---

2. O'Neill, "Hoover"; Vollenweider, "Der „Raub""; cf. Hellerman, "Μορφη Θεου,"
787–88n22; Holloway, *Philippians*, 121n38. Shaner thinks that O'Neill was right and
should have had the courage of his convictions ("Rape and Robbery," 349).

3. Martin, "ἁρπαγμός Revisited."

4. BDAG s.v. ἁρπαγμός, 133. It has also been argued that *harpagmos* can mean
"rape" or "abduction marriage" (e.g., Plutarch, *[Lib. ed.]* 15; Vettius Valens 2.38; Pausanias, *Descr.* 1.20.3) after the manner of the gods: Christ is in the form of God, he
takes on human form, but not for the purpose of rape or abduction. Shaner properly
emphasizes the pre-Chalcedonian social-political context of the encomium: "cities like
Philippi were filled with images of gods, even images of imperial divine men whose
power is confirmed through aesthetically beautiful depictions of military victory and
domination of female bodies representing conquered nations" ("Rape and Robbery,"
345–46). But she can make *harpagmos* mean "rape and robbery" only by substituting
the context of imperial iconography for the actual context of the encomium, in which it
would appear to have to do with *seizing power* rather than with *seizing a woman*, whether literally or figuratively. Fletcher-Louis intends in a forthcoming study to develop the
argument of Fredrickson that it means "erotic abduction, kidnapping for marriage":
"Christ reckons that the character of divine being is not to violently seize humans out of
erotic desire for them" ("Being," 617n121). It is difficult to see why the denial *specifically*
of erotic intent on Christ's part would be relevant here, even if he is conceived as a "god"
who has taken human form, or why such a course of action would be countered with
the statement about becoming a slave.

5. LSJ s.v. ἅρπαγμα 1, 245.

6. Wright notes the "incidental advantage" of Hoover's interpretation that it accounts
for the position of *ouch* at the beginning of the clause rather than immediately before the
verb, modifying the whole expression (*Climax*, 79); cf. Martin, *Confession*, 22.

construction the active and passive forms are interchangeable. The meaning of the expression is that the thing or situation is considered "exploitable" or an "opportunity to be taken advantage of."[7]

The evidence for the idiomatic usage comes from a small collection of texts that date from the third to fifth centuries AD. Three of the instances are clustered in two consecutive chapters of a romantic novel known as the *Aethiopica* by Heliodorus of Emesa; the others are found in patristic texts. There are six examples with *harpagma*, two with *harpagmos*. We will consider the texts somewhat independently of Hoover's analysis, taking into account both the scant criticism of the proposal in the literature and Martin's defence of Hoover. I will suggest that the linguistic argument is essentially sound. The problems arise when we come to the application of the idiomatic meaning to the Philippians text by Hoover, Wright, and others. The difficulties have not gone unnoticed—by Martin, for one, who has proposed a refinement of Hoover's solution that makes the context, and not the idiom alone, decisive for christological meaning.

The Texts

The Idiom with Harpagma

The *Aethiopica* of Heliodorus of Emesa (third or fourth century AD) tells the story of Chariclea, an Ethiopian princess, raised in Egypt to avoid the scandal of her surprisingly white complexion, who becomes a priestess at Delphi, where she meets and falls in love with a Thessalian nobleman called Theagenes; after many perils and twists of fortune they marry. The scenes that concern us are set in Memphis. Theagenes, it so happens, is also being pursued by Arsace, the daughter of the satrap Oroondates, with help from her scheming handmaid Cybele. There are three *harpagma* incidents. First, Cybele happens to learn from the verger at the temple that Theagenes and Chariclea are in need of accommodation and regards this "happy circumstance" (*xyntychian*) as *harpagma* and "as the beginning of a way of ensnaring" the couple (*Aeth.* 7.11).[8] Later she upbraids Theagenes for disregarding the advances made by Arsace: "A young man so handsome and in his prime

---

7. Hoover, "*Harpagmos*," 106. Cf. Foerster, "ἁρπάζω," 473: "'to take up an attitude to something as one does to what presents itself as a prey to be grasped, a chance discovery, or a gift of fate, i.e., appropriating and using it, treating it as something desired and won.' What is regarded as gain may be something which is already present and is utilised, or a possibility which is about to eventuate and is not to be let slip. Materially, therefore, the sense is no less 'to utilise' than 'to take.'"

8. Cf. Smith, *Greek Romances*, 160: "The old woman, thinking this an admirable occasion to spread her nets and prepare her snares . . . ."

thrusts away a young woman of similar qualities who yearns for him, and does not regard the matter as *harpagma* nor even as a piece of good luck (*hermaion*) . . . " (7.20).[9] Theagenes continues to spurn Arsace's attention, so Cybele suggests to her mistress that they should contrive to have Chariclea killed in the hope that Theagenes will "despair of obtaining her, and surrender himself to your desires." Consumed with jealousy and anger, Arsace regards this proposition as *harpagma*.[10] "You have spoken well," she says, "I shall take care to command that the offending female be done away with" (8.7). In each of these incidents an advantageous circumstance or turn of events is presented, which is considered—or not considered—as something to be seized on and exploited for benefit. The clustering of the texts is striking, no doubt reflecting the fact that opportunism and fortuity are stock features of the romance genre.

Now we turn to the patristic texts. In an account of the deaths of martyrs in Antioch Eusebius writes that some were tortured "not to the point of death, but with a view to lengthy punishment"; others, fearful of falling into the hands of their enemies and suffering the same torments, threw themselves from the roofs of high buildings, "thinking death to be *harpagma* in preference to the savagery of impious men" (*Hist. eccl.* 8.12.2*). The meaning here seems clear: the second group considered death something to be seized *while the power was still in their hands* in order to escape the worse fate of protracted torture suffered by the first group. In this case, suicide is a course of action available *at the moment* that is eagerly taken advantage of.

In his *Life of Constantine* Eusebius records the emperor's order that exiled Christians should be allowed to return to their homes and that those "who have lived destitute lives for a long time . . . , if they consider such a return *harpagma* and if from now on they lay aside their anxieties, may live among us without fear" (*Vit. Const.* 2.31.2). The return home is not something already possessed; it is an opportunity presented by the decree; the exiles may or may not choose to take advantage of it.[11]

In an exposition of Phil 2:6 Isidore of Pelusium, who died around 450, discusses Christ's motivation in humbling himself. If he had considered being equal with God a "windfall" (*hermaion*)—as a matter of good fortune—he would not have jeopardized his newly acquired status, as it would have been, by taking the form of a slave. Isidore explains: "For a slave who was set free and honoured with sonship, because he considers

---

9. For the translation see Hoover, "*Harpagmos*," 105.

10. Cf. Smith, *Greek Romances*, 189: "Arsace eagerly seized upon this idea . . . ."

11. Hoover understands *harpagma* here as "something to take advantage of" ("*Harpagmos*," 110).

(*hēgēsamenos*) his status *harpagma* or a windfall (*heurema*), would not submit to doing household work" (*Ep.* 4.22). In other words, because he was already a "genuine son," Christ did not do what a slave would naturally do: he did not regard equality with God an opportunity that has been seized and that must be jealously guarded, a windfall that would be squandered by reverting to the condition of a slave.

Hoover, in fact, thought that this last passage was an exception to his rule that when *harpagma* and *harpagmos* occur in a double accusative construction, "they carry senses different from those conveyed when they are otherwise employed." He translates *harpagma* as "booty", on the assumption that "sonship" is something that the slave has seized for himself.[12] The admission was flagged up by O'Neill, who insisted that the "exception is fatal to the rule." Martin has since defended the idiomatic interpretation, maintaining that there is nothing in the context to preclude the sense "something to seize upon, to take advantage of." He notes that the translation "booty" makes little sense, in any case: in Isidore's argument, and no doubt generally, adoptive sonship is not stolen or seized but bestowed as a privilege and honor—a godsend or windfall, perhaps, but not booty.[13] There seems no reason, therefore, to view this passage as an exception to the emerging pattern: *harpagma* casts the thing considered as *something to be used or exploited to advantage*. Martin later finds in this passage evidence that the idiom can entail the thought that the thing to be exploited is already in the person's possession, which will become a critical consideration for determining the Christology of Phil 2:6. We will be obliged at that point to look a little more closely at Isidore's statement.

The Idiom with Harpagmos

Hoover cites two texts where the idiomatic expression occurs with *harpagmos*, as in Phil 2:6, rather than *harpagma*. The first is a comment by Eusebius on the martyrdom of Peter, who "considered death on a cross *harpagmon* because of the hope of salvation" (*Comm. Luc.* 6*). The meaning is partly suggested by the further remark that the apostles "did not suffer these things against their will (*ou para gnōmēn*), reckoning the hope in the promises of salvations as sweet as any pleasure" because Jesus had "taught them to rejoice on account of their sufferings." Presumably, in Eusebius's view, Peter regarded his death by crucifixion as *something to be embraced willingly* (i.e., he did not suffer *para gnōmēn*) because it offered

12. Hoover, "*Harpagmos*," 117 and n33.
13. Martin, "ἁρπαγμός Revisited," 181–82.

the opportunity to suffer not only for Christ's sake but also *in the same manner as Christ suffered.*[14] Eusebius underlines this point by stressing that the apostles in their deaths exhibited the "purity and steadfastness of their obedience" to the words of Jesus.

The second passage is Cyril of Alexandria's (fifth century AD) discussion of Lot's offer of hospitality to the angels, which Hoover renders: "He did not regard [their] polite refusal as something to take advantage of . . . as if . . . from a listless and feeble heart" (*De ador.* 1.25; cf. Gen 19:1–4).[15] There will be more to say about this passage later, but for now I suggest that the point is this: Lot offers hospitality at some risk to himself; the angels turn down the offer and propose to spend the night in the town square; but Lot does not *take advantage of* their "polite refusal" (*paraitēsin*) to escape the dilemma and renews the invitation.

Conclusions from the Texts

Hoover has constructed a careful case for thinking that *harpagma* and *harpagmos* are interchangeable in the idiom: 1) the Greek Fathers read Phil 2:6 as though it had *harpagma* in the place of *harpagmos*;[16] 2) the distinction in classical Greek between nouns in *-ma* and *-mos* was often not observed in the Hellenistic period, though *harpagmos* occurs too infrequently to be sure that it was "employed in both active and passive senses"; 3) *harpagma* is used in the Septuagint and Plutarch in both the active and passive senses, suggesting that the formal distinction no longer applied in this case; 4) both terms are used synonymously by Eusebius with reference to the same object and in constructions that are precisely parallel to the construction in Philippians 2:6; and 5) in a passage in which Cyril of Alexandria discusses Lot's offer of hospitality to the angels we have a plausible example of the use of the idiomatic expression with the active form *harpagmos.*[17]

O'Neill concedes that *harpagma* and *harpagmos* "could be synonyms, as far as we know" but takes issue with Hoover over the interpretation of

14. The Latin translation in *PG* 24.538 is imprecise: "Petrus autem regnum rapuit per crucis necem cum spe salutari" ("Peter however seized the kingdom through death on a cross with hope of salvation"); but it suggests that *harpagmon* was understood as an act of seizing ("rapuit").

15. Hoover, "*Harpagmos*," 110–11; Wright, *Climax*, 85.

16. Foerster says that patristic expositions mostly conform to the understanding of *harpagmos* as a gain not to be let slip or not used: "Particularly those which consciously or less consciously give an independent paraphrase, i.e., one which is not dependent on the word group ἁρπάζειν [*harpazein*] etc., point in this direction" ("ἁρπάζω," 474).

17. Hoover, "*Harpagmos*," 107–114.

the two supposedly synonymous passages in Eusebius, arguing that in both cases *harpagmos* has the normal sense of "robbery."[18] First, with regard to the statement in Eusebius's commentary on Luke, he objects that Peter was not in a position to "regard death by crucifixion as an advantage to be seized."[19] Rather Peter seized death by crucifixion "because of the saving hopes that accompanied it." On the face of it, this is little different from the idiomatic sense: O'Neill rather muddies the waters by putting the phrase "the act of reaping an advantage" in interpretive apposition to "robbery." Moreover, as we have seen, the wider context suggests that Peter regarded such a death not as a means of gaining salvation but as an opportunity to emulate Christ's suffering. Secondly, O'Neill prefers the Loeb translation of the line about the martyrs in Antioch: "regarding death as a prize snatched from the wickedness of evil men" (Eusebius, *Hist. eccl.* 8.12.2). But the genitive construction with *mochthērias* ("depravity") seems an unlikely way of specifying the people *from whom* the prize has been snatched; the phrase makes more sense as a genitive of comparison (BDF §185.1), which is how Hoover has taken it ("in comparison with the depravity of ungodly men"). O'Neill is also unconvinced by Hoover's translation of the only other passage where *harpagmos* is used "as part of a double accusative after a verb of considering." In the end, he settles for "Lot did not consider the angels' refusal as an occasion for reaping an advantage."[20] Again, there seems little difference as far as the meaning of *harpagmon* is concerned.[21]

Grammatically, therefore, the conclusion that *harpagma* and *harpagmos* were interchangeable in Hellenistic Greek seems reasonably secure.[22] The inconsistency is perhaps attributable to the fact that the first accusative in the construction is effectively the object of both actions—the considering and the "seizing." The natural construction, given the preponderance of instances with the passive form, would be "the martyrs

18. O'Neill, "Hoover," 446. Moule also insisted, before the publication of Hoover's article, that the formal distinction holds and translates "he did not regard equality with God as *consisting in* snatching" ("Reflections," 266, his emphasis).

19. O'Neill, "Hoover," 446.

20. O'Neill, "Hoover," 447.

21. Cf. Martin, "ἁρπαγμός Revisited," 189: "Here again, we encounter a gloss for 'robbery'—'reaping an advantage'—that is essentially no different from Hoover's 'something to seize upon, to take advantage of.'"

22. Vincent says that "In this condition of the evidence it is certainly straining a point . . . to insist on making the rendering of the passage turn on the active meaning of ἁρπαγμὸν [*harpagmon*]" (*Philippians*, 58). He cites several examples of comparable active forms with a passive meaning. BDAG s.v. ἁρπαγμός, 133, suggests *himatismos* for comparison. See also Lightfoot, *Philippians*, 111, and the discussion in Keown, *Philippians 1:1–2:18*, 395.

considered death *harpagma* . . . ": "death" is the object of the considering but the *subject* of the passive verbal idea conveyed by *harpagma*. But since the subject of the two verbal ideas is the same person, it is easy to see how the idiom might oscillate between the passive and active forms. So Peter "considered death *harpagmon* . . . ": in this case death is the object of both actions. The point is not so much that the two *forms* are interchangeable but that the idiom is inherently ambiguous.[23]

Hoover traced the idiomatic double-accusative interpretation back to Werner Jaeger, who had identified a cluster of texts in which *harpagma* occurs with verbs of considering and a set of words suggesting good fortune (*hermaion, heurēma, eutychēma*).[24] Jaeger concluded that in such expressions *harpagma* was synonymous with these words: to consider something *harpagma* was to consider it a stroke of luck, a windfall, a godsend. He had some difficulty applying the sense to Phil 2:6.[25] Hoover acknowledged the association but took pains to differentiate between *harpagma* and the notion of "windfall." In both *Aethiopica* 7:20 and Isidore's Fourth Epistle *harpagma* is directly related to *hermaion* or *heurēma*: Theagenes "does not regard the matter as *harpagma* nor even as a piece of good luck (*hermaion*)"; the freed slave regards his new status "as *harpagma* or a windfall (*heurema*)." An element of fortuity may also be observed in the other examples. Hoover makes the point, however, that a logical distinction may be made between the opportunity presented, whether by chance (*hermaion, heurēma, eutychēma*) or by design (for example, Cybele's proposal to eliminate Chariclea), and the metaphorical seizing of it.[26]

Support for this is drawn from the metaphorical use of the verb *harpazō* for the *seizing* of a fortuitously presented opportunity. For example, Timoleon sent a letter to Corinth urging the city to send settlers to re-found Syracuse, but the Corinthians "did not seize the advantage" (*ouch hērpasan . . . tēn pleonexian*); they did not exploit the opportunity for self-aggrandizement (Plutarch, *Tim.* 23). With Sparta in a state of confusion,

---

23. We find a similar ambiguity with a verbal noun in -*mos* with *hēgeomai* in Heb 11:26*: Moses "considered the reproach of the Christ (*hēgēsamenos . . . ton oneidismon tou Christou*) greater wealth than the treasures of Egypt, for he was looking to the reward." In this case the action is probably active primarily (cf. Ps 88:52 LXX), but the reproaching of the Christ as direct object is also the reproach which the Christ suffered.

24. Hoover, "*Harpagmos*," 95–98; Glasson finds the idea first in Lightfoot, *Philippians*, 111 ("Two Notes," 133–34).

25. Hoover, "*Harpagmos*," 96–98.

26. Hoover says that the "meaning conveyed by ἅρπαγμά τι ποιεῖσθαι [*harpagma ti poieisthai*] is related to the meaning conveyed by ἕρμαιον, εὕρημα, εὐτύχημά τι ποιεῖσθαι [*hermaion, heurēma, eutychēma ti poieisthai*], not because the nouns are synonymous, but because a stroke of luck is 'something to seize upon'" ("*Harpagmos*," 106).

Philopoemen "seized the moment" (*harpasas ton kairon*) to launch an assault on the city (Plutarch, *Phil.* 15.2). Having learned of the absence of Dionysius, the soldiers of Dion were eager to "seize the moment" (*harpasai ton kairon*) and urged him to lead them to Syracuse (Plutarch, *Dion* 26.2). Josephus says that when Alexandra fell sick, her son Aristobulus "seized the moment" (*ton kairon harpasas*) and took possession of all the fortresses (*J.W.* 1:117*). When Herod was running around the palace, tormented by suspicions about his wife, his sister Salome "took the occasion" (*ton kairon . . . harpasasa*) to slander the woman (*J.W.* 1:443*). Athena says to Odysseus "my eye is on you as you prowl about to snatch (*harpasai*) some opportunity against your enemies" (Sophocles, *Aj.* 1–2). Xenophon has Socrates speak of the mind as something that might have been "snatched up by lucky accident" (*eutychōs synarpasai*) (*Mem.* 1.4.8*).[27] Finally, lowering the tone of the conversation, we have this protest about the misappropriation of a dildo in Herodas, *Mimes* 6.27–31*: "Ladies, this woman will be the death of me yet. Fed up with her persistent entreaties, I gave it her, Metro, before using it myself. But seizing it as a windfall (*hō<s>per heurēm' harpasa<sa>*), she gives it to others without permission."

This survey of the small number of texts cited by Hoover has broadly confirmed the philological argument. The double accusative construction with a verb of considering and either *harpagma* or *harpagmos* conveys the idea that a person *thinks that a circumstance or opportunity presented may be exploited for benefit or taken advantage of.*

There is the obvious problem that the parallels are late, but there is no positive reason to think that the idiom was not current in the first century, and the much earlier comparable metaphorical expressions with *harpazō* may indicate that the word-group was readily used for the seizing of an opportunity.[28] There must also be some suspicion that the idiom belongs a very different type of literature, in which it functions as a vulgar way of speaking about "opportunities to be seized for *sex and crime*."[29] Vollenweider thinks that this jars with the solemn and elevated style of the Christ encomium. The use of the expression by ecclesiastical writers may have been

---

27. Hoover, "*Harpagmos*," 96.

28. Vollenweider argues that the *harpazō* word group is always negatively marked in the Septuagint and that the sense of "forcibly taking away" has to be seriously considered for the interpretation of Phil 2:6 ("Der „Raub"," 268–69); cf. Yarbro Collins, "Origins," 367. But in the *metaphor* of seizing an opportunity, the idea of violence is naturally diminished.

29. Vollenweider, "Der „Raub"," 266–67. Also Reumann, *Philippians*, 347. Jaeger originally suggested that the idiomatic expressions (specifically with the sense of "windfall") arose in common speech and were assimilated into literary usage through the romance literature (Hoover, "*Harpagmos*," 96).

influenced by familiarity with the Philippians text, but it is quite possible that popular usage has colored the meaning of the idiom. So when Isidore of Pelusium tells a story about a freed slave who regards his status as *harpagma* or "windfall," we may wonder whether as a young man in Alexandria he read too many romantic novels. The idiom may have acquired the scurrilous connotations after the New Testament period. But we should also allow for the possibility that the first paragraph of the encomium echoes a less solemn, less elevated, more popular, more prosaic reconstruction of the story of Jesus than is usually assumed.

Has Hoover Settled the Christological Argument?

We now come to Hoover's application of the idiomatic meaning to Phil 2:6, which he translates "he did not regard being equal with God as something to take advantage of" or "as something to use for his own advantage."[30] From this he draws a direct christological conclusion: this understanding of the statement "carries with it the assumption that τὸ εἶναι ἴσα θεῷ [*to einai isa theōi*] represents a status which belonged to the pre-existent Christ," because the idiomatic expression with *harpagmos* "refers to something already present and at one's disposal." This solution has been enthusiastically endorsed by N. T. Wright, who takes Hoover's "strongest point" to be that the idiom "assumes that the object in question—in this case equality with God—is already possessed."[31] According to Wright's rather unwieldy definition, *harpagmos* "refers to *the attitude one will take towards something which one already has and holds and will continue to have and hold*, specifically, to the question of whether that attitude will or will not consist in taking advantage of this possessed object."[32] He reckons that all other proposed interpretations, though in any case intrinsically faulty, are hereby "undercut at a stroke." When applied to Phil 2:6 it gives the simple meaning: Jesus had equality with God, but he did not exploit it or use it for his own ends. "Over against the standard picture of oriental despots, who understood their position as something to be used for their own advantage, Jesus understood his position to *mean* self-negation, the vocation described in vv. 7–8."[33] The

---

30. Hoover, "*Harpagmos*," 118.

31. Wright, *Climax*, 82. The section on *harpagmos* (62–90) is an updated reprint of Wright, "ἁρπαγμός." See also Bockmuehl, *Philippians*, 129–31; Fee, *Philippians*, 206; Oakes, *Philippians*, 193n67, 198; Jipp, *Christ is King*, 129; Hellerman, *Honor*, 133–35.

32. Wright, *Climax*, 78 (his emphasis).

33. Wright, *Climax*, 83.

proposal has since been widely accepted and put to good use in defence of a high christological reading of Phil 2:6.

The flaw in the argument at this point, however, is glaring. In the shift from philological definition to christological exposition the idea of an *opportunity unexpectedly presented or newly contrived*, which has appeared integral to the idiomatic expression, has been replaced by the idea of an *attribute or status already possessed*, a thing which *belongs* to the pre-existent Christ.[34] The substitution of the vague "something" in the translation for "opportunity" has facilitated the slide towards an interpretation that falls outside the field of usage so meticulously delineated in Hoover's article.[35] Interpretation of the expression cannot be reduced to the choice between what is not possessed and must be grasped and what is possessed and may be exploited. Hoover states that "in every instance . . . this idiomatic expression refers to something already present and at one's disposal," but an *opportunity* is not something already secured and possessed. It is something made present or discovered *at the moment*—when a stratagem is proposed, when a chance meeting occurs, when a letter is received, when an attractive woman offers herself, when a decree is issued, when an invitation is declined, when a sex toy is shown off—demanding a prompt response; and the idea of *seizure* is relevant because the opportunity might as quickly vanish. The basic meaning of the verb *harpazō* remains operative in the idiomatic expression. You do not *seize*—even metaphorically—something that you already possess.[36] Actually, in none of the passages put forward as evidence for the idiom is the object considered *harpagma/harpagmos* something that was in the person's possession *prior to the narrative moment that elicits the statement*. There is no example of a person taking or not taking advantage of something—a material object, a status, a course of action—which was not *at that moment* made available or exploited. Even in the case of the martyrs at Antioch, it is not Eusebius's point that the opportunity of suicide had been *in their possession* for some time.

Wright considers three patristic texts which he thinks lend support to his contention that the *harpagmos* clause in Phil 2:6 makes equality with

34. Glasson argues for the sense "did not regard it as a piece of good fortune," without referencing Hoover, but also concludes that "the pre-existent Christ already had equality with God" ("Two Notes," 134, 136).

35. Hoover earlier summarized Lohmeyer's criticism of Jaeger's thesis: "on the occasions Jaeger noted that which is regarded as ἕρμαιον [hermaion], etc., is always seen as something which has come to the person from outside; being equal with God, however, cannot be an external fortuity but is a quality of which one is bearer" (Hoover, "Harpagmos," 100). This precisely identifies the false move that Hoover makes.

36. Cf. Martin, *Confession*, 20.

God an attribute that is already possessed by Christ.[37] But in each case his interpretation seems forced. Eusebius's reference to Phil 2:6 in the context of an account of the experience of the martyrs in Gaul provides a good illustration of Hoover's argument: "And they carried so far their zeal and imitation of Christ, 'who being in the form of God, thought it not *harpagmon* to be equal with God,' that for all their glory, and though they had testified not once or twice but many times . . . , they neither proclaimed themselves as martyrs, nor allowed us to address them by this title" (*Hist. eccl.* 5.2.2). Wright thinks that Eusebius "clearly regards them as martyrs anyway; there is no question of their refusing to grasp at a glory they did not possess, or of actually giving up one they did." So they did not use the fact that they were *already* martyrs "as something to take advantage of." But this misrepresents the analogy. Just as Christ was "in the form of God," these people had attained honor, which is the thing possessed. Just as Christ did not consider *harpagmon* being equal with God (Eusebius does not attempt to interpret Paul's words), so they refused to take the *opportunity of being known or acclaimed as* "martyrs."

The second passage is the story of the martyrs in Antioch (Eusebius, *Hist. eccl.* 8.12.2), which we have looked at already. Wright argues that death was not something that they might have actively seized; in effect, they already possessed it: "instead of regarding that death as something to be feared or shunned, they regarded it as something to be taken advantage of, to the extent that they were prepared to anticipate their execution by committing suicide." But again he has missed the point of the story. Perhaps death was inevitable—though it was hardly in their possession in the way that Wright thinks that equality with God was in Christ's possession.[38] But they *grasped the opportunity* to throw themselves from their roofs while they still had the freedom *rather than suffer drawn-out torment at the hands of cruel men.* What they regarded as *harpagma* was the avoidance of torture, not the attainment of death.

Wright's brief discussion of Cyril of Alexandria's comments on the visit of the angels to Lot, thirdly, is inconsequential. He does not explicitly claim that the angels' refusal was something in Lot's possession rather than an opportunity presented to him.

---

37. Wright, *Climax*, 85.

38. Cf. Dunn, *Theology*, 285n87: "the critical point is surely that death was not something already possessed by the would-be martyrs, but something they eagerly grasped at"; and Reumann, *Philippians*, 347.

Martin's Refinement of Hoover's Thesis

The inconsistency in the application of the lexicological argument to the statement about Christ in Phil 2:6 is noted by Martin in a vigorous defense of Hoover against the criticisms made by O'Neill.[39] He sets Wright's insistence on the "already possessed" character of Jesus' equality with God against the counterclaim made by Dunn that the idiom makes equality with God (in Martin's words) "a nonpossession that Christ was tempted to grasp," and suggests that they have got hold of opposite ends of the same stick. He argues that "the idiom apart from context does not speak positively or negatively to the subject's possession of the object deemed ἅρπαγμα/ ἁρπαγμός [*harpagma/harpagmos*]." Outside of the idiom, *harpagma* would imply non-possession of an object that needs to be seized. But in the idiom this "seizing" has become metaphorical: "the object deemed ἅρπαγμα/ ἁρπαγμός is not something literally seized as a newly claimed possession; rather, it is something seized metaphorically as an opportunity."[40] We must rely, therefore, on context to determine whether or not the object is already in the person's possession, whether it is merely to be exploited as an advantage or to be seized. Martin suggests that most of the examples considered fall into the latter category: "the object in view is most certainly not a possession of the subject, either because it belongs to another or because it cannot in any proper sense be considered a possession." This is fully consistent with the meaning that we have determined for the expression. In two instances, however, he argues that the object is already in the possession of the subject. These texts need to be re-examined.

The argument from Isidore of Pelusium (*Ep.* 4.22) is weakened, in the first place, by the fact that this is a fifth-century discussion of the Pauline text and is likely to have been influenced by fifth-century theological interests. The analogy that Paul establishes between Christ and the Philippians would be invalid, Isidore thinks, if Christ "was not equal" to God. That begs the question. But the larger argument of the letter, in any case,

---

39. Martin points out that in the same paragraph Hoover both affirms, on the strength of his analysis of the idiom, that equality with God "belonged" to Christ and states that in every instance considered the question is "not whether or not one possesses something, but whether or not one chooses to exploit something" ("ἁρπαγμός Revisited," 190, with reference to Hoover, "*Harpagmos*," 118). This may misread Hoover's argument, which is that the idiomatic expression 1) *assumes* that the thing is in the person's possession rather than asserts the fact, and 2) raises the question instead of whether what is possessed will be exploited. But the basic criticism is valid.

40. Martin, "ἁρπαγμός Revisited," 191. It is not clear that the distinction between a literal seizing "as a newly claimed possession" and a metaphorical seizing "as an opportunity" can be sustained. A metaphorical seizing is still a seizing.

suggests that there is little difference in Isidore's mind between *harpagma* and *heurēma* ("piece of good luck, windfall") or *hermaion* ("unexpected piece of luck, godsend, wind-fall, treasure-trove").[41] He first says of Christ that if he had "considered the being-equal a windfall (*hermaion*), he would not have humbled himself, lest the submission caused prejudice to his dignity." But he had equality and nobility by nature; they had not been given to him according to grace; therefore, he did not decline to humble himself. Significantly, Isidore does not entertain the thought that Christ might have "considered the being-equal *harpagma*." Of the slave who *was* set free and adopted as a son Isidore then says: "having considered the dignity *harpagma* or *heurēma*, he would not submit to doing household work." Given what was said about Christ, it seems likely that the main thought here is that the slave regarded the *past events* of manumission and adoption as having been a gift of good fortune, an opportunity to be seized. So *harpagma* here neither means "booty," something seized from someone else (as Hoover and O'Neill), nor refers to something—sonship—that was already in the former slave's possession at the moment when he was required to perform a degrading task (Martin).[42] Rather it *looks back to the moment in the past* when the opportunity was presented to him and he gladly took it.

The second example is Cyril's discussion of the story of Lot and the angels, which also dates from the fifth century (*De ador.* 1.25). Martin's translation of the relevant sentence is unconvincing: "He did not regard his entreaty as a thing to use for advantage's sake, as if it were from a listless and wishywashy heart."[43] That is, Lot had not invited the "men" to his home in an insincere and half-hearted fashion merely to save face and escape an awkward situation. Even if we allow that *paraitēsis* refers to Lot's "entreaty" rather than to the angels' "polite refusal," it is difficult to see how the invitation to the angels to stay under his roof would count as an object in Lot's possession that he might, or might not, exploit or use to his advantage. The question is whether he can use it to his advantage *in the present*. But in any natural reading of the passage, it is not the invitation, however half-hearted it may have been, that offered a potential get-out but the "excuse, apology," "declining," "begging off" of the angels.[44] On the whole, it appears that *paraitēsis* is better suited to the angels' negative reaction than to Lot's simple request that they come to his house. Martin argues that Hoover's translation

41. LSJ s.v. εὕρημα II.1, 729; ἕρμαιον, 690 (emphasis removed).

42. The Latin translation in *PG* 78.1071 has "pro praeda quasi aut re inventa" ("as a sort of booty or thing found") for *hate harpagma ē heurema*.

43. Martin, "ἁρπαγμός Revisited," 189.

44. LSJ s.v. παραίτησις, 1311.

of *paraitēsis* as "polite refusal" requires him to supply an unstated "his invitation had come."[45] But the phrase "as from a weak and watery mind" need only qualify the verb *epoieito* ("he considered"), which it encloses (*hōs ex adranous kai hydaresteras epoieito phrenos*): he was not so pusillanimous as to seize the opportunity of their "begging off" in order not to pursue this course of action. It was not the *original* invitation that was from a weak mind but the *subsequent* thought that he might use the angels' refusal to accept the invitation as an excuse to stay out of trouble.

There seems no reason, therefore, to yield to Martin's insistence on neutrality. Neither of the examples cited supports the claim that in the idiomatic construction *harpagma/harpagmos* may refer to an object that is already in the person's possession. In fact, both passages conform to the interpretation proposed here, which is that the expression most naturally speaks of *something presented, perhaps unexpectedly, as an opportunity that might be exploited to that person's advantage.*

The Being Equal to a God/God

Before we work out exactly what to do with this rather nuanced understanding of the *harpagmos* expression, we need to consider the meaning of the object of the seizing: *to einai isa theōi* ("the being equal to a god/God"). We should take care not to read this unthinkingly as a matter of identity or ontology, a condition of *being divine*. The phrase *isa theōi* is adverbial: a person or object typically is treated—honored, reverenced—as though equal to a god;[46] and again we note that in a pagan environment the affirmation, whether positively or negatively made, is characteristic of colorful histories and legends.[47] Fletcher-Louis has recently re-evaluated the use made of the grammatical argument for the interpretation of Phil 2:6, and I will get to his objections shortly. For now, let me list a few examples of the adverbial construction tracked down through the dictionaries and other sources, with enough context added to gain a sense of the manner of narrative.[48]

---

45. Martin, "ἁρπαγμός Revisited," 189.

46. Cf. Murphy-O'Connor, "Anthropology," 39: "The adverb *isa* . . . conveys only that Christ is 'like' God . . . . The force of *Phil.*, II, 6*b* is that Christ did not regard his right to be *treated* as if he were god as something to be used to his own advantage." Also Reumann, *Philippians*, 344, noting especially Job 11:12 LXX: "a mortal, born of woman, is like a desert ass (*isa onōi erēmitēi*)." And Hellerman, "Μορφη Θεου," 789; Hellerman, *Philippians*, 111–13; Focant, "La portée," 285.

47. Reumann notes, too, the relevance of "civic traditions" in which heroes and rulers are honored, which would have been "at home in Philippi" (*Philippians*, 345).

48. For a comprehensive catalogue see Fletcher-Louis, "Being," 595–611, who has

The Meaning of the Adverbial Expression

Odysseus is advised by his son that the people of Ithaca now look upon the suitor Eurymachus "as equal to a god" (*isa theōi*). The adverbial expression qualifies not the *person* Eurymachus but the "beholding" or perception of him (Homer, *Od.* 15.520*).[49] Pythagoras was honored among the Crotonians "in the manner that the gods" (*isa theois*) were honored (Diodorus Siculus, *Bib. hist.* 10.9*). Beare quotes the pseudo-Platonic Axiochus (364 A), who says of Heracles that "he was honoured on an equality with the gods (*isa theois*)." Beare is careful to deny that the Christian encomium is in any way dependent on a pagan myth, but he is inclined to agree with Knox's assessment that Paul "had in fact described Jesus in terms which represented Him in very much the same light as some of the most popular cult-figures of the hellenistic world."[50] The best legislators, according to Iamblichus, were from the school of Pythagoras and "obtained from their citizens honors equal to the gods (*isotheōn timōn*)" (*Vit. Pyth.* 30.172*).[51] Nicolaus of Damascus describes the murder of Julius Caesar: when the bloodied body was carried through the forum, "no one was tearless, seeing the one recently honored even like a god (*isa kai theon*)" (*FGrH* fr. 130.26*). Caesar was deified after his death, but before he died, he had been revered by the populace *as though* he were a god. Philo says of Augustus that "the whole of the rest of the habitable world (*oikoumenē*) had decreed him honours equal to those of the Olympian gods (*isolympious*)" (*Embassy* 149).

According to the second-century AD geographer Pausanias the Corinthians were instructed by the Pythian priestess to discover a certain tree associated with Dionysus and "worship it as though it were the god (*isa tōi theōi*)" (*Descr.* 2.2.6–7*). The priestess does not mean that the tree was actually "equal to" the god or possessed the real attributes of the god but that it was to be afforded the same display of reverence as the wooden image of Dionysus that stood in the marketplace. Another geographer, Dionysius of Byzantium, described Byzas, the son of Keroessa and Poseidon, who gave his name to Byzantium, as "a man honored like a god (*isa theōi*)" (*Anaplus* 24). Justinian required members of the Senate to do obeisance to

---

sorted 149 texts into six syntactical types: attributive statements, predicative statements, the substantival adjective, adverbial statements in which a person is the object of honor, adverbial statements in which he or she is the subject of the verb, and statements in which a person is said to have been "made equal" to a god or God.

49. See also Murphy-O'Connor, "Anthropology," 39.

50. Beare, *Philippians*, 80; Knox, "Divine Hero," 231.

51. In this case the adverbial element is implicit in the adjective; the verbal idea is in *timōn*. See Fletcher-Louis, "Being," 601.

his wife Theodora "as though she were a god" (*isa theōi*) (Procopius, *Secret History* 10.6). The Goths reverenced Totila "equally with God" (*isa theōi*) as long as he was invincible, but when he met with a reverse, "they did not feel it improper to inveigh against him" (Procopius, *History of the Wars* 7.24.29). Finally, the idea is flipped on its head by Arrian, who objects both to the elevation of mortals to the status of gods and to the denigration of the gods "by honouring them in the same way as men (*isa anthrōpois*)" (*Anab.* 4.11.3–4). The gods are not actually reduced to human status but are *treated as though* they have been.

In Phil 2:6 we have the simple *einai* ("to be") rather than any verb of honoring, but the strong pattern of usage suggests that *to einai isa theōi* compresses something like "being regarded as one equal to a god" or "being in a position equal to that of a god."[52] Murphy-O'Connor paraphrases: "Christ did not regard his right to be *treated* as if he were a god as something to be used to his own advantage."[53] That rather conflates "being in the form of a god" and having equal status with a god/God. I suggest that we hold to the thought that a *new opportunity* was unexpectedly presented to the one who was in the form of a god. But the central emphasis is correct: the opportunity is not to *be* a god but to be in the position of a god, to exist as a god exists, and, implicitly, to be revered accordingly.

Jewish Rejection of Divine Kingship

The evidence has been brought forward here primarily in support of the grammatical argument about the adverbial phrase. It evokes a lively pagan background to the idea that a person might be granted godlike status and honors without being or becoming a god.[54] Fletcher-Louis's suggestion that Paul's *to einai isa theōi* ultimately echoes *isa theoisi(n)* in *Iliad*

52. Adverbial expressions with the singular *ison* are also common: Ulysses tells Achilles that the Achaeans will "honor you like a god (*ison . . . theōi*)" (Homer, *Il.* 9.603; cf. 9.616; Euripides, *Hel.* 801). Likewise *ex isou*: Pericles was marveled at by the Athenians "as being like the gods" (*ex isou tois theois*) (Aelius Aristides, *Orat.* 46 244; cf. Aeschines, *Tim.* 1.28; Demosthenes, *Fals. leg.* 280; Dio Cassius, *Roman History* 51.20).

53. Murphy-O'Connor, "Anthropology," 39, his emphasis. Yarbro Collins comments on the decision of the Roman senators to include the name of Caesar "in their hymns equally with those of the gods (ἐξ ἴσου τοῖς θεοῖς)" (Dio Cassius, *Roman History* 51.20): "presumably they did not think that the living Octavian was equal, for example, to Zeus in any strong sense. Their intention apparently was that he should be honored in the same way as the gods are honored because of his beneficial accompaniments" ("How on Earth," 63).

54. See Strait, "Wisdom," 611–12, on the "hybrid iconography" (Galinsky) of the imperial cults.

5.441–2 and would have "sounded archaic, perhaps even Homeric" may be an overstatement, but it serves to underline the distinctively Hellenistic tone of his language.[55] But the *repudiation* of such an elevation in Phil 2:6 brings into consideration, too, the extensive Jewish obverse of the tradition, which protested in the strongest terms against the conferment of such status and honors on humans.[56]

There are some obvious antitypes to the Christ who eschewed equal honors with a god/God. The king of Babylon is condemned for wanting to set his throne "above the stars of God" and be "like the Most High" (Isa 14:13–14 LXX). The Adam-like ruler of Tyre declared himself to be a god but is told, "you are human and not a god, and you rendered your heart as a god's heart" (Ezek 28:2 LXX). Antiochus Epiphanes will be "exalted over every god and will speak strange things against the God of gods," but the hour of his "consummation" will come (Dan 11:36, 45 LXX). Legend has it that at the end of his life he came to the realization that "It is right to be subject to God and for one who is mortal not to think godlike thoughts (*isothea phronein*)" (2 Macc 9:12*).[57] In the New Testament Herod does not reject the acclamation, "The voice of a god, and not of a man!" and pays the price for his vanity (Acts 12:22–23; cf. Josephus, *Ant.* 19:345); and Paul warns of the coming of a "man of lawlessness," who "opposes and exalts himself against everything called god or object of worship, in order to take his seat in the temple of God, exhibiting himself as a god" (2 Thess 2:3–4*). Philo was greatly exercised by Caligula's efforts to style himself as a god (*Embassy* 77, 80, 110, 114). In Sibylline Oracles 5:33–34* the expectation is expressed that Nero "will return, making himself equal to a god (*isazōn theōi*): but (God) will prove that he is not." It seems highly likely that Phil 2:6 was composed with this tradition in mind.

The Argument Against the Ruler Cult Background

Fletcher-Louis has raised a number of objections to the argument—associated with Hellerman in particular—that the adverbial expression points to

55. Fletcher-Louis, "Being," 610.

56. Cf. Reumann, *Philippians*, 345: "2:6 reflects the positive Gk. sense ('like God') and the OT-Jewish view (Jesus did not treat it as *harpagmon*)"; Yarbro Collins and Collins, *King and Messiah*, 114–16; Hellerman, "Μορφη Θεου," 788–89; Jipp, *Christ is King*, 129–32.

57. Fletcher-Louis says that *isothea* is "best explained as an adverbial neuter plural accusative modifying the verb φρονεῖν [*phronein*]" ("Being," 605). No interest is expressed in divine status or cultic honors; rather the king should "not think in a manner equal to God."

an interest in a *status* analogous to that of divine rulers rather than Christ's divine *being*.[58] Briefly: 1) the adjective *isos* is sometimes used for "equality of character, nature, or composition"; 2) it is inappropriate to say that the pre-existent Christ *in heaven* was accorded a *social* status equal to God; 3) for grammatical reasons *to einai isa theōi* must mean something like "being (that is) in a manner equal to God" (emphasis removed)—"an existence characterized by equality with God's own manner of being, *but not a status*"; 4) the argument for status has tended to over-generalize from a wide range of Greek "equality" expressions; 5) sometimes ancient rulers were regarded as actually divine, not merely *accorded* divine status; 6) the critical language of "honor" is missing from Phil 2:6; and 7) there is "nothing in the rest of Paul's letter that means v. 6c has to be a status statement." His proposal instead is that the phrase signifies "a particular kind, or way of being, or of living—a dynamic, incarnational, divine ontology."[59]

It is not clear to me, in the first place, that the passages discussed attribute an *actual* divine character or quality to the person said to be equal to a god/God.[60] Certainly, the focus on status is too narrow for our purposes, but a person may have a "godlike" power, disposition, grace, or beauty without being divine; if a person is said to be "god-equal" or "godlike" it is because he or she is *not* a god. Darius was "godlike" (*isotheos*) because he governed well, but he was not a god (Aeschylus, *Pers.* 852–56). Sappho speaks of the man who sits opposite a beautiful woman, with whom she herself is smitten, as being "equal to the gods" (*isos theoisin*) (Sappho 31.1–2). Fletcher-Louis suggests that he "perhaps has a divine beauty—a quality," but the point surely is that he is blessed, "as fortunate as the gods" (Loeb), not that he shares some intrinsic quality with the gods; it is the woman who is beautiful, not the man. The epigrammatic "What is a god? Exercising power. What is a king? One who is equal with a god" (*P.Heid.* 1716) is taken to mean that "a king is equal to god by virtue of his supreme power—an attribute." But the king is not a god; he is equal to a god *only in the sense that he exercises a comparable power* in the earthly sphere. It is too much to infer that he was thought to possess actual divine power or to share in a divine ontology.

The second objection is irrelevant if the decision is made not in heaven but in the course of Jesus's earthly ministry and if "being equal to a god/God" is not something already possessed but an opportunity that might be seized. We are working towards a reconstruction of the *harpagmos*

58. Fletcher-Louis, "Being," 587–95.

59. Fletcher-Louis, "Being," 581.

60. Fletcher-Louis, "Being," 596–99.

incident in which what status and authority he would have, how he would be honored among the nations, without actually—ontologically—being a god/God, are very much to the point.

Thirdly, indeed, *isa theōi* is adverbial and cannot be construed as an adjectival predicate with *einai*; but *being in the manner of a god* does not need to be understood ontologically, particularly if it is given the sort of dynamic or active sense that Fletcher-Louis thinks it should have in Phil 2:6. He cites as key evidence *Homeric Hymns* 5 (To Aphrodite) 200–214*. The flaxen-haired youth Ganymede, one of those mortals "close to the gods in appearance and stature," has been seized (*hērpasen*) by Zeus to serve drinks in his house, and his grieving father is assured that he "is immortal and ageless in a manner equal to the gods (*isa theoisin*)." The issue is not how Ganymede is perceived or honored, but *isa theoisin* preserves the ontological distinction: only *in the particular respect of the immortality granted to him in order to fulfil his task* does he have a godlike existence.[61] Likewise, Jesus was presented with the opportunity to enjoy an existence or position which *in some particular respect*, which we will come to, would have been considered on a par with the life of the gods.

The diversity of grammatical form, fourthly, would appear to demonstrate chiefly that comparison with the gods was a popular, lively, and well-worked theme. The examples given of the specific adverbial construction with the god-equal person as the subject of the verb, other than the Ganymede story, are of the type: a person thinks, feels, or acts in a manner equal to the gods.[62] Much is made of the fact that Antiochus Epiphanes thought and planned to act as though he were equal to the one true God (*isothea*), consistent with a well-established Hellenistic tradition traceable back to Homer (2 Macc 9:12). There is no suggestion of a "claim to a divine status or God-equal cultic honours," but this does not obviate the argument that Jesus was presented with the opportunity to attain a god-equal position as a king, and to think and act as such. At the end of his life, Antiochus comes to the belated realization that to "think godlike thoughts" is what a mortal does; he would not have expressed it in such terms if his intention had been to affirm an essential divinity.

The fifth objection is difficult to assess because it is not clearly indicated which of the 149 texts surveyed presuppose the belief that rulers were sometimes divine "in identity, nature, and conduct, not just in

---

61. According to Fletcher-Louis, the adverbial "equal to the gods" modifies *eoi* (from *eimi*) and therefore signifies a "god-equal manner of existence" ("Being," 603). More accurately, *isa theoisin* modifies "immortal and ageless": it is not Ganymede's "life" that is "equal to the gods" but his immortality.

62. Fletcher-Louis, "Being," 602–10.

status."[63] I think that we can discount the *P.Heid.* 1716 epigram. Appeal is later made, in support of a "divine nature" interpretation of Phil 2:6, to Musonius Rufus, *That Kings Should Also Study Philosophy* 8.8, but the "superior nature" with which a king is endowed is juxtaposed with a good education and the possession of the best human virtues, which hardly suggests that a divine nature is in view.[64] The last two criticisms are correct but beside the point if the implicit narrative that pivots around the opportunity to attain a god-equal existence has more to do with the exercise of sovereignty and rule (cf. Phil 2:9–11) than with the status and honor that went with it. Ganymede was equal to the gods because, and inasmuch as, he had been granted immortality; status and honor may then have followed, but that is not the point of the story.

I suggest, therefore, that we do not have to abandon the view that the "being equal to God" is explained by appeal to a popular motif best illustrated by stories of the hubris of rulers such as Antiochus Epiphanes: a person is treated, or expects to be treated, as one who has a standing or authority equal to that of a god.[65] But we do need to explore the narrative setting of Jesus' decision not to exploit the opportunity presented to him.

The Opportunity Presented in the Wilderness

The Articular Infinitive

At this point, the article with the infinitive (*to einai*, "the being") becomes a matter of interest. According to Wright, the article refers back epexegetically to "being in the form of God" with the result that the two expressions are more or less synonymous—"*this* divine equality."[66] Daniel Wallace

63. Fletcher-Louis, "Being," 594. Levene, "Defining the Divine," is referenced in a footnote (594n47), but Levene's argument for a real rather than a relative status distinction *in Rome* between humans and gods has nothing to say about the phrase *to einai isa theōi* or the Latin equivalent.

64. Fletcher-Louis, "Being," 618–19n124.

65. In an attempt to bring "Platonic ontology" into the equation, principally as a distinction between "being" and "becoming," Fletcher-Louis says that the statement in verse 6c "denotes an innate, pre-incarnate, or metaphysical identity and way of being, not one that is earned, acquired, ascribed, or inherited" ("Being," 618). But the *harpagmos* clause must introduce the possibility of acquisition, either before or after the decision, which seems also to make the whole "Platonic ontology" argument redundant.

66. Wright, *Climax*, 83 (emphasis added); cf. O'Brien, *Philippians*, 216; Fee, *Philippians*, 207; Hawthorne and Martin, *Philippians*, 114–15: "The definite article in τὸ εἶναι [*to einai*], 'the being,' implies that this second expression is closely connected with the first; for a function of the definite article here is to point back to something previously mentioned . . . ." Also Gorman, "Form of God," 155; Hellerman, *Honor*, 134; Keown,

disagrees: "As attractive as this view may be theologically, it has a weak basis grammatically. The infinitive is the object and the anarthrous term, ἁρπαγμός [*harpagmos*], is the complement. The most natural reason for the article with the infinitive is simply to mark it out as the object."[67]

Examples of the construction with *hēgeisthai* and an articular infinitive object abound, and it is apparent that the object *may* have reference back to something that has already occurred or is otherwise presupposed in the narrative. But while this may provide the *occasion* for the statement, it does not account grammatically for the definite article. Josephus says that some Jews, offended by Herod's determination to impose Hellenistic customs, "considered the destroying (*to kataluesthai . . . hēgoumenoi*) of ancestral things the beginning (*archēn*) of great evils" (*Ant.* 15:281*).[68] In this case, *to kataluesthai* with the article is the object, *archēn* without the article is the complement. They had in mind the recent building of theatres and introduction of Greek games (15.267–76), but the sentiment expressed is the general one: it was a matter of principle for devout Jews that the abandonment of ancestral custom would lead to catastrophe. There is a relevant narrative context, therefore, but there is no need to attribute a specific anaphoric function to the article.

One example of the articular infinitive with *hēgeisthai* is of particular interest for us. According to Josephus, it was Nimrod who persuaded the post-flood generation to abandon the task of cultivating the whole earth and to construct the tower of Babel. He "stirred them up to insolence and contempt of God," and as a result the "multitude was willing to obey the decrees of Nimrod, considering it slavery to yield to God (*douleian hēgoumenoi to eikein tōi theōi*)" (*Ant.* 1:113–15*).

This constitutes a rather close grammatical parallel to Paul's *ouch harpagmon hēgēsato to einai isa theōi*, but it is also thematically relevant. Nimrod does not aspire to a godlike mode of being, but the whole enterprise is driven by an ambition to get the better of God: he was determined to avenge himself on God for having destroyed their forefathers in the flood. So Nimrod and his people considered it slavery to yield to God, and Nimrod exalted himself

---

Philippians 1:1—2:18, 393. On the anaphoric article see BDF §399. Dunn thinks that the article refers to the familiar motif of the "Adamic temptation 'to be like God'" (*Theology of Paul*, 285n89). This is nearer the mark.

67. Wallace, *Grammar*, 220. Burke says that "the article with the infinitive functions primarily as a syntactical marker" ("Articular Infinitive," 260); also Hellerman, "Μορφη Θεου," 788n23; and Focant, "La portée," 286. For a detailed assessment see Weymouth, "Christ-Story," 260–76.

68. The construction is also found in Let. Aris. 124; Philo, *Confusion* 160; *Abraham* 258; *Sacrifices* 50; Josephus, *Ant.* 4:187; 11:48; 18:363; *J.W.* 1:361.

against God. According to Philo, "Moses calls the seat of Nimrod's kingdom Babylon" (*Giants* 66). He was the archetypal opponent of God: the impious man who contends against God is spoken of proverbially "as a second Nimrod" (*QG* 2 82). Jesus is the opposite. He did not consider being equal to a god/God an opportunity to be seized and instead humbled himself, taking the form of a slave. If in the first instance the matter of principle (it is slavery to yield to God) alludes to the revolt on the plain of Shinar that resulted in the construction of the tower, the obvious narrative reference in Phil 2:6 would be to the tradition of Satan's proposition, in the wilderness, to give Jesus the authority and glory of the kingdoms of the *oikoumenē*, which had been handed over to him, if Jesus would simply "worship before" him (Luke 4:6–7; cf. Matt 4:8–9). The articular expression *to einai isa theōi* then would indeed be in this broader sense anaphoric; but it would refer back not to the being *en morphēi theou*, which in any case is incompatible with the understanding of the *harpagmos* clause developed here, but to the remembered incident when *the* opportunity to be equal to a god—perhaps even to the God of Israel—was put before Jesus by Satan.

A Short Cut to Godlike Power

If "being in the form of a god" reflects a peculiarly Greek perspective on the wonder-working Jewish hero, then we have no reason to imagine something akin to the opportunity presented to Satan himself in the heavenly court in Job 1:6–12. The lexicological evidence has suggested quite strongly that the idiomatic expression belongs not to apocalyptic or metaphysical discourse but to animated, down-to-earth storytelling, with or without the vulgar connotations. It typically captures a decisive moment in a drama, whether that drama is an Old Testament legend, a romantic adventure, an account of martyrdom or political dealings, or the parable of a freed slave. Vollenweider's argument about genre cuts both ways. The testing in the wilderness is the only known moment when Jesus chose to reject something that could, on biblical terms, be construed as being godlike.[69] It exactly fits the literary and linguistic requirements of the idiomatic

---

69. Brown proposes that "the temptation 'to be like God' is another form of the tradition preserved in the temptation narratives of Matt. and Luke. It also echoes charges that Jesus was putting himself in God's place (Mark 2:8; John 5:18), and that he was a seducer empowered by an alien deity (Matt. 10:24; 12:24; Mark 3:22; Luke 11:15; cf. Lev. 20:27; CD 12:2–3)" ("*Kyrios* Jesus Revisited," 27–28). The view was also espoused by J. Ross, "ἁρπαγμός, Phil ii.6," *JTS* 10 (1909), 573 (noted by Keown, *Philippians 1:1–2:18*, 395).

expression, which expects a *timely opportunity presented*, not the exploitation of an existing condition or possession.[70]

Colin Brown has proposed a reading along these lines. He argues that "the image/Adam allusion should be recognized," but he thinks that *en morphēi theou* develops the idea of being "in the image of God" in the direction of being a *visible* manifestation of God on earth. In that case, the obvious background to the temptation to "be like God" is the testing of Jesus in the wilderness—the offer of Adam's original dominion in return for "obeisance to Satan."[71] The "being in the form of God," therefore, may be the counterpart to "if you are the Son of God," on the grounds that "image of God" connotes "kingship and the role of God's representative." Brown notes further that in Luke's narrative, between the pronouncement about the "beloved Son" at Jesus's baptism and the testing of the Son of God in the wilderness, we have a genealogy that goes back all the way to "Adam, the son of God." Given the charge that Jesus had entered into a pact with Satan or Beelzebul (Matt 10:25; 12:24; Mark 3:22; Luke 11:15), the encomium can be understood as a direct defense against such accusations: "Jesus did not seek to exploit his status and authority to be 'like God' in the manner to which Adam succumbed and to which Satan sought to induce him. Nor was he guilty of the charges levelled against him."

This needs some amendment, however. The original dominion of Adam was over living creatures (Gen 1:26, 28; cf. Ps 8:6–8). What Satan offers Jesus is rule over the kingdoms of the Greek-Roman *oikoumenē* (Luke 4:5) or of the "world" (Matt 4:8). This is political and historical, not creational and cosmic. It brings to mind Daniel's account of the transference of sovereignty over the nations from the beast-kingdom to the "one like a son of man," representing in some capacity the "holy people of the Most High" (Dan 7:13–14, 27 LXX). But the proposition also anticipates, in a "faint echo,"[72] the realization of the divine promise of Ps 2:7–8: "I will tell of the decree: The LORD said to me, 'You are my Son; today I have begotten you. Ask of me, and I will make the nations your heritage, and the ends of the earth your possession.'"

Daniel's account of the fourth and most destructive beast is brought up to date in the vision of Rev 13. John sees a beast emerging from the sea "with

70. I find it remarkable that Martin can interpret the *harpagmos* clause with reference to Jesus's decision to "forgo the opportunity to use a prize that is held out in prospect" or the "opportunity for advancement that lay in his power" and even identify the dilemma as "temptation" (*Hymn of Christ*, lxix), and yet not see the connection with the temptation in the wilderness.

71. Brown, "*Kyrios* Jesus Revisited," 27–28.

72. Green, *Luke*, 194.

ten horns and seven heads, with ten diadems on its horns and blasphemous names on its heads," part leopard, part bear, part lion. The dragon, which is "that ancient serpent, who is called the devil and Satan, the deceiver of the whole *oikoumenēn*," the accuser of believers, has given his power, authority and great throne to the beast, making it indomitable (Rev 12:9-10; 13:1-4). The beast, of course, is Rome; one of the horns was Caligula, another Nero, presumably the one with the "mortal wound."[73] It is just this power, authority, and great throne that is offered, in effect, to Jesus in the wilderness. He is given the opportunity to emulate the pagan king who would make himself equal to God and exercise a brutal, exploitative beast-like rule over the nations of the *oikoumenē*. He does not take advantage of the opportunity. He will usurp Caesar's honor and rule—he will inherit the nations, he will be confessed as Lord—by other means.[74]

Three more stories, two from Josephus, one from another romantic novel, help to bring out the energy and direction—and something of the polemical force—of the narrative tradition that has been so artfully compressed into this expression of Jesus's refusal to take the way of selfish ambition and vainglory put before him by Satan.

The first two briefly illustrate the suitability of the *harpazō* word-group in relation to the pursuit of political ambitions. Antipater complains that Archelaus is seeking the "shadow" of kingship, the substance (*sōma*) of which he has already "seized (*hērpasen*) for himself" (Josephus, *J.W.* 2:28).[75] The seizure of kingship is not so far removed from seizing or taking advantage of *the opportunity of kingship that has been presented*. Secondly, we have an intensified form of *harpazō* in this sarcastic rebuke to a priest in another romantic novel, *The Adventures of Leucippe and Clitophon*: "Better

73. Nero committed suicide by driving a "dagger into his throat" (Suetonius *Nero* 49.3-4). Victorinus identified this head with Nero (*Comm. Apoc.* XIII and XVII.3). "The healing of the mortal wound is probably an allusion to the legend of the return of Nero" (Aune, *Revelation 6-16*, 736-37).

74. The relation between divine form and kingship is illustrated in a third- or second-century BC treatise attributed to Diotogenes: "the king who has an absolute rulership, and is himself Animate Law, has been metamorphosed (*pareschēmatistai*) into a deity among men" (Stobaeus, *Anth.* 4.7.61). Having rejected such a model of kingship, Jesus is "found in *schēmati* as a man" (Phil 2:7). For the quotation and discussion see Litwa, "Deification," 12.

75. The contrast here between "shadow" and "body" is similar to that between "form" and equality in Phil 2:6. Philo's account of the appointment of Moses also bears comparison: he received "authority and kingdom" over them "not having gained it like some men who have forced their way to power and supremacy by force of arms and intrigue . . . , but having been appointed for the sake of his virtue and excellence . . . ; and, also, because God, who loves virtue, and piety, and excellence, gave him his authority as a well-deserved reward" (*Moses* 1 148).

still, claim a position above mankind altogether; have worship paid to you along with Artemis, for it is her honour that you have usurped (*exērpasas*)" (Achilles Tatius, *Leuc. Clit.* 8.8.8).[76] By *snatching* Artemis's honor from her the priest has, in the eyes of the malevolent Thersander, made himself equal to the goddess. Jesus refused to usurp by impious means a godlike rule that would bring him great worldly honor.

The third—and more intriguing—passage is Josephus's account of the attempted seduction of Joseph by the wife of Potiphar (*Ant.* 2:41–42*). She has fallen in love with him not least because of his "beautiful form" (*eumorphian*) and determines to seduce him, assuming that, being in the *schēma* of a slave, "he would consider it a stroke of good fortune (*eutychēma*) that his mistress should proposition him." She does not reckon, of course, with his high moral character. So we have a person of beautiful *morphē*, who is nevertheless in the position of a slave, who is unexpectedly presented with an alluring opportunity. The construction with *hēgeomai* and the articular infinitive is close to Paul's statement if *harpagmon hēgeomai* is a rough idiomatic equivalent to *eutychēma hēgeomai*. The *temptress* imagined that Joseph would consider the proposition a piece of good fortune. Satan thought that Jesus might consider "being like a god/God" a golden opportunity to be seized. The well-formed Joseph is already a slave—this is not something that he chooses; but otherwise the narrative parallelism is remarkable. The compact drama, which may well have been popular with Hellenistic-Jewish moralists and familiar to the author of the encomium, provides an efficient literary model for a telling of the story about Jesus, on Hellenistic terms, that could be used—whatever else is going on—for a precise ethical purpose: "Do nothing from selfish ambition or vainglory, but . . . have this mind among yourselves . . . " (Phil 2:3, 5*).

He Emptied Himself

We still have to explain, of course, the transition from verse 6 to verse 7. In the purview of the encomium the one now confessed and acclaimed as exalted Lord was, to begin with, not the Son sent to redeem those under the Law but a wonderworker who appeared to the pagan mind to have been "in the form of a god." This perception already invites various plausible narrative developments—the divine man is honored, the god is offered sacrifices. But what the apostolic tradition remembers is that the Spirit-endowed Jesus immediately faced a dilemma that would have been construed in quite different ways by pagans and Jews. In the testing in the wilderness he was

---

76. See Vollenweider, "Der „Raub"," 278.

"fortuitously" presented with the opportunity to acquire a status equal to that of a god/God, in the manner of pagan rulers from the king of Babylon and the prince of Tyre to Augustus and Caligula. To gentiles the prospect was commonplace; to Jews it was an abomination.

Jesus turned the opportunity down, citing Deut 6:13 (Luke 4:8). It is convenient for my overall argument that this verse belongs to the immediate development of the Shema. The Lord our God is one Lord, therefore love the Lord your God with your whole mind, etc., and when you enter the land, do not go after other gods. "The Lord your God you shall fear, and him you shall serve, and to him you shall cling, and by his name you shall swear" (LXX). As a summary of the drama of the charismatic demagogue who rejects a blasphemous ambition out of loyalty to the Lord his God and chooses the way of disgrace and suffering, the first part of the encomium is an affirmation of the Shema on its original terms. In the second paragraph, however, a radically new possibility is entertained. *At some point in the future* people will not swear by God's name, but it will be at the name of Jesus that "every knee shall bow and every tongue shall acknowledge God" (Isa 45:23 LXX), confessing Jesus as Lord to the glory of God the Father, finally bringing about the comprehensive victory over pagan idolatry foreseen in Isa 45:14–25.

In the meantime, Luke says that when the devil had finished testing Jesus, he "departed from him until an opportune time" (Luke 4:13), and both Peter's rebuke and Jesus's wavering in Gethsemane can be seen as revisiting the original "temptation," if not the opportunity that it presented. His whole ministry was a determined and difficult living out of the consequences of the decision made in the wilderness. In that respect, we do not have to think in terms of a strict narrative sequence from being in the form of a god, to rejecting Satan's enticing proposition, to taking the form of a slave. But "form of a god" and "form of a slave" are not mutually compatible modes of existence: having the form of a slave is not a way of being in the form of a god.[77] At some point in his ministry Jesus *lost* the outward appearance of a god; he "emptied himself" and assumed the outward appearance of a slave. The emphasis is less on the "powerful, divinely beautiful male" body than on charisma, wisdom, and marvelous works, but Shaner is right in this much: "the *body* of a god takes on one bodily shape and the *body* of a slave takes on a different shape." There is in the encomium an argument "about the visual form of Christ's body."[78]

77. Against Bockmuehl, *Philippians*, 133–34; Gorman, "Form of God," 157; Focant, "La portée," 286: the "revolutionary" revelation is that the "divine condition . . . expresses itself in humanity and takes the condition of a slave."

78. Shaner, "Rape and Robbery," 361. Being like a divine emperor is *what Jesus turns*

Whether the "slave" is in some sense, at some remove, the "servant" (*pais*) of Isa 52:13—53:12 remains an open question.[79] We should note the attention paid to the *appearance* of Isaiah's servant. Foreign peoples and kings would be shocked by his shameful "appearance" (*eidos*); he had no "form (*eidos*) or glory," no "form (*eidos*) or beauty" (Isa 52:14—53:2 LXX).[80] Does this partly account for the gentile perspective of Phil 2:6–8? The peoples and authorities of the Greek-Roman world look on this god-like figure turned slave, subjected to a dehumanizing execution, and are frankly shocked by his "outward appearance," disturbed by the trans-*form*-ation. But the slave is not the servant-child (*pais*); rather, he seems now to be a degraded version of the son sent to the vineyard of Israel to do the work—and suffer the fate—of a prophet. The slave is what the charismatic servant-child *became*. Arguably, Jer 7:25–26 LXX has influenced Paul's language: "I have also sent out all my *slaves* (*doulous*) the prophets to you . . . , and they did not obey me."

The suggestion that "he emptied himself" echoes "he poured out his soul to death" (Isa 53:12) is also attractive, but in the encomium it precedes taking the form of a slave and does not appear to stand as a metaphor for death.[81] Another proposal may connect better with the narrative that has emerged so far. Philo says that Moses "led away (his people) from the harm-ful customs of the cities into the wilderness that he might empty (*kenōsei*) their souls of unrighteous deeds" (*Decalogue* 13).[82] We would have to sup-pose that "emptying the soul" in the desert was a familiar religious trope, but we may imagine that the physical and spiritual trial was the means by which Jesus *emptied himself* of the "selfish ambition" (*eritheian*), "vainglory" (*kenodoxian*), and self-interest that now distracts the Philippians from their

---

down, not what he has when "in the form of a god."

79. For discussion of the relation between Phil 2:7 and the description of the ser-vant in Isa 52:13—53:12 see Cerfaux, *Christ*, 377–82; Jeremias, "Zu Phil 2:7"; Talbert, "Problem," 152–53; Murphy-O'Connor, "Anthropology," 40–41; O'Brien, *Philippians*, 220, 268–71; Kuschel, *Before All Time*, 253–55; Bockmuehl, "Form of God," 12–13; Hurst, "Preexistence," 87; Hamerton-Kelly, *Pre-Existence*, 159; Hawthorne and Martin, *Philippians*, 119; Keown, *Philippians 1:1–2:18*, 355–56, 405–6.

80. Aquila has *horasis autou, kai morphē autou* in Isa 53:14 for the LXX *to eidos sou kai hē doxa sou*. In this context "glory" is to be understood as a reference to the physi-cal beauty and nobility of a person; cf. the *morphē* that Tobit had in the eyes of king Enemessaros (Tob 1:12–13).

81. See, for example, Jeremias, "Zu Phil 2:7," 183–84; Martin, *Hymn of Christ*, 182–83; Keown, *Philippians 1:1–2:18*, 405–6.

82. Cf. Philo, *Sacrifices* 50: the shepherd Moses led his passions like sheep "from the tumultuous vexations of political affairs into the desert, for the purpose of avoiding all temptation to injustice."

calling (Phil 2:3–4).[83] In Paul *eritheia* normally has the general sense of "strife, contentiousness" (Rom 2:8; 2 Cor 12:20; Gal 5:20; Phil 1:17; cf. Jas 3:14, 16), but before the New Testament it is found only in Aristotle, where it "denotes a self-seeking pursuit of political office by unfair means."[84] Philo says that Caligula "ought not to be likened to any god, and not even to any demi-god . . . ; but appetite as it seems is a blind thing, and especially so when it takes to itself vain-gloriousness (*kenodoxian*) and ambition in conjunction with the greatest power" (*Embassy* 114). The terms lose their edge somewhat in the parenetic setting of Paul's letter, but the political connotations would be entirely appropriate in the language domain of a post-pagan, Hellenistic-Christian reflection on the earthly pre-existence of the exalted Lord who would eventually rule the nations. Jesus emptied himself of the corrupting passions that characterized pagan government.

Being Human

If so far only the career of the earthly Jesus has been in view, however, why do we have such a strong emphasis on his being human in Phil 2:7–8*: "in likeness of humans . . . in the characteristic appearance (*schēmati*) of a human person"?[85] We saw in our discussion of Gal 4:4 that the aorist participle *genomenos* need only mean that he *was* or lived prior to the present moment; it neither is a reference to the event of his birth nor speaks of his *becoming* human.[86] Rather, "having been in the likeness of human persons" underlines the point that the one now known and encountered through the Spirit as the transcendent heavenly Lord, who appeared for a while to be in the form of a god, was indeed only another concrete instance of ordinary

83. Cf. Keown, *Philippians 1:1–2:18*, 401: "Rather than seek personal glory, esteem, status, and honor by the pursuit of self-aggrandizement, the Philippians are to emulate the Christ, who emptied himself of all such claims."

84. BDAG s.v. ἐριθεία, 392. In the Loeb edition *eritheia* is translated "election intrigue" (Aristotle, *Pol.* 5.2 1302b5; 1303a16).

85. Cf. Strimple, "Philippians 2:5–11," 258.

86. Against Dunn, "Preexistence," 78; Loke, *Origin*, 32. Holloway says that *ginomai en* must speak of "entry into a new condition" (*Philippians*, 123). He gives the example of L.A.E. 17:1: "Then Satan appeared in the form (*eidei*) of an angel and sang hymns to God, just as (do) the angels" (Evans). If so, then the clause underlines the contrast between being in the form of a god and taking, being transformed into, the form of a slave. A slave is never godlike, merely human. But the meaning "be changed into a new condition" is not inevitable. To take a couple of examples from the same paragraph in BDAG, Paul says, according to Luke: "It happened that . . . I was in a trance" (*Egeneto . . . genesthai me en ekstasei*) (Acts 22:17*); similarly, John says, "I was in the Spirit *egenomēn en pneumati* on the Lord's day" (Rev 1:10). In both cases the aorist may be taken as constative rather than as actually signifying the process of becoming.

humanity. Perhaps we are to hear an inversion of the axiomatic "God is not as a man"—the "principal fact which ought to be remembered concerning God," according to Philo.[87] Jesus comes to be found no longer in the form of a god but *as a man*. We may also recall the flatterers of Herod Agrippa, who cried out, "calling him a god, 'Be well disposed to us'; and saying, 'If indeed until now we feared you *as a man*, henceforth we confess you as superior to mortal nature" (Josephus, *Ant.* 19:345*, emphasis added). Perhaps the Philippians encomium would have been heard by some as an ironic take on just this sort of two-stage adulation. In any case, once Jesus chose not to pursue the path of divine kingship, with all the authority and glory that went with it (cf. Matt 4:8; Luke 4:6), once he dropped the semblance of a super-human wonderworker, he was found to have the characteristic identity and frailty of a human person, and in that condition humbled himself and was obedient to the point of death on a Roman cross.[88]

Who Wrote It?

A speculative afterthought. The second part of the encomium is undoubtedly Jewish in its language and thought. My argument has been, however, that the first paragraph captures, in a distinctly Hellenistic idiom, something of the perspective of gentiles who have "turned to God from idols to serve the living and true God, and to wait for his Son from heaven, whom he raised from the dead, Jesus who delivers us from the wrath to come" (1 Thess 1:9–10). How might they have looked back on the perhaps thinly and ambiguously delineated earthly life of this Son? The acclamation of Paul and Barnabas at Lystra as gods who "have come down to us in the likeness of men" does not explain everything, but it may have been a paradigmatic experience. According to Luke, Paul will pass through Lystra again after the Jerusalem council, before directly crossing to Philippi in Macedonia. On this occasion he picks up the gifted, young disciple Timothy, whose mother was a Jewish believer, his father a Greek (Acts 16:1–3). Timothy is named as a co-sender of the letter to the Philippians—like Paul, a "slave" of Christ. We may

---

87. Philo, *Sacrifices* 94; *Unchangeable* 53, 62, 69; *Drunkenness* 30; *Confusion* 98; *Migration* 42; *Dreams* 1 237; *Moses* 1 283; *Decalogue* 32; cf. Num 23:19; Jdt 8:16; T. Jos. 2:5.

88. According to Lohmeyer, *schēmati heuretheis hōs anthrōpos* is impossible in Greek, and *hōs anthrōpos* translates the Aramaic *kbar ᵓenash* in Dan 7:13 (see Brown, "*Kyrios* Jesus Revisited," 13; Hamerton-Kelly, *Pre-Existence*, 159). If this is correct (the argument is rejected by O'Brien [*Philippians*, 227n147] and Reumann [*Philippians*, 351]), the latent narrative of Phil 2:6–8 would run through to the disclosure that Jesus is the Son of Man who must suffer many things before he comes in the glory of his Father (Mark 8:31—9:1).

conjecture, at least, that the uncircumcised half-Greek, half-Jewish Timothy, or someone like him, had a hand in the composition of this half-Greek,
half-Jewish panegyric. Perhaps the production of compositions celebrating
Christ was the "gift," or an element of the gift, confirmed by prophecy and
imparted by the laying on of hands, that he is urged not to neglect in 1 Tim
4:14 (cf. 2 Tim 1:6). Even if not the work of Paul, the Pastoral Letters may
accurately recall such details about Timothy. He is told to "practice (*meleta*)
these things," and the verb *melō* features prominently in the Psalms and
Wisdom literature with the sense "meditate upon." These lines, for example,
are suggestive: "May those who want my vindication rejoice and be glad,
and let those who want the peace of his slave say ever more, 'Let the Lord be
magnified.' And my tongue shall declaim (*meletēsei*) your righteousness, all
day long your commendation" (Ps 34:27–28 LXX). In this case, the psalmist
meditates upon and gives voice to his own vindication as a "slave" and the
praise of God as *kyrios*, but it would be natural to have a "psalmist" meditate
upon the vindication of another "slave" and his exaltation as "Lord"—to the
commendation of the God of Israel.

Since Colossians was also from Paul and Timothy (Col 1:1), the further possibility arises that Timothy had a hand in the composition of our
final passage—the Christ encomium of Col 1:15–20, an excellent example
of letting "the word of the Christ dwell in you richly, in all wisdom teaching
and warning one another, in psalms, hymns, spiritual songs" (Col 3:16*; cf.
1 Cor 14:26). Anyway, that is where we head next.

9

The Colossians Encomium and the Beginning of a New World Order

THE CHRIST ENCOMIUM OF Col 1:15–20 is directly connected to the preceding prayer ("... the Son of his love, in whom we have redemption ..., who is image of the invisible God ..."), and this prayer is *oriented firmly towards a future outcome*. The message of the gospel which they received was centrally that there was a "hope stored away for you in the heavens" (Col 1:5*). This was not the hope of *going to heaven*, whatever the personal implications may have been; it was the hope, made certain by God, that eventually the "wrath of God" would come upon a religiously and morally bankrupt pagan order, Christ would be revealed to the world, and they would be vindicated for their belief in this stunning bouleversement (3:4–6).[1] Because this day may have been some way off, Paul—let us say—prays that they will be strengthened "for all endurance and patience with joy," being thankful that they have been qualified to share in the future inheritance (1:9–12*; cf. Eph 1:11–14). Their expectation, in other words, was to inherit the world to come (cf. Rom 4:13). It was in anticipation of this outcome that God delivered them from the authority of darkness and "removed" (*metestēsen*) them into the "kingdom of his beloved Son," in whom they have "the redemption, the forgiveness of sins" (Col 1:14). We have a straightforward analogy in Josephus: the Assyrian king Tiglath-Pileser took the Israelites captive and "transplanted (*metestēsen*) them into his own kingdom" (*Ant.* 9:235). The difference is that the "saints and faithful brothers" in Colossae have been

---

1. Cf. Barth and Blanke, *Colossians*, 155: "Col does not offer a determination for conceptualizing 'heaven' as a place in which hope would fulfill itself after death .... Rather, it deals with the place where the Messiah 'sits at the right hand of God.'" Gen 49:10 LXX is a close parallel: "A ruler shall not be wanting from Judah ... until the things stored up (*ta apokeimena*) for him come, and he is the expectation of nations" (NETS modified). But note the reference in 2 Macc 12:45 to "the splendid reward that is laid up (*apokeimenon*) for those who fall asleep in godliness."

transferred into a kingdom-in-waiting, a presumptive kingdom. But it will be a *kingdom* nevertheless.

The phrase "Son of his love" (*tou huiou tēs agapēs autou*) may be an allusion to "Ephraim my beloved son (*huios agapētos . . . emoi*)," who is heard mourning, who will be returned to the land (Jer 38:20 LXX = 31:20 MT; cf. 4Q475 f1:7), especially in view of the earlier statement about "Ephraim my firstborn" going with weeping into exile (Jer 38:9* LXX). In Psalms of Solomon the persecuted righteous Jew is being disciplined as a "son of love" (*huion agapēseōs*), who is also the "firstborn" (*prōtotokou*) (Pss. Sol. 13:9; cf. 18:3–4).[2] Israel is especially loved when under stress and is given assurance of restoration. Given the prominence of the kingdom motif in Col 1:13–14, however, the characteristic New Testament use of Ps 2:7–9 is likely to be pertinent: the Son "begotten" on the day of his resurrection will inherit and rule over the nations (cf. Acts 13:33; Rom 1:4; 15:12; Heb 1:5; 5:5; Rev 2:27; 12:5; 19:15). If the heavenly announcements regarding the "beloved Son" in the Gospels are also to be heard (Matt 3:17; 17:5; and parallels), then the point would be that the anointed Son who was sent as a servant to Israel has now received (or perhaps will receive) the inheritance of the kingdom, which was his by right. This Son is then eulogized in the lines that follow.

At its simplest structural level the encomium falls into two balanced paragraphs, each consisting of a compressed description of the Son and a longer explanatory statement beginning with "because" (*hoti*).[3] The first paragraph presents the Son in relation to "all things," the second in relation to the church; in both paragraphs he is "firstborn" (*prōtotokos*), and the repetition gives the word an obvious thematic prominence.[4] The possibility that pre-existence is being attributed to the Son arises at three points.[5] First, does "image of the invisible God" identify the Son with some eternal aspect of the divine, perhaps the wisdom of God? Secondly, should "firstborn of every

2. In Pss. Sol. 18:4 the reference is to Israel: "Your discipline for us (is) as (for) a firstborn son (*huion prōtotokon*), an only child (*monogenē*), to divert the perceptive person from unintentional sins."

3. Cf. Lohse, *Colossians and Philemon*, 41–45. Analyses that assume that the passage is hymnic are inevitably more complex, requiring perhaps a middle stanza (Barth and Blanke, *Colossians*, 227–32; Bruce, *Colossians*, 54–57) or excisions. See also Wright, *Climax*, 99–106.

4. Cf. Michaelis, "πρῶτος," 879: "it is surprising that a rare NT word like πρωτότοκος should occur twice in Col. 1:15–20, and that, coming each time in the second statement of the two parts of the hymn, it should help to determine the structure, so that the two occurrences are not unrelated"; and McKnight, *Colossians*, 144.

5. Kuschel argues that in this post-Pauline text we have for the first time in the New Testament "a bold and audacious protological confession" regarding Christ (*Before All Time*, 337); cf. Fee, *Christology*, 504–5.

creature" or "of all creation" be understood in temporal terms—firstborn in time, *before* all creation? Thirdly, is the creation of all things "in him . . . through him and for him" a reference to the original act of creation, with Christ as the pre-existent Son taking over the function of wisdom in Jewish thought? Did Christ, like wisdom, exist "before all things" in time?

The Image of the Invisible God

The expression "image (*eikōn*) of the invisible God" has numerous points of contact with Hellenistic-Jewish thought, which can be sorted into two broad categories. On the one hand, an image may convey something of the unseen nature of God, either abstractly as a lively wisdom or concretely in the form of humanity.[6] On the other, an image may be a false representation of divinity.

A person is in the "image" of the creator as a son is in the "image" of his father (Gen 1:27; 5:1–3; 9:6 LXX; Wis 2:23; Sir 17:3). Humanity, according to Philo, having been granted supremacy over all earthly creatures in imitation of the power of God, is "a visible image of the invisible nature" (*Moses* 2 65*). But because the human person is rational, the image is also readily equated with the wisdom of God, which is a "reflection of eternal light and a spotless mirror of the activity of God and an image (*eikōn*) of his goodness" (Wis 7:25–26). Philo says that the "ethereal and heavenly wisdom" is variously called "beginning and image (*archēn kai eikona*) and vision of God" (*Alleg. Interp.* 1 43*). Divine reason or the Logos is the image of the invisible God (*Confusion* 97; *Dreams* 1 239) stamped upon the soul (*Creation* 31, 69; *Worse* 86; *Planting* 18; *QG* 1 4, 8). The intersection of sonship and wisdom themes in the "image" motif is remarkably illustrated in a passage in which Philo contrasts the polytheistic "sons of men," who are ignorant of "the one Creator and Father of all things," with those whom Moses calls "sons of God" (*Confusion* 144–47). He doubts that anyone yet qualifies to be designated a "son of God" in this regard, but men should strive nevertheless to be adorned "according to his first-born (*prōtogonon*) word, the eldest of his angels." In other words, people are not fit to be called children of God himself but may at least be known as children of "his eternal image, the most sacred word; for an image of God is the most ancient word."

An image, however, may also epitomize the corruption or distortion of the representation of the invisible being or nature of God. An artisan

---

6. Lohse, *Colossians and Philemon*, 46–47: "When the word εἰκών [*eikōn*] is defined as the 'image' of the invisible God, the Hellenistic understanding of this term is to be assumed. God is invisible, but he allows himself to be known wherever he wills to be known, i.e. he is revealed in his 'image.'"

fashions an "image" for people to worship (Isa 40:19 LXX). A father may create an "image" (*eikona*) of a dead child and now honor "as a god what was once a dead human being" (Wis 14:15). A "visible image (*eikona*)" of a ruler is set up in a distant part of his territory so that people may honor him in his absence, but this leads first to worship of the human king, then to bestowing "on stones and pieces of wood the incommunicable name" (14:17–21*).[7] These are the stages of the "invention of idols" (14:12). The author of Sibylline Oracles 3 draws attention to the irony that despite being in the image of God, humanity pays no heed to the creator. There is "one God, monarch, ineffable, living in the ether, self-grown, invisible"; no sculptor's hand made him, nor does an "image (*typos*) of gold or ivory by the skills of man reveal him." But people, who have "a God-molded form in an image" (*theoplaston . . . , en eikoni morphēn*), nevertheless wander aimlessly, disregarding the creator (Sib. Or. 3:8–12*).[8] Rom 1:18–32 is Paul's version of this analysis. The "invisible things" of God have always been apparent in the created order but the Greeks inexcusably chose to exchange "the glory of the immortal God for a likeness of an image (*eikonos*) of a mortal person and of birds and animals and reptiles" (Rom 1:20–23*).[9] The image of a singular "mortal person" is somewhat dissociated grammatically in Paul's statement from the image of other living creatures, and the possibility arises that a now *immortal* person might legitimately function as a true image of the invisible God.

Not all of this is necessarily relevant for the interpretation of "image of the invisible God" in Col 1:15, but it establishes a field of meaning that comfortably encompasses both sonship and wisdom—both the eschatological *kingdom* theme of a coming day of wrath against pagan ignorance, when the Son and his brethren would inherit the nations, and the explicitly *creational* language of the rest of the first paragraph.[10] The words of the Persian Chiliarch Artabanus to the Greek Themistocles illustrate how readily the two

7. See Strait on Ps.-Solomon's critique of the Roman imperial cults ("Wisdom," 617–19). His argument is that "the Areopagus speech's diction of polemic against idols is not politically innocuous when read alongside the literary culture of early Judaism" (619).

8. Cf. Sib. Or. 21:7–8, 19–22, 27: mortals exalt themselves, taking no account of the "one God, sole Sovereign, excellent in power, unbegotten, almighty, invisible." Instead of worshiping the true God they have made "sacrifices to the deities in Hades."

9. For the focus on Greek culture, see Perriman, *Future of the People of God*, 53–54; Perriman, *End of Story*, 97–101.

10. Dunn thinks that verse 16 precludes an allusion to Adam; he attributes the thought instead to the Wisdom tradition, arguing that this "raises the possibility that already the thought is of the exalted Christ": "Only of the Christ crucified and exalted would Paul say 'he is the image of the invisible God'" (*Christology*, 188–89).

themes converge: "in our eyes, among many fair customs, this is the fairest of all, to honour the King, and to pay obeisance to him as the image of that god who is the preserver of all things" (Plutarch, *Them.* 17.3).

Image and Suffering

There is more to be said, however, about the content of this "image" in a text that purports to have been written by Paul. In 2 Cor 4:4–5 Christ is said to be the "image of God" (*eikōn tou theou*) in connection with a reference to "the gospel of the glory of Christ" and the apostolic proclamation of "Jesus Christ as Lord." The thought is not so remote from that of Col 1:12–15, pulling together "gospel," "image of (the invisible) God," and the belief that the exalted Son would eventually be recognized and served as Lord or king. The context, however, is different, adding two quite distinctive emphases to the "image of God" motif.

First, the Christ who is the "image of God" is specifically the template for the transformation of the apostles. They "share abundantly in Christ's sufferings"; they are afflicted for the sake of the "comfort and salvation" of believers; they carry the treasure of the gospel in "jars of clay"; they are afflicted in every way, perplexed, persecuted, struck down; they carry in the body the dying (*nekrōsin*) of Jesus, "always being given over to death for Jesus' sake" (2 Cor 1:8–10; 4:7–12). But it is precisely in this respect that they are being "transformed into the same image (*eikona*)" (3:18): they *embody* in themselves the dying of Jesus. Any allusion to Adam or to an ideal humanity in the image of God is heavily overlaid—perhaps to the point of obliteration—with this typology of suffering and vindication. So too in Romans: those who share in Christ's sufferings—not the general pains of human existence but the suffering of persecution and martyrdom—are being "conformed to the image (*eikonos*) of his Son" (Rom 8:29).[11] Jesus, therefore, is no longer the only one to suffer and be glorified: he is now the "firstborn (*prōtotokon*) among many brethren" who will follow him down this painful path, the apostles foremost among them. In this argument "firstborn" denotes the resurrected Jesus, as it does in Col 1:18, and we find that Paul's treatise on the resurrection in 1 Cor 15 follows the same line of thought. He expects the dead in Christ—those who have fallen asleep in him (1 Cor 15:18, 20)—to be raised at the *parousia*. Whether these dead suffered directly on account of Christ is perhaps uncertain, but Paul's reference to his own experience as an apostle introduces persecution into the narrative, even if it is expressed metaphorically: "I protest, brothers . . . ,

---

11. See Perriman, *Future of the People of God,* 117–21.

I die every day! What do I gain if, humanly speaking, I fought with beasts at Ephesus?" (1 Cor 15:31–32). Christ in this case is "firstfruits" (*aparchē*) rather than "firstborn" of those who will be raised at the *parousia*, but there is the same thought that they will be conformed to his glorified likeness, they will "bear the image (*eikona*) of the man of heaven" (15:20–23, 49). So too in Hebrews the "assembly of the firstborn who are enrolled in heaven" is the persecuted and painfully disciplined community (Heb 12:3–17, 23). The relevance of this theme is driven home when we get to Col 1:24, where Paul speaks frankly about making up the deficit between his own suffering in the flesh and that of Christ for the sake of the church.[12]

Secondly, in the 2 Corinthians passage Jesus is said to be the "image of God" against the backdrop of concern for the authenticity of the apostolic testimony. Paul has to convince his readers that an apostolic ministry characterized by suffering, disgrace, and a seeming lack of sophistication is authenticated precisely by its *Christlikeness*. Under these circumstances it is not immediately apparent to skeptical observers that God, who after all is *invisible*, is present and active in the apostolic program: the "god of this world" has blinded minds to keep people (Paul is thinking primarily of the Jews) from seeing the truth. But the hidden God has caused a light to shine in the hearts of the apostles to give "the light of the knowledge of the glory of God in the face of Jesus Christ," and so they proclaim the crucified Jesus as Lord (2 Cor 4:4–6).

To say, therefore, that the "Son of his love" is the "image of the invisible God" is likely to bring into play the thought that *under the current eschatological conditions* the glory of God is revealed through the suffering and vindication of Jesus, which constitute, secondarily, the prototype for the suffering and vindication of the apostles and the churches.[13] What will enhance the reputation of the God of Israel among the nations? Not

12. See Perriman, "Pattern," 62–68. The assertion that the "new person" is being "renewed in knowledge according to the image (*kat' eikona*) of the one who created it" (Col 3:9–10*) is probably a reference only to Gen 1:27 and the more general regeneration of the person in Christ (cf. Lohse, *Colossians and Philemon*, 142; O'Brien, *Colossians*, 191).

13. Northcott argues that *eikōn* in Col 1:15 signifies "representative rulership for its bearers" ("King of Kings," 212; cf. Barth and Blanke, *Colossians*, 249; McKnight, *Colossians*, 147). He insists that the whole phrase "image of God" must be interpreted with reference to its context in Gen 1. But the phrase is not "image of God." It is "image of the invisible God," and there is reason to think that the appropriate context is eschatological and polemical rather than creational. What is at issue in the encomium is not the rulership of humanity over creation but the rulership of Christ over the new post-pagan order or kingdom, made a possibility through his death and resurrection. See also the argument of Hellerman that Paul modeled his portrayal of Christ in Phil 2:6–8 on the humiliation of the apostles at Philippi as described in Acts 16:11–40 ("Vindicating").

Torah-observance but, in the long run, in this eschatological transition, the faithful Christ-like suffering of the apostles and of the churches.

Firstborn of Every Creature

The closest parallel to the expression "firstborn of *pasēs ktiseōs*" in Hellenistic-Jewish literature is to be found in a claim made by Jacob in the first century AD text Prayer of Joseph A.[14] Jacob identifies himself as the earthly incarnation of "Israel, an angel of God and a ruling spirit," the "first minister before the face of God" (Pr. Jos. A 1:3, 8). The angel, it turns out, had descended to earth and had "tabernacled among people" under the name Jacob. The name Israel means "a man seeing God," and it was bestowed on the angel by God because he was "first-born of every living creature living from God" (*prōtogonos pantos zōiou zōoumenou hypo theou*) (1:1–2*).[15] In the ensuing dispute with Uriel he also claims to be "an archangel of the power of the Lord and *archichiliarchos* among sons of God . . . the first minister before the face of God" (1:7–8*). It is not part of the argument, however, that the angelic Israel *preceded in time* either the other heavenly "sons of God" or all earthly creatures. What accounts for the use of the *prōtogonos* ("first-born") metaphor in this context is the intimacy of Israel with God in that he has uniquely seen God (cf. Gen 32:28, 30) and that he is pre-eminent with respect to other beings.[16] It is also said that Abraham and Isaac were "pre-created (*proektisthēsan*) before every work" (Pr. Jos. A 1:2), and presumably Israel was also "pre-created," but this is not what the *prōtogonos* metaphor means.

This speculative development of the motif has its origins in the biblical idea that Israel as a people is YHWH's "firstborn" (e.g., Exod 4:22; Jer 38:9 LXX; cf. Hos 11:1; Sir 36:11; Jub. 2:20; 4 Ezra 6:58–59; 4Q504 f1–2iii:6).[17]

14. Smith, in Charlesworth, *OT Pseudepigrapha* 2, 703n22, cites Windisch and Moule for the comparison. See also Hengel, *Cross*, 45–46; Chester, *Messiah*, 391.

15. Smith emphasizes the affinity of the work with "Jewish and Christian texts from a Greco-Egyptian provenance" (Charlesworth, *OT Pseudepigrapha* 2, 700–705, this quotation 703). Cf. Philo, *Flight* 208: "seeing is the inheritance of the legitimate and first-born (*prōtogonos*) son, Israel; for the name Israel, being interpreted, means 'seeing God'"; and *Confusion* 146*: the Logos is "first-born . . . , the eldest of angels, as being archangel of many names; . . . beginning and the name of God and word and a human according to image, and he who sees, Israel." *Prōtogenēs* is not used metaphorically in the Septuagint, but the mother of the king addresses her son as *prōtogenes* in Prov 31:2; *prōtogonos* is not found in the Septuagint.

16. Cf. Kim, "Firstborn Son," 189: "Every living being should be subjugated to Israel/Jacob as the angels should be submitted to Israel/Jacob who is the first minister of God."

17. Cf. Hengel, *Cross*, 46.

But the figure may also be applied to certain individuals in the biblical tradition. First, the king is God's "firstborn." The psalmist says that YHWH will crush David's enemies before him, truth and mercy will be with him, his horn will be exalted; YHWH will establish his rule from the sea to the rivers; David will call upon God as "My Father"; God will "make him a firstborn (*prōtotokon*), high among the kings of the earth"; and his descendants and his throne will be established forever (Ps 88:24–30 LXX = 89:23–29 MT).[18] Secondly, the righteous person, who in this case happens to be the king, is disciplined through affliction because he is a "son of love" (*huion agapēseōs*) and "firstborn" (*prōtotokou*) (Pss. Sol. 13:9*; cf. 18:4; Heb 5:8).

Again, it is apparent from these examples that the "firstborn" son metaphor does not itself convey the idea of temporal precedence. Only the notion of special status, which in literal usage derives from being *first* born, is retained.[19] Israel does not precede in time other sons of YHWH. The point is rather that God established a relationship specifically with Israel (Jer 38:9 LXX); therefore, Israel has a privileged status as a priestly people among the nations (cf. Exod 19:5–6; Deut 7:6). The firstborn, therefore, is a uniquely qualified *member of a group*: angelic Israel is pre-eminent among living beings, heavenly and earthly. The people of Israel belongs to a group of nations that includes Egypt and Babylon but as firstborn is uniquely related to the living God. Israel's king is firstborn only because there are other kings who do not have the same relationship with YHWH as Father.[20] If chronology is relevant at all, it is in the *story* of the firstborn's triumph and rule among the nations, not in his ontology: there is currently opposition and conflict, God *will make* his king firstborn.

All Creation or Every Creature?

There is some debate, of course, about the meaning of *pasēs ktiseōs*. Is this a reference to "every creature" or to "all creation"? Larry Helyer has made

---

18. The note of belligerence in the metaphor is underlined by Deut 33:17 LXX: Joseph is a "firstborn (*prōtotokos*) of a bull—his beauty! His horns are horns of a unicorn; with them he will gore nations, all at once as far as earth's end."

19. Cf. Barth and Blanke, *Colossians*, 248: "In the transmitted sense, the Israelite people are called the 'first-born' of God . . . in which the component that these people are the '*first*-born,' foremost among the other 'brothers,' is not an important factor anymore." Also MacDonald, *Colossians and Ephesians*, 58–59; McKnight, *Colossians*, 149; Northcott, "King of Kings," 221. Against this see Fowl, *Story of Christ*, 108: the phrase reflects "the supremacy and sovereignty over all creation that is Christ's by virtue of his temporal precedence."

20. See Michaelis, "πρῶτος," 873–74.

the case for the collective sense at some length, but the reasoning is flimsy.[21] First, if *pasēs ktiseōs* equates to the "all things" of verses 16–17, we have to reckon with the fact that the "all things" are narrowly defined as "thrones or lordships or rulers or authorities." Helyer rejects the argument that "every creature" belongs to "an entirely distinct class of creatures (the angel powers)," but the description of angelic Israel as "first-born of every living creature" in Prayer of Joseph A suggests that this is not such an implausible interpretation. Something less than "all creation" seems to be at issue. Secondly, the appeal to the inclusion of the "inanimate realm" in *ktisis* in Rom 8:18–23 does not work. In this passage Christ is "firstborn" in relation to "many brothers," who will also be revealed as "sons of God" (8:29); and this group is *part* of "the creation," which, figuratively speaking, groans in the pains of childbirth.[22] Paul's argument is precisely that Christ *shared in* the mortality of the suffering believers and in the perishability of created things; and these hope to share in his resurrection to imperishable life. Thirdly, the argument strains the sense of "firstborn." An individual may be firstborn among many brothers (Rom 8:29) or firstborn of a family. But a family is only a *collection* of related individuals—parents and children.[23] To be firstborn of "all creation," therefore, would require "creation" to be understood as a collection of appropriate individuals—in effect, of "every living creature," as in Prayer of Joseph A.

Elsewhere it is normal to affirm that *God* is sovereign with regard to "all creation" (e.g., 3 Macc 2:2; 4 Bar. 9:6). The possessive "your" with *pasēs ktiseōs* and *pasa hē ktisis* makes "your whole creation" more likely (Jdt 9:12; 16:14).[24] In Ben Sirach's catalogue of Old Testament heroes, however, it is said that Shem and Seth were "glorified among people, and Adam was above every living thing in the creation (*hyper pan zōion en tēi ktisei*)" (Sir 49:16).

---

21. Helyer, "Arius Revisited," 62–63.

22. Helyer notes that ordinarily "adjectival *pas* used with an anarthrous noun in the singular signifies 'every' or 'each,' emphasizing the individual members of the class denoted by the noun" ("Arius Revisited," 62). The distinction between the anarthrous *pasēs ktiseōs* in Col 1:15 and *pasa hē ktisis* in Rom 8:22 may, therefore, be significant.

23. In his rebuttal of Eunomius Gregory of Nyssa addresses just this opinion: "every first-born is the first-born not of another kind, but of its own" (*Against Eunomius* 4.3).

24. That said, there is an individualizing force in the context. Judith prays to God who is "master of the heavens and earth, creator of the waters, king of your *pasēs ktiseōs*" (Jdt 9:12). The sequence (heavens and earth, waters, *pasēs ktiseōs*) suggests a reference to the "life forms" (*ōn zōsōn*) that are brought forth from the waters and on the earth in Gen 1:20–25. In Jdt 16:14 it is said of "all your creation" that "they came into being. You sent your spirit, and it built them up, and there is no one who will withstand your voice."

In this case, it is not the relation of God to "all creation" that is in view but the relation of an individual person to other living beings.[25]

Finally, Helyer rejects the interpretation of "firstborn of every creature" as a partitive genitive on the grounds that it reduces Christ "to the status of a created being."[26] The argument is, on the one hand, that "full deity is ascribed to Christ" elsewhere in the passage, and on the other, that a partitive genitive would highlight the element of "birth," which is not emphasized in the New Testament (excepting Luke 2:7).[27] Whether or not the passage as a whole makes Christ the agent of the original creation will be considered in due course, but there is no reason why Paul should not say something here, in connection with the affirmation about the kingdom of the beloved Son, about the favored status of the resurrected *man* Jesus in relation to the rest of creation. Michaelis's argument about the partitive genitive, which Helyer briefly summarizes, is not easy to unpick. He assumes that *prōtotokos pasēs ktiseōs* is explained by the statement in verse 16 that "Christ is the Mediator at creation to whom all creatures without exception owe their creation." The phrase cannot be saying both that Christ is the mediator of creation and that he was "created as the first creature"; and in any case, "the *-tokos* is never emphasised in the NT in passages which speak of Christ" (note especially Col 1:18). Therefore, the genitive must be understood hierarchically: "What is meant is the unique supremacy of Christ over all creatures as the Mediator of their creation."[28] But the separation of the two components in "first-born" seems contrived in light of the metaphorical usage of the term. Israel as "firstborn" is neither first in time nor born, merely found or rescued in Egypt: "I became a father to Israel, and Ephraim is my firstborn" (Jer 38:9 LXX; cf. 2 Sam 7:14).

Firstborn and Kingdom

What may we conclude so far about the description of the "Son of his love," who has a kingdom, as "firstborn of every creature"? While "firstborn of every creature" conforms most closely to "first-born of every living creature" in Prayer of Joseph A, nothing in the Colossians text indicates a prior existence

25. The expression *diakrisis pasēs ktiseōs* in T. Adam B 2:6 is obscure, but is perhaps to be translated "judgment of every creature," corresponding to "presentation" (*parastasis*) of the angels.

26. Helyer, "Arius Revisited," 63.

27. Helyer, "Arius Revisited"; cf. Michaelis, "πρῶτος," 878.

28. Michaelis, "πρῶτος," 878–79.

analogous to that of angelic Israel.[29] On the contrary, the encomium describes the *current* post-resurrection status of the exalted Son, not a status acquired by descent from heaven and dwelling among people. The verb *estin* in the opening relative clause makes it emphatically a present statement about the Son who now has a kingdom: he *is* "image of the invisible God" and "first-born of every creature" in the same way that he *is* "head of the body," "beginning" and "firstborn from the dead" (Col 1:18).

The oracular pronouncement in Ps 88:21, 27–28 LXX (= Ps 89:20, 26–27 MT) concerning Israel's "anointed" (*echrisa*) king, who will be made "firstborn, high among the kings of the earth," is readily transferred to the resurrected Christ—especially when we take into account the fact that it is expressly *political* entities that are created in him (Col 1:16).[30] In the second half of the Colossians encomium the Son is identified as "beginning, firstborn from the dead" (*archē, prōtotokos ek tōn nekrōn*). This presumably overlaps in meaning with "firstfuits" (*aparchē*) in 1 Cor 15:23: Christ is the first of many who will be raised from the dead, who have suffered for his sake and will therefore be glorified with him—making him the "firstborn among many brothers" (Rom 8:29).[31] It is in this respect that he is "the head of the body of the church" and has "first place among all" (Col 1:18*).[32] In this other use of the metaphor, the temporal aspect appears to remain active: as "firstborn" *Son* Jesus is preeminent above all creatures in the new political-religious order; as "firstborn from the dead," however—that is, as "firstfruits" or as "firstborn" *brother*—the point is less that he is preeminent than that he *precedes* those of his "family" who will likewise suffer and be

29. Noting the close link between "first-born of all creation" and "first-born of every living thing" in Pr. Jos. A 1:2, Chester suggests that the writer of Colossians is "engaged in arguing against the view that Christ is only one of several angelic or heavenly beings, but to do so he has to use angelological themes and terminology" (*Messiah*, 391).

30. The thought may be echoed in 4Q369 f1ii, which speaks of God's "firstbo[rn] son" as one who has been given the "glory of your earthly land," who is a "prince and ruler in all your earthly land," and to whom God's love cleaves forever. For the translation and comment, see Evans, "First-Born Son," 194, 198.

31. This would mean that "image of the invisible God" and "firstborn of all creation" are not in "synthetic parallelism" (against, e.g., Northcott, "King of Kings," 221).

32. Cf. Barth and Blanke, *Colossians*, 247: "The hymn in its further statements does not deal with the theme of Christ's pre-existence; rather, it emphasizes the superiority of the Messiah, the creator over all creatures. Thus, the concept 'first-born' is most likely a designation of rank"; MacDonald, *Colossians and Ephesians*, 59: "The focus is on Christ's primacy; . . . he stands beyond the created world as the agent through which everything came into existence"; and Kim, "Firstborn Son," 189: "this stresses the notion of the firstborn son who has rulership and supremacy over every creature." Feník and Lapko argue that the theme of Christ's primacy carries greater weight in Colossians than the assertion of his lordship ("Reign").

raised in him, and, indeed, who will judge and rule with him in the age to come (cf. Matt 20:21; 1 Cor 6:3; 2 Tim 2:12; Rev 20:4).

Usage elsewhere in the New Testament accords well with this reading. Revelation speaks of Jesus as "the faithful witness, the firstborn of the dead, and the ruler of kings on earth" (Rev 1:5). Hebrews describes the Son begotten by the power of the resurrection, the exalted and enthroned Jesus, as the "firstborn" brought into the *oikoumenē*—that is, I think, into the Greek-Roman political-religious sphere—to be worshiped by angels (Heb 1:5–6; cf. Ps 2:7). So the one who through suffering and vindication is the "image of the invisible God" in the clash with pagan idolatry becomes "high among the kings of the earth" by virtue of his resurrection from the dead, beyond "every creature."

It is possible, therefore, to discern a coherent eschatological narrative running through the dense clumping of heavily freighted terminology. The beloved Son has acceded to a kingdom of light, in contrast to the *present* age of darkness to which Paul and his readers have died; and they are confident that at some *future* juncture, on a day of God's "wrath," Christ will be revealed to the world and those who have believed in this coming transformation will be vindicated (Col 2:20—3:7). The beloved Son, however, not only has a kingdom; he is also the one through whom they have the redemption, the forgiveness of sins. He is a king who has suffered. This antithesis between suffering and glory is also implicit in the other two terms if the wider resonances are heard. On the one hand, the "firstborn of every creature" is both the king exalted above all other powers and the righteous son who suffers and is disciplined. On the other, the phrase "image of the invisible God" fuses the Jewish Wisdom motif with a type of suffering sonship which for Paul is exemplary for the apostles and churches.

The reconciliation of "all things, whether on earth or in heaven," with which the encomium ends includes the reconciliation of the gentile Colossian believers to the God of Israel (Col 1:21–22; cf. Eph 2:11–12). They will be presented before him holy and blameless, on the day when wrath comes upon the pagan order, if they do not shift from "the hope of the gospel that you heard" (Col 1:23; 3:6). If this is the same "hope" as in Rom 15:12–13, it is oriented towards a political outcome—the rule of the root of Jesse over the nations. But this gospel has been "proclaimed *en pasēi ktisei* under heaven" (Col 1:23). This is another way of saying that the gospel has been proclaimed "in the whole world" (1:6), but the expression attracts attention given the preceding description of the Son as "firstborn of every creature." It further aligns the scope of this created sphere with the reach of Paul's message concerning the government of the nations from Jerusalem to Spain (Rom 15:18–21, 24).

We should also note, belatedly, the characterization of wisdom in Prov 8, which was "created . . . as the beginning of his ways for the sake of his works," founded in the beginning before the age, begotten before the making of land, sea, and mountains (Prov 8:22 LXX). The relation of created wisdom to the rest of creation is not that of a firstborn to every creature. Wisdom is conceived as a "way" or "work" ahead of the subsequent works of God in creating, and it is the scenery that is in view (seas, mountains, heavens), not living creatures (Prov 8:24–29). In the Hebrew text wisdom is the "first of his acts of old." Philo, however, picks up on the thought of wisdom's primeval birth: "And who is to be considered the daughter of God but Wisdom, who is the first-born mother of all things and most of all of those who are greatly purified in soul?" (*QG* 4 97; cf. *Drunkenness* 31). Since Paul then accounts for the Son's firstborn status in terms that strongly evoke the creation-wisdom motif, we should probably allow that this thought is at least latent in the expression "firstborn of every creature."[33]

In Him Not All Things Were Created

The Son who suffered and who has received a kingdom is "image of the invisible God" and "firstborn of every creature" *because* (*hoti*) "in him were created all things in the heavens and on the earth, the visible and the invisible, whether thrones or lordships or rulers or authorities; all things through him and for him have been created" (Col 1:16*). The question is whether the "all things" created in the Son are the entire cosmos, the original creation as described in Gen 1, or something lesser and later.

The creation of all things "in him" or "through him" has the form of a wisdom statement.[34] Philo says, for example, that God is the "father of all

33. Dunn says that it is "hard to imagine any first-century reader interpreting the first strophe except as a reference to the 'old' creation, particularly in view of the Wisdom and Stoic parallels" (*Christology*, 190; cf. Dunn, *Colossians and Philemon*, 90). See also Lohse, *Colossians and Philemon*, 48; Bruce, *Colossians*, 59–60; Hamerton-Kelly, *Pre-Existence*, 172; O'Brien, *Colossians*, 44–45; Chester, *Messiah*, 390–91; Foster, *Colossians*, 181–82. Note Zeller, "Christology," 325: "Because attributes and functions of the 'Son' in Heb 1.2–3 or the 'firstborn' in Col 1.15 are identical with those of the personified Wisdom or the Philonic Logos who is called πρωτόγονος [*prōtogonos*], there are good reasons to surmise that those Christians . . . in their christological predications were inspired by wisdom theology." But I disagree that "from the Davidic representative of divine power grew a universal mediator in creation and redemption." Not the whole of creation but a new political order is in view. Against the wisdom thesis see Roon, who argues instead for a purely messianic understanding of "firstborn of all creation" ("Relation," 232–39).

34. Cf. Lohse, *Colossians and Philemon*, 50; Dunn, *Colossians and Philemon*, 91; O'Brien, *Colossians*, 46. There are also Stoic parallels, but it seems correct to give

things" and wisdom the mother "through whom the all came into being" (*Flight* 109*). Presumably influenced by Prov 8:22–31, *Targum Neofiti* Gen 1:1 reads: "From the beginning, with wisdom, the Lord created and finished the heavens and the earth." Dunn draws attention to the parallel with Ps 103:24* LXX (= Ps 104:24 MT; cf. Prov 3:19; Wis 9:2; Philo *Worse* 54; *Heir* 199; *Flight* 109): "How magnified were your works, Lord! You made all things in wisdom; the earth was filled with your possessions (*ktēseōs*)." This need not mean, in his view, that pre-existent wisdom is identified with the pre-existent Christ; rather the writer may be saying that the creative force of God's wisdom has found its supreme expression in Christ. "If then Christ is what God's power/wisdom came to be recognized as, of Christ it can be said what was said first of wisdom—that 'in him (the divine wisdom now embodied in Christ) were created all things.'"[35]

If the creation of all things "in him" (*en autōi*) is not simply equivalent to "through him" (*di' autou*), the idea that Paul conceived of the exalted Son, who had been revealed to him from heaven (Gal 1:16), as "the 'sphere' within which the work of creation takes place" seems improbable.[36] Stephen Fowl argues, for example, that "God's creation finds its coherence in Christ because Christ is the 'sphere' in which creation took place."[37] The intensity of Paul's personal relationship to the Christ who suffered and was glorified, not least in Colossians (cf. Col 1:24), is such that we should assume that at the forefront of his mind is Christ the *person*, seated at the right hand of God, who eventually will appear in glory with his "brothers" (Col 1:2; 3:3–4; cf. Rom 8:29–30).[38] In that case, the prepositional phrase "in him" is more likely to have in view the Son who at this moment is understood to be "image of the invisible God, firstborn of every creature." The aorist *ektisthē*, then, at the beginning of verse 16 would refer to a specific act of creation *in the moment of becoming firstborn of every creature* through his resurrection from the dead. The perfect *ektistai* at the end of the verse emphasizes the effects of this new creation for Paul's present: "all things through him and for him

---

priority to the Jewish traditions (O'Brien, *Colossians*, 45–46).

35. Dunn, *Christology*, 190; cf. McGrath, *Only True God*, 44–46. Zeilinger argues for a fully eschatological reading of the Colossians encomium, as an assertion of the new creation that has come about in Christ, since this is the only way to resolve the problem of explaining why a cosmos created in Christ is in need of redemption (*Erstgeborene*, 195–200). Christ is "the firstborn from the dead, the beginning and root of a new world, owner and master of a whole creation, which he already contains as a corporate archetype" (189).

36. Bruce, *Colossians*, 61–62; cf. O'Brien, *Colossians*, 45; McKnight, *Colossians*, 150–51.

37. Fowl, *Story of Christ*, 109.

38. See Perriman, "Pattern".

have been created." The change in tense is, in fact, rather important because it suggests that what is in view is a created reality that is directly relevant to the circumstances celebrated in the encomium.[39]

I agree, therefore, with Dunn that Paul does not mean that "the Christ known to his followers during his ministry in Palestine was as such God's agent in creation," but not exactly with his alternative reading—that the creative wisdom of God, through which the world came into being, "is now to be seen as embodied in Christ, its character now made clear by the light of his cross and resurrection."[40] The point is not that the act of creation was *Christlike*, rather the reverse: recent events have been *creation-like*. The death and resurrection of Jesus are represented as the profoundly creative event, in which the wisdom of God is again dynamically engaged, by which a new world order has come about. It is, therefore, this new "all things" that is subsequent to him and that holds together in him (Col 1:17).[41] Admittedly *ta panta* is part of the wisdom formula: "*the* all things" are everything that makes up the cosmos. But in the present context, at the climax to the prayer of 1:9–14, the reference seems to be more narrowly to the novel and ambitious "inheritance," brought about by the execution of Jesus, in which the Colossians now have a share (1:12). I argued much the same in chapter 3 with regard to 1 Cor 8:6 and the application of the formula to God in Rom 11:36. Paul uses the cosmological-wisdom motif as a lens to focus the creative activity of the living God *on the present historical moment*.

To what extent the statement about Christ was meant as a rebuff to Augustan propaganda is difficult to say. Paullus Fabius Maximus famously declared that the birthday of the most divine Caesar could justly be considered "equal to the beginning of all things (*tēi tōn pantōn archēi isēn*), if not in terms of the natural order (*physei*), then in terms of practicality (*chrēsimōi*); when everything was falling apart and passing into disarray, he restored order and gave another aspect to the whole world"

39. The writer to the Hebrews quotes Ps 8 to the same end: "the world to come" and "all things" have been subjected to Christ (Heb 2:5–8). Note Dunn, *Christology*, 110–11, 190.

40. Dunn, *Colossians and Philemon*, 91.

41. The statement in Col 1:17 that "in him all things hold together" (*ta panta en autōi synestēken*) is Stoic but has probably come by way of Hellenistic-Jewish Wisdom thought; for example: "the spirit of the Lord fills the world and that which holds all things together (*to synechon ta panta*) has knowledge of what is said" (Wis 1:7); see Dunn, *Colossians and Philemon*, 93; O'Brien, *Colossians*, 47–48. The context, however, is political rather than cosmological. The work begins with an appeal to those who judge the earth to love righteousness, seek the Lord, and pursue wisdom; their unrighteous and impious thoughts and deeds will not escape detection (Wis 1:1–11).

(*OGIS* 458.4–9*).[42] Here too we have a cosmological trope that has been repurposed, in this case explicitly, to speak of a startling transformation in the sphere of history, and a lofty reference to a god-equal ruler whose contemporaneous career is the beginning of *ta panta* and the renewal of the world. I would venture to suggest, moreover, that the pragmatism expressed by the proconsul would not go amiss in interpretation of the Colossians encomium. Christ was viewed as the beginning of all things not as an emperor on earth but as a king of kings in heaven, elevated to a position of supremacy above all living beings. But the rule that would eventually be actualized, when he would be confessed as Lord by the nations, would be more in terms of practicality than of nature, a matter of history rather than of cosmology, contingent rather than absolute.

Thrones, Lordships, Rulers, and Authorities

The fact is that any interpretation that takes verse 16 to be a reference to the original creation has to account for the narrow range of created things explicitly listed.[43] There is no reference to the creation of heaven and earth, light and darkness, sea and dry land, lights in the heavens, vegetation, or living creatures, which we might have expected if the thought of Ps 103:24 LXX were in the background. What was made "in wisdom" (*en sophiai*) are the creatures of the sea, which look to God to "give them food in due season," which return to the dust when they die but are created again so that the face of the earth is renewed (Ps 103:24–30).[44] The Colossians verse mentions only the creation of political entities—thrones, lordships, rulers and authorities, visible and invisible—either in the already existing heaven or on the *already existing and, presumably, populated* earth. What this speaks of is a new governmental order consisting of both invisible-heavenly and visible-earthly entities.[45]

42. For the text see also Sherk, *Roman Documents*, 329–30. For discussion see Harrison, "Imperial Gospel," 88–90; Klauck, *Context*, 297–98; Buxton and Hannah, "*OGIS* 458," 294–95; Reid, "'Savior' and 'Lord,'" 53–54; Winter, *Divine Honours*, 33–36.

43. O'Brien sees in the reference to cosmic powers a narrowing of the creation theme in order to address the Colossian heresy (*Colossians*, 46); but 1) grammatically the powers are the "all things," not a subset; and 2) these are both heavenly and earthly powers—thrones, kingdoms, governing authorities. Cf. Bruce, *Colossians*, 63; MacDonald, *Colossians and Ephesians*, 60.

44. Wright maintains that "the language of v.16, and its background in Proverbs 8 and Genesis 1" do not leave open the option of understanding these verses as a reference to new creation (*Climax*, 114). But neither of these Old Testament passages prepares the reader for the exclusive focus on political structures that we find in Col 1:16.

45. Kuschel discusses the view of Merklein regarding the "political origins" of

A limited but instructive parallel is found in Similitudes of Enoch. God sets his Elect One "on the throne of glory" to carry out judgment. On the one hand, "all the forces of the heavens . . . the cherubim, seraphim, ophanim, all the angels of governance . . . , and the other forces on earth (and) over the water" are summoned for judgment and will bless the name of the Lord of the Spirits.[46] On the other, the Lord commands kings, governors, high officials and landlords (perhaps "those who possess the land"[47]): "Open your eyes and lift up your eyebrows—if you are able to recognize the Elect One!" (1 En. 61:8, 10; 62:1). They will plead for mercy but they will be delivered "to the angels for punishments in order that vengeance shall be executed on them—oppressors of his children and his elect ones" (1 En. 62:11). So the consequence of the exaltation of the Elect One or Son of Man is that powers of government both in heaven and on earth are overhauled. Jesus, in effect, is the "Elect One" of Jewish apocalyptic vision, who has been seated at the right hand of God as judge and ruler of the nations, who will eventually be acknowledged by earthly authorities—real kings, governors, high officials, and landlords (cf. Rom 15:12).

In the roughly parallel narrative in Ephesians the thought is that "all things" are to be "recapitulated" in him, "things in heaven and things on earth," as part of God's purpose for the management of the "fulness of time" (Eph 1:9–10). There is no *creation* of "all rule and authority and power and lordship" in Christ; rather he is seated at the right hand of God in the heavenly places *far above these powers*. "All things" have been put under his feet; he has been given as "head over all things to the church" (1:21–22). Those who have now been saved by grace and seated with him, however, are "his work, created in Christ Jesus for good works" (2:6–10*). In this case, what has been *created* through the eschatological process is not yet the political order but the community that will serve God in advance of it. But arguably, what must be "made known to the rulers and to the powers in the heavens through the church" is the same *reconciliation* of rule in heaven and rule on earth (3:10*). Paul's task as an apostle—in his own words, or in the words of

---

Christ's pre-existence—that the belief arose not from vague reflection on the "Easter experience" but specifically from "criticism of Temple and Torah, the conflict of the Nazarene with the Jewish establishment," as an attack on the establishment view that pre-existent divine wisdom was embodied in Torah (*Before All Time*, 264–66). Later he emphasizes the wider political aspect: "Given the swords of Roman military power, there could be no doubt which thrones and principalities, dominions and powers ruled the world. And what could stand against them?" (338). But Paul expects more than this, I think: the *actual* reconciliation and consolidation of political power in earth and heaven.

46. Cf. T. Levi 3:4–8; 2 En. 20:1.

47. Nickelsburg and VanderKam, *1 Enoch*, 79–80.

an imitator—was to proclaim to the nations the "unfathomable riches" of the Christ, who would head up this new unified government (3:8–10*).

The relation of the Colossians encomium to the letter to the nearby Laodiceans in Rev 3:14–22 (and note the instructions in Col 4:16) also bears consideration. In the prescript Jesus is described as "the Amen, the faithful and true witness, the beginning (archē) of the creation of God" (Rev 3:14*). In this context the phrase "faithful and true witness" recalls Christ's sufferings (cf. 2:13; 17:6). If we are right to discern a Wisdom background to "the beginning of the creation of God," we might understand Jesus as the "wisdom" established by God as the paradigm for his subsequent works: "The Lord created (ektisen) me as the beginning of his ways, for the sake of his works" (Prov 8:22; cf. Wis 6:22; Sir 24:9).[48] Aune thinks that the phrase may be dependent on "firstborn of all creation" in Col 1:15, bearing in mind that archē and prōtotokos are effectively synonyms in 1:18.[49]

The corresponding promise to the "one who conquers" at the end of the letter is that he will sit with Jesus on his throne, "as I also conquered and sat down with my Father on his throne" (Rev 3:21), which serves to associate "the beginning of the creation of God" not only with resurrection but also with the rule of the exalted Christ at the right hand of God. Earlier, the enthroned Jesus is said to be "the faithful witness, the firstborn (prōtotokos) of the dead, and the ruler of kings on earth" (1:5). The progression is from faithful suffering to resurrection to kingdom, and finally he will come with the clouds to be seen not only by those who pierced him but by "all tribes of the earth" (1:7). At the end of the book Jesus is "the Alpha and the Omega, the first and the last, the beginning (archē) and the end" (22:13). The "one like a son of man" in the opening vision claimed to be "the first and the last, and the living one," who died and is now alive for evermore, having the "keys to Death and Hades" (1:17–18), a theme repeated in 2:8: "The words of the first and the last, who died and came to life." It seems not unreasonable, therefore, to conclude that the terms "Alpha," "first," and "beginning" refer to the resurrection. If this may be regarded as an informed reading of the Colossians passage, it confirms the conclusion that what was created in and through and for Christ was the impending *political* state of affairs brought about by his suffering, death, resurrection, and exaltation.

48. See Dunn, *Christology*, 247.
49. Aune, *Revelation 1–5*, 256.

New Creation, New Moons, and Sabbaths

In the closing chapters of Isaiah we have an account of the restoration of Jerusalem that utilizes explicitly new creation language. YHWH has spread out his hands all day to a disobedient people; he will repay them for their iniquities, but for the sake of his servants he will not destroy them all; he will bring forth offspring from Jacob and Judah, and they will possess his mountains (Isa 65:1–9). The renewal of Jerusalem will be the creation of new heavens and a new earth *in the sense that* the "former things shall not be remembered" (65:17). But there is also a judgment of the pagan nations to come (66:15–17). YHWH will gather all nations and tongues, and "they shall come and shall see my glory" (66:18). He will "send survivors" to declare his glory among the nations, and foreigners will facilitate the repatriation of scattered Israel.[50] The descendants of those Israelites brought back will stand for as long as "the new heavens and the new earth that I make" remain. Finally, it will be that "from moon to moon and from Sabbath to Sabbath all flesh shall come to worship before me, says YHWH" (66:23*).

What we have here, then, is a "new creation" consisting in the forgiveness and restoration of God's people, a judgment against "all flesh," the sending of envoys, perhaps proselytes, to proclaim YHWH's glory to the nations, the establishment of Jerusalem as a glorious, prosperous, and peaceful political-religious center, with the expectation that all flesh—presumably including non-Israelites—will come every Sabbath and every new moon to celebrate holy days and festivals. Now, I suggest that reflection on this narrative, or a polemical tradition derived from it, lies behind Paul's argument in Colossians and that it gives us further reason to interpret the act of creation described in the encomium in less than cosmic terms. He is writing to converts from paganism, who have acquired a "share in the inheritance of the saints in the light" (Col 1:12*) who have been transferred to the kingdom of the beloved Son, and who, therefore, will share in the glory of the Son that will be manifested when the wrath of God comes upon the nations (1:13–14; 3:3–7). In chapter 2 he reiterates the point, made in the encomium about the firstborn Son, that the "fullness of deity dwells bodily" in Christ, who has become "the head of all rule and authority": all hostile forces of governance having been disarmed through the cross (2:9–10, 15). Behind this is the affirmation that the "all things" that are "thrones or lordships or rulers or authorities" have

50. As the text stands, the words "some of them also I will take for priests and for Levites" (Isa 66:21) more likely refer to returning Jews than to the gentiles who escort them home (Watts, *Isaiah 34–66*, 940). Blenkinsopp, *Isaiah 56–66*, 314–15, however, thinks that verse 20 is an interpolation to correct the impression that some of the proselytes sent to declare God's glory to the nations would be taken as priests and Levites (cf. Isa 56:1–8).

been created in Christ. Paul then warns the Colossians: "Therefore let no one pass judgment on you in questions of food and drink, or with regard to a festival or a new moon or a Sabbath." These are "a shadow of the things to come, but the substance belongs to Christ" (2:16–17).

So Isaiah speaks of a new creation that will be expressed conspicuously in the participation of all flesh in Jewish holy days, and we may imagine a Jewish-Christian campaign to accommodate the religious practice of the Colossian converts to this paradigm. If as gentiles they have come to participate in the new creation, in a decisive restoration of Israel like that envisaged by Isaiah, it is only right that they should also worship the God of Israel from "new moon to new moon, and from Sabbath to Sabbath." There is no reference to "food and drink" here, but we find close at hand Isaiah's sharp censure of those who eat the flesh of pigs and broth of unclean meat (Isa 65:4; 66:17), who, therefore, will be excluded from the new heavens and new earth of Israel's restoration. But Paul insists that the participation of gentile Colossians in the eschatological process should *not* be expressed in the observation of Jewish customs. The story in Isaiah about the remaking of the heavens and the earth is only a foreshadowing of the transformation that has come about in Christ. Jerusalem-centered Torah observance was no longer required of proselytes because they had been "circumcised with a circumcision made without hands," the "record of debt . . . with its legal demands" had been annulled, and they had died to the religious regulations that held sway in that present age (Col 2:11, 14, 20–23).

A New Political-Religious Order

The emphasis on political entities and realities in verse 16 carries over into verse 20: the "all things" on earth and in heaven that were reconciled to God are the powers of "government" that had for ages been contesting human history *from the perspective of the Jews*. In simple terms, the pagan nations had long been at war with YHWH: "The kings of the earth set themselves, and the rulers take counsel together, against the LORD and against his Anointed" (Ps 2:2; cf. Acts 4:26). Jesus's death brought about "peace," the reconciliation of kingdom on earth with kingdom in heaven; and by his resurrection he became the Son who in due course would receive the nations as his heritage, to rule them with a "rod of iron" (Ps 2:7–9; cf. Acts 13:33; Heb 1:5; 5:5; Rev 2:27; 12:5; 19:15). The powers of kingdom and empire, both human and super-human, which condemned and executed Jesus, had been put to shame (cf. Col 2:15), shown to be ineffectual, powerless to prevent the outworking of *Gottesreichgeschichte*, by the resurrection of the beloved Son and his elevation to a position of kingship "far above all rule and authority and power and lordship, and above every name that is named, not only in this age but also in the one to come" (Eph 1:21). As a visible image of the invisible God and firstborn of every creature the crucified and resurrected Son now held together in himself—embodied the reconciliation of—rule on earth and rule in heaven. A descendant of David had finally overcome the age-old disjunction between the unseen rule of God in heaven and the hostile and impious rule of the kings of earth. It was only a matter of time before this *belief* would become a solid reality.

A new civilization was coming into existence, in which kings and emperors, governments and bureaucracies, economies and judicial systems, would be explicitly ordered under the rule of God through his Son at his right hand. The kingdom of the world would become "the kingdom of our Lord and of his Christ, and he shall reign forever and ever." The nations raged, but the wrath of God came, "destroying the destroyers of the land" (Rev 11:15–18*). This was the good news, Paul goes on to say, that was being "proclaimed to every creature under heaven"—that Jesus has been "appointed Son of God in power . . . by resurrection from the dead" (Col 1:23; Rom 1:4*). All government has been subjected to him. It was, therefore, with this *political-religious* outcome in view that the gentile believers in Colossae were personally reconciled to the living God, along with Jewish believers (Col 1:21–23), and relocated from the kingdom of darkness to the kingdom of God's Son. For the Colossians the overriding and pressing significance of the distant death of Jesus was that a deeply antagonistic civilization had been, was being, and would be subdued and reconciled to God. Because they believed in this new future, Israel's God was prepared to overlook or forgive their sins; they would be justified by this risky faith.

Conclusion

The problem to which Col 1:15–20 is Paul's answer is encapsulated by the despairing author of 4 Ezra. Writing after the war against Rome, he asks why God's people, "whom you have called your firstborn, only begotten (*primogenitum, unigenitum*)," have been given into the hands of their enemies. Why do the nations, who are mere spittle, "a drop from a bucket" (cf. Isa 40:15), "domineer over us and devour us"? "If the world has indeed been created for us, why do we not possess our world as an inheritance?" (4 Ezra 6:58–59). The implicit answer given by the author of the encomium was that the historical resolution had been preempted in Christ. The "saints and faithful brothers in Christ at Colossae" (Col 1:2) had been transferred to the kingdom of the Son and therefore would inherit the *kosmos*, the *saeculum* (cf. Rom 4:13). This eventual inheritance would indeed entail a radical transformation of the political-religious landscape of the world as seen from the historical standpoint of Second Isaiah or Paul or the author of 4 Ezra. The domineering idol-worshiping nations would at last be subjected to the wrath of God on account of their "sexual immorality, impurity, passion, evil desire, and covetousness, which is idolatry" (Col 3:5–6), and actual rule over them would be put in the hands of the "firstborn from the dead," who is the "beginning" of a new order, thus consolidating government on earth and government in heaven under the God of Israel.

10

A Christological Opportunity
to be Grasped . . .

I WILL BE BRIEF. Going back to the question with which we began, it turns out that the answer is no: Paul does not express the belief that *before* his life as a Roman era Jew, Christ Jesus existed actually and personally in heaven from eternity. Asking the question, though, has opened up a line of enquiry that, I suggest, has not only cast unexpected light on some major exegetical difficulties but also allowed us to see rather more clearly how—and with what end in view—Paul told the story of Jesus.

In the first place, he understood the career of Jesus not in transcendent and cosmological terms but as an urgent matter of Jewish history. Jesus had been "sent out" by God, much as Moses and the prophets were sent out, at a decisive and climactic moment not for a universal redemptive purpose but in a last ditch attempt to rescue Israel from the political-religious crisis of the "evil age" that had come upon it. That he was sent "in the likeness of sinful flesh" reflects a contemporary Jewish judgment on his efforts. He was a "sinner" not as a human person but as an offensive, transgressive first-century Jew, and he suffered the extreme penalty of repudiation and execution on a tree, cursed according to the Law. The problematics of incarnation are beside the point. There is no descent of a heavenly man. There is no existentially necessary incursion from outside the domain of human history to accomplish the salvation of humanity. That is not Paul's perspective as someone deeply implicated in the events, to whom the *personal* reality of the resurrected and exalted Son has been revealed.

This controversial and paradoxical redemption was interpreted at a number of points by appeal to Wisdom traditions: it was an act of new creation, on the one hand; it was a moment of effective eschatological intervention, on the other. If the eschatological framework, which is at the same time a historical framework, is allowed to fade from view, the association with wisdom is easily misconstrued as an affirmation of Christ's real primordial role in creation. But I have argued that both in 1 Corinthians and Colossians the traditional language is applied to Christ in order to bring out the profoundly *transformative* impact of an event that was a stumbling block to Jews and folly to Greeks. In other words, the dynamic Word or Wisdom by which God first created the world—already a complex *figurative* notion in Jewish thought—had become flesh in this particular individual and had set about a new creative program.

The community in Corinth now expressed in its own weakness and faithfulness the wisdom that would bring the current age to an end and usher in a new age. They defiantly acclaimed, and called upon the name of, the "one Lord" to whom the "one God" had given all necessary authority—first, to execute judgment on the old order, then to rule over formerly pagan nations until the last enemy has been destroyed and the one God becomes again all in all. In the argument of Colossians the strange wisdom exhibited in the cross and in the suffering of the apostles and the churches was the means by which rule in heaven and rule on earth would be united under a single government.

The prospect of this unified rule is also the climax of the Philippians encomium, when every knee "in heaven and on earth and under the earth" would bow down at the name of Jesus, but our focus has been on the beginning of the story. The exemplary decision and its fateful consequences, I have argued, are presented in a Hellenistic idiom and from a pagan or post-pagan point of view. The only understanding of Christ's being *en morphēi theou* that does not put the expression under impossible strain is that, in the early stages of his ministry, he would have appeared to most Greeks as a person "in the form of a god"—that is, godlike in outward appearance and behavior—much as the people of Lystra mistook Barnabas and Paul for Zeus and Hermes. We have been able to fill out the narrative details of the terse reconstruction. In the wilderness Jesus was presented with the opportunity to attain the god-equal status of a pagan ruler over the nations of the Greek-Roman world, though the moral tension appears to have stayed with him throughout his career—the rebuke of Peter, the prayer in the garden. He did not consider Satan's proposition an opportunity to be grasped at. To the contrary, he emptied himself—perhaps of just those destructive passions that typically drove the acquisition and exercise of pagan rule—and in an act of self-abasement took the "form for a slave." At this point, it becomes apparent that he had to follow his path as an ordinary human person—born of a woman, subject like any Jew to the Law and to those who enforced it—obedient to the will of his Father, through to death on a cross.

What determines the shape of the encomium is not a "cosmograph" of descent and ascent. *Both* movements have been imposed for theological reasons on what is in fact a quite *flat* narrative. It is the unfolding *perception and judgment* of the converted gentiles in the Pauline communities: a godlike wonderworker turns his back on the offer of Caesar-like rule over the nations of the pagan world to become the degraded, unsightly, slave-like casualty of Roman violence, with nothing to recommend him other than his obedience to the calling of God; but after death his reputation is transformed, even among the Greeks, and the prospect arises that in time the nations, and the kings of the nations, will abandon their gods and acclaim him as Lord, thus reconciling government in heaven and government on earth. In this way, the gentile perspective of verses 6–8 is assimilated to the Jewish perspective of verses 9–11.

We are reminded here, finally, that Paul and his colleagues looked back on Jesus's career from the context of the mission to the gentiles. The *reality* for them and for their Spirit-filled churches was their consciousness of the risen and exalted Christ as a *Spirit*-person, a *sōma pneumatikon*, seated at the right hand of God, to whom they might pray and who would come in some sense, eventually, to deliver them from the wrath of God. For both gentile and Jewish believers in the cities of Asia Minor and Greece, knowledge of the pre-exalted Jesus may have been, in this early period, little more than hearsay. It seems likely, therefore, that if the humanity of the Jewish Jesus is oddly emphasized in the texts, the contrast is not with a hypothetical heavenly pre-existence but with a powerfully experienced heavenly *post-existence*. But the fundamental ethical significance of the insight lay in the fact that their vocation consisted in a close alignment with the path of Jesus. The eschatological wisdom of God was being expressed in them not through any godlike attainment but precisely through their Christlike suffering.

Bibliography

Achtemeier, Paul J. "Gospel Miracle Tradition and the Divine Man." *Interpretation* 26 (1972) 174–97.

Allen, Leslie C. *Ezekiel 20–48*. Word Biblical Commentary. Grand Rapids: Zondervan, 1990.

Aune, David E. *Revelation 1–5*. Word Biblical Commentary. Grand Rapids: Zondervan, 1997.

———. *Revelation 6–16*. Word Biblical Commentary. Grand Rapids: Zondervan, 1998.

Barker, Margaret. *The Great Angel: A Study of Israel's Second God*. London: SPCK, 1992.

Barth, Markus, and Helmut Blanke. *Colossians: A New Translation with Introduction and Commentary*. AB. New Haven, CT: Yale University Press, 1974.

Bates, Matthew W. *The Birth of the Trinity*. Oxford: Oxford University Press, 2015.

———. "A Christology of Incarnation and Enthronement: Romans 1:3–4 as Unified, Nonadoptionist, and Nonconciliatory." *Catholic Biblical Quarterly* 77 (2015) 107–27.

———. *Gospel Allegiance: What Faith in Jesus Misses for Salvation in Christ*. Grand Rapids: Brazos, 2019.

Bauckham, Richard. *Jesus and the God of Israel: God Crucified and Other Studies on the New Testament's Christology of Divine Identity*. Grand Rapids: Eerdmans, 2008.

———. *God Crucified: Monotheism and Christology in the New Testament*. Grand Rapids: Eerdmans, 1999.

Beare, F. W. *The Epistle to the Philippians*. BNTC. London: A. & C. Black, 1959.

Behm, J. "μορφή, μορφόω, μόρφωσις, μεταμορφόω." In *TDNT*, edited by Gerhard Kittel, and Geoffrey W. Bromiley, 4:742–59. Grand Rapids: Eerdmans, 1964.

Betz, Hans Dieter. *Galatians: A Commentary on Paul's Letter to the Churches in Galatia*. Hermeneia. Minneapolis: Fortress, 1979.

Betz, Hans Dieter, ed. *The Greek Magical Papyri in Translation*. Chicago: University of Chicago Press, 1986.

Bird, Michael F. *Jesus the Eternal Son: Answering Adoptionist Christology*. Grand Rapids: Eerdmans, 2017.

Blackburn, Barry. *Theios Anēr and The Markan Miracle Traditions: A Critique of the Theios Anēr Concept as an Interpretative Background of the Miracle Tradition used by Mark*. Wissenschaftliche Untersuchungen zum Neuen Testament 2.40. Tübingen: Mohr Siebeck, 1991.

Blenkinsopp, Joseph. *Isaiah 56–66: A New Translation with Introduction and Commentary*. AB. New Haven, CT: Yale University Press, 1974.

Bockmuehl, Markus N. A. *The Epistle to Philippians*. BNTC. London: A. & C. Black, 1997.

———. "'The Form of God' (Phil 2:6): Variations on a Theme of Jewish Mysticism." *JTS* 48 (1997) 1–23.

Bowman, Robert M., Jr., and J. Ed Komoszewski. *Putting Jesus in His Place: The Case for the Deity of Christ*. Grand Rapids: Kregel, 2007.

Boyarin, Daniel. *The Jewish Gospels: The Story of the Jewish Christ*. New York: The New Press, 2012.

———. "Two Powers in Heaven: Or, the Making of a Heresy." In *The Idea of Biblical Interpretation: Essays in Honor of James L. Kugel*, edited by Hindy Najman and Judith H. Newman, 331–70. Leiden: Brill, 2004.

Branick, Vincent P. "The Sinful Flesh of the Son of God (Rom 8:3): A Key Image of Pauline Theology." *Catholic Biblical Quarterly* 47 (1985) 246–62.

Brown, Colin. "Ernst Lohmeyer's *Kyrios* Jesus Revisited." In *Where Christology Began: Essays on Philippians 2*, edited by Ralph P. Martin and Brian J. Dodd, 6–42. Louisville: Westminster John Knox, 1998.

Brown, Raymond E. *An Introducton to New Testament Christology*. London: Geoffrey Chapman, 1994.

Bruce, F. F. *1 and 2 Thessalonians*. Word Biblical Commentary. Waco, TX: Word Incorporated, 1982.

———. *The Epistle to the Galatians: A Commentary on the Greek Text*. Exeter: Paternoster, 1982.

———. *The Epistles to the Colossians, to Philemon, and to the Ephesians*. NICNT. Grand Rapids: Eerdmans, 1984.

Budd, Philip J. *Numbers*. Word Biblical Commentary. Nashville: Thomas Nelson, 1984.

Bultmann, Rudolf. *Theology of the New Testament vol. 1*. London: SCM, 1952.

Burke, Denny. "On the Articular Infinitive in Philippians 2:6: A Grammatical Note with Christological Implications." *Tyndale Bulletin* 55 (2004) 253–74.

Buxton, B., and Robert Hannah. "*OGIS* 458, the Augustan Calendar, and the Succession." In *Studies in Latin Literature and Roman History XII*, edited by Carl Deroux, 290–306. Brussels: Éditions Latomus, 2005.

Byrne, Brendan. "Christ's Pre-Existence in Pauline Soteriology." *Theological Studies* 58 (1997) 308–30.

———. *Romans*. Sacra Pagina. Collegeville, MN: Liturgical, 1996.

Campbell, Douglas A. "The Story of Jesus in Romans and Galatians." In *Narrative Dynamics in Paul: A Critical Assessment*, edited by Bruce W. Longenecker, 97–124. Louisville: Westminster John Knox, 2002.

Capes, David B. *The Divine Christ: Paul, the Lord Jesus, and the Scriptures of Israel*. Grand Rapids: Baker Academic, 2018.

———. "Pauline Exegesis and the Incarnate Christ." In *Israel's God and Rebecca's Children: Christology and Community in Early Judaism and Christianity: Essays in Honor of Larry W. Hurtado and Alan F. Segal*, edited by April D. DeConick et al., 135–54. Waco, TX: Baylor University Press, 2007.

Cerfaux, Lucien. *Christ in the Theology of St. Paul*. New York: Herder and Herder, 1959.

Charlesworth, James H., ed. *The Old Testament Pseudepigrapha vol. 1*. London: Darton, Longman & Todd, 1983.

———. *The Old Testament Pseudepigrapha vol. 2*. London: Darton, Longman & Todd, 1985.

Chester, Andrew. "High Christology—Whence, When and Why?" *Early Christianity* 2 (2011) 22–50.

———. *Messiah and Exaltation: Jewish Messianic and Visionary Traditions and New Testament Christology*. Tübingen: Mohr Siebeck, 2007.

Ciampa, Roy E., and Brian S. Rosner. *The First Letter to the Corinthians*. PNTC. Grand Rapids: Eerdmans, 2010.

Collins, John J. *Jewish Wisdom in the Hellenistic Age*. Louisville: Westminster John Knox, 1997.

Conzelmann, Hans. *1 Corinthians: A Commentary on the First Epistle to the Corinthians*. Philadelphia: Fortress, 1975.

Copenhaver, Brian P. *Hermetica: The Greek Corpus Hermetica and the Latin Asclepius in a New English Translation, with Notes and Introduction*. Cambridge: Cambridge University Press, 1992.

Craigie, Peter C. *Psalms 1–50*. Word Biblical Commentary. Waco, TX: Word Incorporated, 1983.

Crossan, John Dominic, and Jonathan L. Reed. *In Search of Paul: How Jesus' Apostle Opposed Rome's Empire with God's Kingdom*. London: SPCK, 2005.

Crowther, Charles. "Inscriptions in Stone." In *Excavations at Zeugma*, edited by William Aylward, 192–219. Los Altos: Packard Humanities Institute, 2013.

Cullman, Oscar. *The Christology of the New Testament*. Philadelphia: Westminster, 1959.

Donahue, John R., and Daniel J. Harrington. *The Gospel of Mark*. Sacra Pagina. Collegeville, MN: Liturgical, 2002.

Dunn, James D. G. *Beginning From Jerusalem: Christianity in the Making vol. 2*. Grand Rapids: Eerdmans, 2009.

———. "Christ, Adam, and Preexistence." In *Where Christology Began: Essays on Philippians 2*, edited by Ralph P. Martin, and Brian J. Dodd, 74–82. Louisville: Westminster John Knox, 1998.

———. *Christology in the Making: A New Testament Inquiry into the Origins of the Doctrine of the Incarnation*. London: SCM, 1980.

———. *The Epistle to the Galatians*. London: A. & C. Black, 1993.

———. *The Epistles to the Colossians and to Philemon: A Commentary on the Greek Text*. Grand Rapids: Eerdmans, 1996.

———. *Romans 9–16*. Word Biblical Commentary. Dallas: Word Books, 1998.

———. *The Theology of Paul the Apostle*. Grand Rapids: Eerdmans, 1998.

Edwards, James R. *The Gospel according to Mark*. PNTC. Grand Rapids: Eerdmans, 2002.

Ehrman, Bart D. *How Jesus Became God: The Exaltation of a Jewish Preacher from Galilee*. New York: HarperOne, 2014.

Evans, Craig A. *Mark 8:27–16:20*. Word Biblical Commentary. Nashville: Thomas Nelson, 1988.

———. "A Note on the 'First-Born Son' of 4Q369." *Dead Sea Discoveries* 2 (1995) 185–201.

Fabricatore, Daniel J. *Form of God, Form of a Servant: An Examination of the Greek Noun μορφή in Philippians 2:6–7*. Lanham, MD: University Press of America, 2009.

Fantin, Joseph D. "The Lord of the Entire World: Lord Jesus, a Challenge to Lord Caesar?" PhD diss., University of Sheffield, 2007.

Fee, Gordon D. *The First and Second Letters to the Thessalonians*. Grand Rapids: Eerdmans, 2009.

———. *The First Epistle to the Corinthians (Revised edition)*. NICNT. Grand Rapids: Eerdmans, 2014.

———. *Pauline Christology: An Exegetical-Theological Study*. Peabody, MA: Hendrickson, 2007.

———. *Paul's Letter to the Philippians*. NICNT. Grand Rapids: Eerdmans, 1995.

———. "Philippians 2:5–11: Hymn or Exalted Pauline Prose?" *BBR* 2 (1992) 29–46.

Feník, Juraj, and Róbert Lapko. "The Reign of Christ in Colossians: A Reassessment." *Catholic Biblical Quarterly* 81 (2019) 495–516.

Fitzmyer, Joseph. *The Acts of the Apostles: A New Translation with Introduction and Commentary*. AB. New Haven, CT: Yale University Press, 1974.

———. *First Corinthians: A New Translation with Introduction and Commentary*. AB. New Haven, CT: Yale University Press, 1974.

———. *Romans: A New Translation with Introduction and Commentary*. AB. New Haven, CT: Yale University Press, 1993.

Fletcher-Louis, Crispin. "'The Being That is in a Manner Equal With God' (Phil. 2:6c): A Self-Transforming, Incarnational, Divine Ontology." *JTS* 71 (2020) 581–627.

———. *Jesus Monotheism. Volume 1—Christological Origins: The Emerging Consensus and Beyond*. Eugene, OR: Wipf & Stock, 2015.

Focant, Camille. "La Portée De La Formule Τὸ Εἶναι Ἴσα Θεῷ En Ph 2.6." *NTS* 62 (2016) 278–88.

Foerster, W. "ἁρπάζω, ἁρπαγμός." In *TDNT*, edited by Gerhard Kittel and Geoffrey W. Bromiley, 1:472–475. Grand Rapids: Eerdmans, 1964.

———. "κύριος." In *TDNT*, edited by Gerhard Kittel, and Geoffrey W. Bromiley, 3:1040–95. Grand Rapids: Eerdmans, 1964.

Fossum, Jarl E. "Jewish-Christian Christology and Jewish Mysticism." *Vigiliae Christianae* 37 (1983) 260–87.

Foster, Paul. *Colossians*. London: Bloomsbury T. & T. Clark, 2016.

Fowl, Stephen E. *Philippians*. Two Horizons New Testament Commentary. Grand Rapids: Eerdmans, 2005.

———. *The Story of Christ in the Ethics of Paul: An Analysis of the Function of the Hymnic Material in the Pauline Corpus*. JSNT Supplement Series. Sheffield: Sheffield Academic, 1990.

Fredriksen, Paula. *Paul: The Pagan's Apostle*. New Haven, CT: Yale University Press, 2017.

Fung, Ronald Y. K. *The Epistle to the Galatians*. Grand Rapids: Eerdmans, 1988.

Garrett, Susan R. *No Ordinary Angel: Celestial Spirits and Christian Claims about Jesus*. New Haven, CT: Yale University Press, 2008.

Gaston, Thomas, and Andrew Perry. "Christological Monotheism: 1 Cor 8.6 and the Shema." *HBT* 39 (2017) 176–96.

Gathercole, Simon J. *The Preexistent Son: Recovering the Christologies of Matthew, Mark, and Luke*. Grand Rapids: Eerdmans, 2006.

Gieschen, Charles. *Angelomorphic Christology: Antecedents and Early Evidence*. Leiden: Brill, 1998.

Gillman, F. M. "Another Look At Romans 8:3: 'In the Likeness of Sinful Flesh.'" *Catholic Biblical Quarterly* 49 (1987) 597–604.

Glasson, T. Francis. "Two Notes on the Philippians Hymn (II. 6–11)." *NTS* 21 (1974) 133–39.

Goldingay, John. *Daniel*. Word Biblical Commentary. Grand Rapids: Zondervan, 1989.

Gordley, Matthew E. *New Testament Christological Hymns: Exploring Texts, Contexts, and Significance*. Downers Grove, IL: IVP Academic, 2018.

Gorman, Michael J. "'Although/Because He Was in the Form of God': The Theological Significance of Paul's Master Story (Phil 2:6–11)." *Journal of Theological Interpretation* 1 (2007) 147–69.

Gourgues, Michel. "La «Plénitude Des Temps», Ou Le Temps Marqué De Façon Décisive Par La Référence À Jésus Christ. Polysémie D'une Formule Néotestamentaire (Mc 1,15; Ga 4,4; Ep 1,10)." *Science et Esprit* 53 (2001) 93–110.

Green, Joel B. *The Gospel of Luke*. NICNT. Grand Rapids: Eerdmans, 1997.

Guelich, Robert A. *Mark 1–8:26*. Word Biblical Commentary. Grand Rapids: Zondervan, 1989.

Hagner, Donald A. *Matthew 1–13*. Word Biblical Commentary. Dallas: Word, 1993.

Hamerton-Kelly, R. G. *Pre-Existence, Wisdom, and the Son of Man*. Eugene, OR: Wipf & Stock, 2000.

Hannah, Darrell D. *Michael and Christ: Michael Traditions and Angel Christology in Early Christianity*. Wissenschaftliche Untersuchungen zum Neuen Testament 2.109. Tübingen: Mohr Siebeck, 1999.

Hansen, G. Walter. *The Letter to the Philippians*. PNTC. Grand Rapids: Eerdmans, 2009.

Harris, Murray J. *The Second Epistle to the Corinthians: A Commentary on the Greek Text*. NIGTC. Grand Rapids: Eerdmans, 2005.

Harrison, J. R. "Paul and the Imperial Gospel At Thessaloniki." *JSNT* 25 (2002) 71–96.

Hawthorne, Gerald F. "In the Form of God and Equal with God (Philippians 2:6)." In *Where Christology Began: Essays on Philippians 2*, edited by Ralph P. Martin and Brian J. Dodd, 96–110. Louisville: Westminster John Knox, 1998.

Hawthorne, Gerald F., and Ralph P. Martin. *Philippians*. Word Biblical Commentary. Grand Rapids: Zondervan, 2004.

Hays, Richard B. *Echoes of Scripture in the Letters of Paul*. New Haven, CT: Yale University Press, 1989.

————. *First Corinthians*. Interpretation. Louisville: Westminster John Knox, 2011.

Heiser, Michael. *The Unseen Realm: Recovering the Supernatural Worldview of the Bible*. Bellingham: Lexham, 2015.

————. "You've Seen One *Elohim*, You've Seen Them All? A Critique of Mormonism's Use of Psalm 82." *FARMS Review* 19 (2007) 221–66.

Hellerman, Joseph H. "Μορφη Θεου as a Signifier of Social Status in Philippians 2:6." *JETS* 52 (2009) 779–97.

————. *Philippians*. Exegetical Guide to the Greek New Testament. Nashville: Broadman & Holman, 2015.

————. *Reconstructing Honor in Roman Philippi: Carmen Christi as Cursus Pudorum*. Cambridge: Cambridge University Press, 2009.

————. "Vindicating God's Servants in Philippi and in Philippians: The Influence of Paul's Ministry Upon the Composition of Philippians 2:6–11." *BBR* 20 (2010) 85–102.

Helyer, Larry R. "Arius Revisited: The Firstborn Over All Creation." *JETS* 31 (1988) 59–67.

Hengel, Martin. *The Cross of the Son of God*. London: SCM, 1986.

————. *Judaism and Hellenism*. London: SCM, 1974.

Hill, Andrew E. *Malachi: A New Translation with Introduction and Commentary*. AB. New Haven, CT: Yale University Press, 1978.

Hill, Brennan R. *Jesus, the Christ: Contemporary Perspectives*. Eugene, OR: Wipf & Stock, 2014.

Holloway, Paul A. *Philippians*. Hermeneia. Minneapolis: Fortress, 2017.

Hooker, Morna D. *From Adam to Christ: Essays on Paul*. Eugene, OR: Wipf & Stock, 2008.

Hoover, Roy W. "The Harpagmos Enigma: A Philological Solution." *HTR* 64 (1971) 95–119.

Horbury, William. *Jewish Messianism and the Cult of Christ*. London: SCM, 1998.

Howard, George. "Phil 2:6–11 and the Human Christ." *Catholic Biblical Quarterly* 40 (1978) 368–87.

Huijgen, Arnold, and Arie Versluis. "'Our God is One': The Unity of YHWH and the Trinity in the Interplay between Biblical Exegesis and Systematic Theology." In *Reading and Listening: Meeting One God in Many Texts*, edited by Jaap Dekker and Gert Kwakkel, 213–25. Amsterdam: 2VM, 2018.

Hurst, Lincoln D. "Christ, Adam, and Preexistence Revisited." In *Where Christology Began: Essays on Philippians 2*, edited by Ralph P. Martin and Brian J. Dodd, Louisville: Westminster John Knox, 1998.

———. "Re-Enter the Pre-Existent Christ in Philippians 2.5–11?" *NTS* 32 (1986) 449–57.

Hurtado, Larry W. *How on Earth Did Jesus Become a God? Historical Questions about Earliest Devotion to Jesus*. Grand Rapids: Eerdmans, 2005.

———. *Lord Jesus Christ: Devotion to Jesus in Earliest Christianity*. Grand Rapids: Eerdmans, 2003.

———. "Pre-existence." In *Dictionary of Paul and His Letters*, edited by Gerald F. Hawthorne et al., 743–46. Downers Grove, IL: InterVarsity, 1993.

Jeremias, Joachim. "Zu Phil 2:7: ΕΑΥΤΟΝ ΕΚΕΝΩΣΕΝ." *Novum Testamentum* 6 (1963) 182–88.

Jervell, Jacob. *Imago Dei. Gen 1, 26 f. im Spätjudentum, in der Gnosis und in den paulinischen Briefen*. Göttingen: Vandenhoeck und Ruprecht, 1959.

Jewett, Robert, and Roy D. Kotansky. *Romans*. Hermeneia. Minneapolis: Fortress, 2007.

Jipp, Joshua W. *Christ is King: Paul's Royal Ideology*. Minneapolis: Fortress, 2015.

Johnson, Luke Timothy. *The Acts of the Apostles*. Sacra Pagina. Collegeville, MN: Liturgical, 1992.

Jowers, Dennis W. "The Meaning of ΜΟΡΦΗ in Philippians 2:6–7." *JETS* 49 (2006) 739–66.

Käsemann, Ernst. "Kritische Analyse Von Phil. 2, 5–1." *Zeitschrift für Theologie und Kirche* 47 (1950) 313–60.

Kennedy, H. A. A. "The Epistle to the Philippians." In *The Expositor's Greek Testament*, edited by W. Robertson Nicoll, 3:399–473. New York: Doran, 1900.

Keown, Mark J. *Philippians 1:1–2:18*. Evangelical Exegetical Commentary. Bellingham: Lexham, 2017.

Kim, Seyoon. *The Origin of Paul's Gospel*. Grand Rapids: Eerdmans, 1981.

Kingsbury, Jack Dean. "The 'Divine Man' as the Key to Mark's Christology—the End of an Era?" *Interpretation* 35 (1981) 243–57.

Klauck, Hans-Josef. *The Religious Context of Early Christianity: A Guide to Graeco-Roman Religions*. Minneapolis: Fortress, 2003.

Kleinknecht, Hermann. "θεός, θεότης, ἄθεος, θεοδίδακτος, θεῖος, θειότης." In *TDNT*, edited by Gerhard Kittel, and Geoffrey W. Bromiley, 4:65–123. Grand Rapids: Eerdmans, 1964.

Klijn, A. F. J., and G. J. Reinink. *Patristic Evidence for Jewish-Christian Sects.* Supplements to Novum Testamentum. Leiden: Brill, 1973.

Knox, Wilfred L. "The 'Divine Hero' Christology in the New Testament." *HTR* 41 (1948) 229–49.

Kuschel, Karl-Josef. *Born Before All Time? The Dispute over Christ's Origins.* London: SCM, 1992.

Lane, William L. *The Gospel of Mark.* NICNT. Grand Rapids: Eerdmans, 1974.

Lee, Aquila H. I. *From Messiah to Preexistent Son: Jesus' Self-Consciousness and Early Christian Exegesis of Messianic Psalms.* Eugene, OR: Wipf & Stock, 2005.

Levene, D. S. "Defining the Divine in Rome." *Transactions of the American Philological Association* 142 (2012) 41–81.

Liefeld, Walter J. "The Hellenistic 'Divine Man' and the Figure of Jesus." *Journal of the Evangelical Theology Society* 16 (1973) 195–205.

Lightfoot, J. B. *Saint Paul's Epistle to the Philippians.* London: Macmillan, 1878.

Linebaugh, Jonathan A. *God, Grace, and Righteousness in Wisdom of Solomon and Paul's Letter to the Romans: Texts in Conversation.* Supplements to Novum Testamentum. Leiden: Brill, 2013.

Litwa, M. David. "The Deification of Moses in Philo of Alexandria." *The Studia Philonica Annual* 26 (2014) 1–27.

———. *Iesus Deus: The Early Christian Depiction of Jesus as a Mediterranean God.* Minneapolis: Fortress, 2014.

———. *We Are Being Transformed: Deification in Paul's Soteriology.* Berlin: De Gruyter, 2012.

Lohse, Edward. *Colossians and Philemon: A Commentary on the Epistles to the Colossians and to Philemon.* Hermeneia. Minneapolis: Fortress, 1971.

Loke, Andrew Ter Ern. *The Origin of Divine Christology.* Cambridge: Cambridge University Press, 2017.

Longenecker, Richard N. *The Epistle to the Romans: A Commentary on the Greek Text.* NIGTC. Grand Rapids: Eerdmans, 2016.

———. *Galatians.* Word Biblical Commentary. Grand Rapids: Zondervan, 1990.

MacDonald, Margaret Y. *Colossians and Ephesians.* Sacra Pagina. Collegeville, MN: Liturgical, 2000.

Marcus, Joel. *Mark 1–8: A New Translation with Introduction and Commentary.* AB. New Haven, CT: Yale University Press, 1974.

———. *Mark 8–16: A New Translation with Introduction and Commentary.* AB. New Haven, CT: Yale University Press, 2009.

Martin, Michael Wade. "ἁρπαγμός Revisited: A Philological Reexamination of the New Testament's 'Most Difficult Word.'" *JBL* 135 (2016) 175–94.

Martin, Michael Wade, and Bryan A. Nash. "Philippians 2:6–11 as Subversive *Hymnos*: A Study in the Light of Ancient Rhetorical Theory." *JTS* 66 (2015) 90–138.

Martin, Ralph P. *2 Corinthians.* Word Biblical Commentary. Waco, TX: Word, 1986.

———. *An Early Christian Confession.* London: Tyndale, 1960.

———. *A Hymn of Christ: Philippians 2:5–11 in Recent Interpretation and in the Setting of Early Christian Worship.* Downers Grove, IL: InterVarsity, 1997.

―――――. *The Spirit and the Congregation: Studies in 1 Corinthians 12–15*. Grand Rapids: Eerdmans, 1984.

Martyn, J. Louis. *Galatians: A New Translation with Introduction and Commentary*. AB. New Haven, CT: Yale University Press, 1974.

McBride, S. Dean. "The Yoke of the Kingdom: An Exposition of Deuteronomy 6:4–5." *Interpretation* 27 (1973) 273–306.

McGrath, James F. *The Only True God: Early Christian Monotheism in its Jewish Context*. Urbana: University of Illinois Press, 2009.

McKnight, Scot. *The Letter to the Colossians*. NICNT. Grand Rapids: Eerdmans, 2018.

Michaelis, W. "πρῶτος, πρῶτον, πρωτοκαθεδρία, πρωτοκλισία, πρωτότοκος, πρωτοτοκεῖα, πρωτεύω." In *TDNT*, edited by Gerhard Kittel and Geoffrey W. Bromiley, 6:865–82. Grand Rapids: Eerdmans, 1964.

Moo, Douglas J. *The Epistle to the Romans*. NICNT. Grand Rapids: Eerdmans, 1996.

Moss, Candida R. "The Transfiguration: An Exercise in Markan Accommodation." *Biblical Interpretation* 12 (2004) 69–89.

Moule, C. F. D. "Further Reflections on Philippians 2:5–11." In *Apostolic History and the Gospel. Biblical and Historical Essays Presented to F. F. Bruce*, edited by W. W. Gasque and Ralph P. Martin, 264–76. Exeter: Paternoster, 1970.

Moulton, James Hope, and George Milligan. *The Vocabulary of the Greek Testament Illustrated From the Papyri and other Non-Literary Sources*. London: Hodder and Stoughton, 1914.

Müller, Ulrich B. "Der Christushymnus Phil 2:6–11." *Zeitschrift für die neutestamentliche Wissenschaft und die Kunde der älteren Kirche* 79 (1988) 17–44.

Murphy-O'Connor, Jerome. "1 Cor., VIII, 6: Cosmology or Soteriology?" *RB* 85 (1978) 253–67.

―――――. "Christological Anthropology in Phil, II, 6–11." *RB* 83 (1976) 25–50.

Nickelsburg, George W. E. *1 Enoch 1: A Commentary on the Book of 1 Enoch, Chapters 1–36; 81–108*. Hermeneia. Minneapolis: Fortress, 2001.

Nickelsburg, George W. E., and James C. VanderKam. *1 Enoch 2: A Commentary on the Book of 1 Enoch, Chapters 37–82*. Hermeneia. Minneapolis: Fortress, 2012.

―――――. *1 Enoch: The Hermeneia Translation*. Minneapolis: Fortress, 2012.

Northcott, Christopher S. "'King of Kings' in Other Words: Colossians 1:15a as a Designation of Authority Rather Than Revelation." *Tyndale Bulletin* 69 (2018) 205–24.

O'Brien, Peter T. *Colossians-Philemon*. Word Biblical Commentary. Grand Rapids: Zondervan, 2000.

―――――. *The Epistle to the Philippians: A Commentary on the Greek Text*. NIGTC. Grand Rapids: Eerdmans, 1991.

O'Neill, J. C. "Hoover on *Harpagmos* Reviewed, With a Modest Proposal Concerning Philippians 2:6." *HTR* 81 (1988) 445–49.

Oakes, Peter. *Philippians: From People to Letter*. Cambridge: Cambridge University Press, 2001.

Oswalt, John N. *The Book of Isaiah Chapters 40–66*. NICOT. Grand Rapids: Eerdmans, 1998.

Pannenberg, Wolfhart. *Systematic Theology vol. 2*. London: T. & T. Clark, 1994.

Pascuzzi, Maria A. "Reconsidering the Authorship of Colossians." *BBR* 23 (2013) 223–46.

Pérez i Díaz, Mar. *Mark, a Pauline Theologian: A Re-reading of the Traditions of Jesus in the Light of Paul's Theology.* Tübingen: Mohr Siebeck, 2020.

Perriman, Andrew. *The Coming of the Son of Man: New Testament Eschatology for an Emerging Church.* Milton Keynes: Paternoster, 2005.

———. *End of Story: Same-Sex Relationships and the Narratives of Evangelical Mission.* Eugene, OR: Wipf & Stock, 2019.

———. *The Future of the People of God: Reading Romans Before and After Western Christendom.* Eugene, OR: Cascade, 2010.

———. "The Pattern of Christ's Sufferings: Colossians 1:24 and Philippians 3:10–11." *Tyndale Bulletin* 42 (1991) 62–79.

Pilgaard, Aage. "The Hellenistic *Theios Aner*—A Model for Early Christian Christology?" In *The New Testament and Hellenistic Judaism*, edited by Peder Borgen and Søren Giverson, 101–22. Aarhus: Aarhus University Press, 1994.

Piñero, Antonio. "Enoch as Mediator, Messiah, Judge, and Son of Man in the Book of Parables: A Jewish Response to Early Jewish-Christian Theology?" *Henoch* 35 (2013) 6–49.

Rastoin, Marc. "Framing Freedom: Galatians 4:1–7 and Pauline Rhetoric." *RB* 121 (2014) 252–66.

Reid, Robert G. "'Savior' and 'Lord' in the Lukan Birth Narrative: A Challenge to Caesar?" *Pax Pneuma* 5 (2009) 46–61.

Reumann, John. *Philippians: A New Translation with Introduction and Commentary.* AB. New Haven, CT: Yale University Press, 2008.

Richard, Earl J. *First and Second Thessalonians.* Sacra Pagina. Collegeville, MN: Liturgical, 2007.

Ridderbos, Herman. *Paul: An Outline of His Theology.* London: SPCK, 1977.

Rillera, Andrew Remington. "A Call to Resistance: The Exhortative Function of Daniel 7." *JBL* 138 (2019) 757–76.

Roon, Aart van. "The Relation Between Christ and the Wisdom of God According to Paul." *Novum Testamentum* 16 (1974) 207–39.

Rose, Charles Brian. "A New Relief of Antiochus I of Commagene and Other Stone Sculpture from Zeugma." In *Excavations at Zeugma*, edited by William Aylward, 220–31. Los Altos: Packard Humanities Institute, 2013.

Rowe, C. Kavin. "Romans 10:13: What is the Name of the Lord?" *HBT* 20 (2000) 135–73.

Sanders, J. A. "Dissenting Deities and Philippians 2:1–11." *JBL* 88 (1969) 279–90.

Schweizer, E. "υἱός, υἱοθεσία." In *TDNT*, edited by Gerhard Kittel and Geoffrey W. Bromiley, 8:334–99. Grand Rapids: Eerdmans, 1964.

Scott, James M. *Adoption as Sons of God: An Exegetical Investigation Into the Background of ΥΙΟΘΕΣΙΑ in the Pauline Corpus.* Tübingen: Mohr Siebeck, 1992.

———. "A Comparison of Paul's Letter to the Galatians with the Epistle of Enoch." In *The Jewish Apocalyptic Tradition and the Shaping of New Testament Thought*, edited by Benjamin E. Reynolds and Loren T. Stuckenbruck, 193–218. Minneapolis: Fortress, 2017.

Seeley, David. "The Background of the Philippians Hymn (2:6–11)." *Journal of Higher Criticism* 1 (1994) 49–72.

Shaner, Katherine A. "Seeing Rape and Robbery: Ἁρπαγμός [sic] and the Philippians Christ Hymn (Phil. 2:5–11)." *Biblical Interpretation* 25 (2017) 342–63.

Sherk, Robert K. *Roman Documents from the Greek East: Senatus Consulta and Epistulae to the age of Augustus*. Baltimore: John Hopkins, 1969.

Silva, Moisés. *Philippians*. Baker Exegetical Commentary on the New Testament. Grand Rapids: Baker Academic, 2005.

Smith, Morton. "Prolegomena to a Discussion of Aretalogies, Divine Men, the Gospels and Jesus." *JBL* 90 (1971) 174–99.

Smith, Ralph L. *Micah–Malachi*. Word Biblical Commentary. Grand Rapids: Zondervan, 1984.

Smith, Rowland. *The Greek Romances of Heliodorus, Longus and Achilles Tatius*. London: George Bell and Sons, 1901.

Söding, Thomas. "Gottes Sohn von Anfang an: Zur Präexistenzchristologie bei Paulus und den Deuteropaulinen." In *Gottes ewiger Sohn: Die Präexistenz Christi in der Diskussion*, edited by Rudolf Laufen, 57–93. Paderborn: Schöningh Ferdinand, 1997.

Steenburg, Dave. "The Case Against the Synonymity of *Morphē* and *Eikōn*." *JSNT* 34 (1988) 77–86.

Sterling, Gregory E. "Wisdom or Foolishness? The Role of Philosophy in the Thought of Paul." In *God and the Faithfulness of Paul*, edited by Christoph Heilig et al., 235–53. Minneapolis: Fortress, 2017.

Stone, Michael Edward. *Fourth Ezra: A Commentary on the Book of Fourth Ezra*. Minneapolis: Fortress, 1990.

Strait, Drew J. "The Wisdom of Solomon, Ruler Cults, and Paul's Polemic Against Idols in the Areopagus Speech." *JBL* 136 (2017) 609–32.

Strimple, R. B. "Philippians 2:5–11 in Recent Studies: Some Exegetical Conclusions." *Westminster Theological Journal* 41 (1979) 247–68.

Stroumsa, Gedaliahu G. "Form(s) of God: Some Notes on Metatron and Christ." *HTR* 76 (1983) 269–88.

Talbert, Charles H. *The Development of Christology During the First Hundred Years and Other essays on Early Christian Christology*. Leiden: Brill, 2011.

———. "The Problem of Pre-Existence in Philippians 2 6–11." *JBL* 86 (1967) 141–53.

Thiessen, Matthew. "'The Rock Was Christ': The Fluidity of Christ's Body in 1 Corinthians 10.4." *JSNT* 36 (2013) 103–26.

Thiselton, Anthony C. *The First Epistle to the Corinthians: a Commentary on the Greek Text*. NIGTC. Grand Rapids: Eerdmans, 2000.

Thurston, Bonnie B., and Judith M. Ryan. *Philippians and Philemon*. Collegeville, PA: Liturgical, 2009.

Tilling, Chris. *Paul's Divine Christology*. Tübingen: Mohr Siebeck, 2012.

Tobin, Thomas H. "The World of Thought in the Philippians Hymn (Philippians 2:6–11)." In *The New Testament and Early Christian Literature in Greco-Roman Context*, edited by John Fotopoulos and David Edward Aune, 91–104. Leiden: Brill, 2006.

Tuckett, Christopher M. *Christology and the New Testament: Jesus and His Earliest Followers*. Louisville: Westminster John Knox, 2001.

Verhoef, Pieter A. *The Books of Haggai and Malachi*. NICOT. Grand Rapids: Eerdmans, 1987.

Veyne, Paul. *When Our World Became Christian: 312–394*. Cambridge: Polity, 2010.

Vincent, Marvin R. *The Epistles to the Philippians and to Philemon*. The International Critical Commentary. Edinburgh: T. & T. Clark, 1897.

Vollenweider, Samuel. "Die Metamorphose des Gottessohns Zum epiphanialen Motivfeld in Phil 2,6–8." In *Horizonte neutestamentlicher Christologie, Studien zu Paulus und zur frühchristlichen Theologie*, edited by Samuel Vollenweider, 285–306. Tübingen: Mohr Siebeck, 2002.

———. "Der „Raub" der Gottgleichheit: Ein religionsgeschichtlicher Vorschlag zu Phil 2,6(–11)." In *Horizonte neutestamentlicher Christologie, Studien zu Paulus und zur frühchristlichen Theologie*, edited by Samuel Vollenweider, 263–84. Tübingen: Mohr Siebeck, 2002.

Waddell, James A. *The Messiah: A Comparative Study of the Enochic Son of Man and the Pauline Kyrios*. London: Bloomsbury T. & T. Clark, 2011.

Wallace, Daniel B. *Greek Grammar Beyond the Basics: An Exegetical Syntax of the New Testament*. Grand Rapids: Zondervan, 2006.

Wanamaker, C. A. "Philippians 2.6–11: Son of God or Adamic Christology." *NTS* 33 (1987) 179–93.

Watts, John D. W. *Isaiah 34–66*. Word Biblical Commentary. Waco, TX: Word, 2005.

Weeden, Theodore J. *Mark—Traditions in Conflict*. Philadelphia: Fortress, 1971.

Weinfeld, Moshe. *Deuteronomy 1–11: A New Translation with Introduction and Commentary*. AB. New Haven, CT: Yale University Press, 1974.

Wenham, Gordon J. *Genesis 16–50*. Word Biblical Commentary. Grand Rapids: Zondervan, 1994.

Weymouth, Richard. "The Christ-Story of Philippians 2:6–11: Narrative Shape and Paraenetic Purpose in Paul's Letter to Philippi." PhD Diss., University of Otago, 2015.

Winter, Bruce W. *Divine Honours for the Caesars: The First Christians' Responses*. Grand Rapids: Eerdmans, 2015.

Wise, Michael, et al. *The Dead Sea Scrolls: A New Translation*. London: HarperCollins-Publishers, 1996.

Witherington, Ben. *Conflict and Community in Corinth: A Socio-Rhetorical Commentary on 1 and 2 Corinthians*. Grand Rapids: Eerdmans, 1995.

———. *Paul's Narrative Thought World: The Tapestry of Tragedy and Triumph*. Louisville: Westminster John Knox, 1994.

Wolfson, Harry A. "The Pre-Existent Angel of the Magharians and Al-Nahāwandī." *Jewish Quarterly Review* 51 (1960) 89–106.

Wong, Teresia Y. "The Problem of Pre-Existence in Philippians 2,6–11." *Ephemerides Theologicae Lovanienses* 62 (1986) 267–82.

Wright, N. T. "Ἁρπαγμός and the Meaning of Philippians 2:5–11." *JTS* 37 (1986) 321–52.

———. *The Climax of the Covenant: Christ and the Law in Pauline Theology*. Edinburgh: T. & T. Clark, 1991.

———. *Paul and the Faithfulness of God III and IV*. London: SPCK, 2013.

Yarbro Collins, Adela. "'How on Earth Did Jesus Become a God?' A Reply." In *Israel's God and Rebecca's Children: Christology and Community in Early Judaism and Christianity: Essays in Honor of Larry W. Hurtado and Alan F. Segal*, edited by April D. DeConick et al., 55–66. Waco, TX: Baylor University Press, 2007.

———. "Mark and His Readers: The Son of God Among Greeks and Romans." *HTR* 93 (2000) 85–100.

———. "Psalms, Philippians 2:6–11, and the Origins of Christology." *Biblical Interpretation* 11 (2003) 361–72.

————. "The Worship of Jesus and the Imperial Cult." In *The Jewish Roots of Christological Monotheism: Papers from the St. Andrews Conference on the Historical Origins of the Worship of Jesus*, edited by Carey C. Newman et al., 234–57. Leiden: Brill, 1999.

Yarbro Collins, Adela, and John J. Collins. *King and Messiah as Son of God: Divine, Human, and Angelic Messianic Figures in Biblical and Related Literature*. Grand Rapids: Eerdmans, 2008.

Zeilinger, Franz. *Der Erstgeborene der Schöpfung: Untersuchungen zur Formalstruktur und Theologie des Kolosserbriefes*. Vienna: Herder, 1974.

Zeller, Dieter. "New Testament Christology in Its Hellenistic Reception." *NTS* 46 (2001) 312–33.

Author Index

Sanders, J. A., 109, 111–13, 111nn8–9, 112nn10–11, 129, 129n72
Scholem, Gershom, 103, 106
Schweizer, E., 21, 21n31, 26, 37, 37n1
Scott, James M., 16n17, 17n19, 21n31, 26, 26n37
Seeley, David, 95n10
Shaner, Katherine A., 155n2, 155n4, 180, 180n78
Sherk, Robert K., 200n42
Silva, Moisés, 154n1
Smith, Morton, 137n14
Smith, Ralph L., 15n15, 43n21
Smith, Rowland, 156n8, 157n10
Söding, Thomas, 9n2, 37, 37n2, 57n62, 76, 76n30
Steenburg, Dave, 84–85, 84n63, 85nn66–67, 86n68, 87nn73–74, 107n67
Sterling, Gregory E., 48n35
Stone, Michael Edward, 118n38
Strait, Drew J., 135n10, 170n54, 188n7
Strimple, R. B., 88, 88n77, 93n4, 154n1, 182n85
Stroumsa, Gedaliahu G., 103–7, 103nn43–44, 104nn48–49, 105nn54–55, 106n61, 107nn62–65, 122

Talbert, Charles H., 39n13, 87n73, 93n2, 130n1, 147, 147nn52–53, 181n79
Taylor, T., 140n26
Thiessen, Matthew, 51n44, 52n45, 54–56, 54n54, 55nn56–56, 56nn57–60
Thiselton, Anthony C., 39n8, 39n10, 47n33, 52n45, 53n52, 54n54
Thurston, Bonnie, 77, 77n35, 154n1
Tilling, Chris, 38n4
Tobin, Thomas H., 65n1
Tuckett, Christopher M., 20n30

VanderKam, James C., 23n34, 118n39, 118n41, 125, 125n60, 201n47
Verhoef, Pieter A., 15n15
Versluis, Arie, 38n4, 139n25
Veyne, Paul, 153n71

Vincent, Marvin R., 74, 75n17, 76, 94n8, 160n22
Vollenweider, Samuel, 109, 126–29, 126nn62–65, 127nn67–69, 128n70, 129, 130, 132, 132n5, 155, 155n2, 162, 162nn28–29, 176, 179n76

Waddell, James A., 10nn3–4, 23n35, 38n4, 51n42, 53n52, 57n61, 110n6, 125nn60–61
Wallace, Daniel B., 174, 175n67
Wanamaker, C. A., 4n7, 47n33, 82n54, 88, 88n78, 93n4
Watts, John D., 203n50
Weeden, Theodore J., 136, 136n13
Weinfeld, Moshe, 38n3
Weiss, Johannes, 39
Wenham, Gordon, 101n34
Weymouth, Richard, 74n16, 154n1, 175n67
Winter, Bruce W., 200n42
Wise, Michael, 102n37
Witherington, Ben, 38n4, 52n45, 154n1
Wolfson, Harry A., 104n49
Wong, Teresia Y., 76, 76n29, 90n82
Wrede, William, 136
Wright, N. T., 16n17, 21n31, 38n4, 151n65, 154n1, 155n6, 156, 159n15, 163–65, 163nn31–33, 165n37, 166, 174, 174n66, 186n3, 200n44

Yarbro Collins, Adela, 10, 20, 27, 43n22, 51n42, 65n1, 116nn29–30, 125n60, 137n15, 141n30, 142, 142n35, 143nn36–38, 145n46, 148n59, 162n28, 170n53, 171n56

Zeilinger, Franz, 198n35
Zeller, Dieter, 27n38, 39n10, 39n12, 45n28, 109n1, 128, 128n70, 137–38, 138n17, 138n20, 139n2, 148, 148nn56–60, 197n33

Ancient Document Index

Pseudepigrapha

Artapanus

2 Baruch

4 Baruch

Demetrius the Chronographer

1 Enoch